The Political Economy of Developmental States in East Asia

"Following the distinguished tradition of research on developmental states, Tian He presents a cogent explanation for how these states have evolved in South Korea, Taiwan, and Singapore, and why this transformation has differed for them due to their respective industrial structure and politics of democratic transition. This book provides a persuasive synthesis and should be read by all students of rising political economies."

—Steve Chan, *College Professor of Distinction, University of Colorado, Boulder, US*

"Tian He has produced a theoretically innovative book that makes a signal contribution to the analysis of East Asian political economy. The central puzzle of this book is why the transformation of the developmental state proceeded so differently within East Asia. It is based on detailed and theoretically informed case studies of Singapore, South Korea, and Taiwan. His complex and sophisticated model is organized around two key interacting explanatory variables: the nature of the democratic transition and the industrial structure of a political economy. It is vital reading for anyone who wants to understand this subject fully."

—Cal Clark, *Emeritus Professor of Political Science, Auburn University, US*

Tian He

The Political Economy of Developmental States in East Asia

South Korea, Singapore and Taiwan

palgrave
macmillan

Tian He
Xi'an Jiaotong-Liverpool University
Suzhou, China

ISBN 978-3-030-59356-8 ISBN 978-3-030-59357-5 (eBook)
https://doi.org/10.1007/978-3-030-59357-5

This Palgrave Macmillan imprint is published by the registered company Springer Nature Switzerland AG
The registered company address is: Gewerbestrasse 11, 6330 Cham, Switzerland

Acknowledgements

This book grew out of years of research into the East Asian model of state-led development and democratic transition. Without the generosity of several individuals and institutions, I would not have been able to turn my interests into a Ph.D. project, finish the doctoral dissertation and subsequently transform it into this book.

This journey began when I was a master's student at Kingston University in England. I would like to express my gratitude to Paul Auerbach, who first sparked my interest in Asian developmental states, patiently guided me through my first research project on East Asian political economy and then pushed me to pursue my Ph.D. Most of the research for this book was done during my Ph.D. studies at the University of Canterbury in New Zealand. During my time there, I was very privileged to be close to a group of fine scholars working in Asia. I am particularly thankful for the wisdom of Alexander Tan, who was instrumental in shaping the theoretical foundation of this book and keeping me on the right track. Anne-Marie Brady offered consistent encouragement and provided useful advice throughout the research and writing process. James Ockey and Naimah Talib also provided help on various occasions during my time at Canterbury.

I am also beholden to the many individuals who, during my field research trips to Singapore and Taiwan, graciously shared their observations on the transformation of the state's economic policy-making. I would like to acknowledge a few in particular. In Taiwan, Yi-Ren Dzeng,

Jenn-Hwan Wang and Yu-Shan Wu contributed extremely helpful views on the transformation of the Taiwanese developmental state over the past two decades. In Singapore, Alan Chong, Gillian Koh, Donald Low, Alexius Pereira and Tan Ern Ser helped me expand my knowledge of the Singaporean developmental state. These individuals' insights were crucial for building the theory of this book.

Since the completion of my doctoral dissertation, several reviewers have read and commented on sections of my work, helping me to sharpen my theoretical arguments and improve my empirical analysis. The two anonymous manuscript reviewers at Palgrave Macmillan provided excellent feedback to improve the book in its final version. The final stage of this book was completed at Xi'an Jiaotong-Liverpool University. I am extremely thankful for the stimulating intellectual environment, as well as the advice and assistance of my colleagues at the XIPU Institution, as I finalised the book. Finally, I thank Rachel Rapaport, who has been a great companion and dedicated editor throughout the preparation of the final book manuscript.

Contents

List of Figures

List of Tables

CHAPTER 1

Unravelling an East Asian Puzzle

An Overlooked East Asian Puzzle

For many years, the concept of Asian developmental states thrived because of its empirical robustness in explaining the East Asian economic miracle. Constructing a Weberian ideal type of interventionist state, the concept of developmental states presents an alternative model of economic development that is neither a socialist central-planning system nor a capitalist free-market economy (Woo-Cumings 1999: 1). The developmental state is 'shorthand for the seamless web of political, bureaucratic and moneyed influences that structure economic life in capitalist Northeast Asia' (Woo-Cumings 1999: 1), and the leadership of the developmental state is 'a central characteristic of these late-late-late industrialisers' (Clark and Chan 2004: 49). The primary characteristics of the state's strategic influence in the economy include a development-oriented government, a competent economic bureaucracy for formulating and executing economic programmes, and the strong ability to insulate economic policy-making from societal pressure (Clark and Jung 2002). The intellectual discussion of the developmental state 'reached something of a climax in the late 1980s and early 1990s' (Stubbs 2009: 2). In 1993, the World Bank—the foremost international developmental agency—for the first time offered its endorsement regarding the concept of the developmental state by recognising that the state plays a role in sustaining high growth (World Bank 1993).

T. He, *The Political Economy of Developmental States in East Asia*,
https://doi.org/10.1007/978-3-030-59357-5_1

The late 1990s was a turning point for the study of Asian developmental states. Not only did the 1997 Asian financial crisis abruptly end the economic miracle of the region, but it also cast serious doubts on the state-led developmental model that most of the region had pursued, and alongside it those theoretical explanations. Although the region recovered quickly at the end of the 1990s, it seemed that 'the most severe and lasting casualty of the 1997 crisis was the East Asian developmental state model itself' (Wong 2004: 345). In the aftermath of the Asian financial crisis, the literature of the East Asian political economy took a sharp turn. On the one hand, some scholars argue that the state's strategic role in the economy led to nothing but institutional corruption and economic inefficiency. As a result, terms like 'crony capitalism' and 'money politics' came to replace those such as the 'East Asian Miracle' (see Kang 2002a, b). On the other hand, it is believed that 'the demise or stillbirth of developmental states was probably more to blame than the creation of competent bureaucracies' (Clark and Jung 2002: 36). This belief led scholars to point to the rise of various social actors to explain the decline of the East Asian state's capability to direct economic development.[1] According to this argument, the principles of the East Asian developmental state manner quickly disappeared in the 1990s.

In regard to the rise and fall of the developmental state, this book addresses an overlooked puzzle by singling out the variations in the transformation of the three most typical Asian developmental states: South Korea, Singapore and Taiwan. These three states represent a particular type of developmental state characterised by an authoritarian political system.[2] All three developmental states emerged out of the desire of authoritarian regimes for political survival in the post-war period (Castells

[1] Studies have argued that other economic forces such as globalisation and industrial upgrading can also weaken the interventionist state. For a general discussion on the impact of these economic forces on the developmental state, see Weiss (2000), Wong (2004), Beeson (2004), and Stubbs (2009). However, as the impact of globalisation and industrial upgrading equally affected the post-war East Asian economies, they thus cannot explain the divergent transformation outcomes of the developmental state across the region. These alternative sources for the transformation of the developmental state will affect the testing of my arguments as they will be excluded through the research design (see the second part of the chapter).

[2] The concept of the 'developmental state' is broad (for a detailed discussion on the concept of 'developmental state', see Haggard 2018). The developmental state I refer to in this paper is a very specific kind of model characterised by an authoritarian political system. It does not include the post-war Japanese developmental state which was governed

1992). Studies have shown that they have had very similar trajectories in terms of directing economic development programmes. Under the leadership of authoritarian governments, the three economies kicked off their rapid economic growth following a switch to an export-led growth model in the early 1960s, pushed for industrial upgrading in the late 1970s, and have embarked on a new post-industrial stage of leading knowledge-intensive, innovation-driven industrial development since the early 2000s (Wade 1990; Haggard 1990; Amsden 1989; Huff 1995; Wong 2011).[3] However, a close examination of the transformation outcomes reveals that transformation processes were significantly varied in these countries. Since the early 1990s, while some analysts have attempted to describe the decline of the developmental state, other analysts have depicted its resilience.

From these divergent narratives arise a series of questions. Why did the South Korean developmental state already show signs of decline even before the country's democratic transition in the late 1980s (E.-M. Kim 1997; Moon 1994)? What led to its rapid decline in the early 1990s, which subsequently resulted in the country's economic disaster during the 1997 financial crisis (Minns 2001; Y.-T. Kim 1999; Heo and Tan 2003; Clark and Jung 2002)? Why did the Korean developmental state manage to achieve a temporary revival in the post-crisis period despite the continuation of the transformation of the developmental state (Cherry 2005; Y.-T. Kim 2005; Hundt 2014; S.-Y. Kim 2018)? Why did the Taiwanese developmental state managed to retain its leadership role in the economy in the 1990s and shelter the country from the financial crisis (Heo and Tan 2003; Tan 2001; Chu 1994; Clark and Jung 2002)? What has caused the rapid decline of the developmental state in the 2000s (Wu

by a democratic political regime. This type of developmental state model emerged in post-war Taiwan, South Korea and Singapore, whereas Southeast Asian countries (e.g. Malaysia, Thailand and Indonesia) never developed the same kind of economic institutions (Doner et al. 2005). Another case that qualifies as per the developmental state model is post-Mao China.

[3] Revisiting the role of the state in more nurturing advanced emerging industries, Wong's (2011) study shows that the developmental state model has proven to be less effective in promoting innovation-driven growth than previous learning-based catch-up growth in all three case countries. It is worth noting that this study does not concern whether or not the developmental state model is effective in generating economic growth. What I am concerned about is if the developmental state model still functions in terms of leading the development process.

2007; Tan 2008, 2009; W.-W. Chu 2011; Lee and Chu 2008; Thurbon 2020)? While these two states have 'mutated into something different' one after another (Y.-P. Chu 2006: 147), the Singaporean developmental state remains in 'good health' (Clark and Chan 2004: 51; Yeung 2005). Despite the belief that the transformation of the developmental state is inevitable, how did the Singaporean state manage to strengthen its position in society and embark on new economic projects (Pereira 2008)?

The experiences of the East Asian developmental state in recent years pose two empirical puzzles for East Asian specialists. The first puzzle concerns the variation in the transformation of the developmental state across the region. Why did some East Asian developmental states transform more rapidly than others despite similar levels of socioeconomic development? The second puzzle concerns the variation in the transformation of the developmental state in one single country. Within national borders, why did the transformation of the developmental state occur more noticeably during some historical periods than others despite a country's consistent performance in socioeconomic transformation? The puzzling variations in the transformation of the three typical East Asian developmental states require an explanation. What lies behind these variations is the main topic that this book addresses.

My overarching argument is that the variations in the transformation of the developmental state have been produced by various levels of policy constraints imposed on the state as it emerges from a state-led developmental process. To account for variations in the levels of policy constraints, I turn to two variables, industrial structure and democratic transition, both of which are shaped by the strategic consideration of the ruling elites. Characterised by three types of indicators—domestic private capital concentration (DPCC), foreign direct investment (FDI) and state-owned enterprises (SOEs), the industrial structure of a country shapes the levels of policy constraints generated by business and labour interests. Playing an even more important role in transforming the developmental state, the democratic transition or the lack of democratic transition of a country affects the political context in which the state's economic policy-making occurs.

Having addressed the main research puzzle of the book, I now turn to literature on the developmental state and its transformation. I will first contend that existing studies lack an explanation for the variations in the transformation of the developmental state. I then offer a theory to account for variations in the state's transformation processes. Finally, I discuss how the empirical evidence presented in the book tests my theory.

Revisiting the Developmental State Model and Its Transformation

What Is the Developmental State Model?

Literature on the developmental state is plentiful. Overall, the main task of studies of the developmental state is to attribute the impressive economic performance of the region to the role of the state in directing overall economic development. Therefore, the thesis of most literature is that the economic development of East Asian countries has been a state-led development process. With consistent commitment to national economic development programmes, highly coherent and autonomous states have been the determining influence in economic decision-making and thus the major forces shaping capitalist development in those countries.

Broadly speaking, literature on the institutional and political profile of the developmental state consists of two important components, in two stages. Ever since Chalmers Johnson (1982) first coined the concept of capitalist developmental state to describe the Japanese state, this notion has been extended by other scholars to the states in Taiwan, Korea and Singapore, and, to some extent, Hong Kong (Wade 1990; Amsden 1989; Haggard 1990). Although individual studies vary in their degree of complexity, the core thesis stresses the state as a unified actor with a cohesive bureaucracy and relative autonomy from social classes (Johnson 1987; Amsden 1989; Wade 1990). In order to link the role of the state in the economy to the economic growth of a country, a key question that developmental state scholars address is how the state engineers the kind of rapid industrialisation that we have seen in East Asia. The answer is the powerful statist arrangements that ensure the strength of the state in directing economic development (Johnson 1982, 1987; Wade 1990, Amsden 1989). The literature's heavy emphasis on the institutional strength of the state in the directing economic development is consistent with Alexander Gerschenkron's (1962) notion that the aggressive intervention of the state in the market provides a necessary thrust to promote economic growth in order to overcome economic backwardness in late-developing countries.

Establishing the theoretical linkage between a country's political institutions and economic performance, scholars have argued that the strength and comprehensiveness of the state's influence in the economy, stemming from statist institutional arrangements, are essential for the state's effective formulation and implementation of growth-promoting industrial policies. In the words of Ziya Onis (1991: 112), state influence in the form of industrial policy is supported by 'specific political, institutional, and organisational arrangements pertaining to both the state apparatus and private business as well as their mutual interaction'. In short, early studies on the developmental state propose that the statist institutional arrangements seen in East Asia produce a kind of state autonomy that can insulate state policy-making from societal pressure in the development process. Such efforts have led some scholars to argue that state institutions in the form of state policy and influence 'should now be accepted as the single most important determinant of East Asian economic miracle' (Appelbaum and Henderson 1992: 23).

While early studies of the developmental state focused on the strength of the state as a key explanatory variable for economic growth, more recent studies of the developmental state have argued that the existence of an autonomous state alone is not a sufficient condition for the operation of the state policy process. It should be noted that early literature emphasising the 'dominance/insulation hypothesis' has resulted in a rigid dichotomy of the state and society, as well as an incomplete conceptualisation of state-society relations (Doner 1992; Moon and Prasad 1998). Pointing out that there are limits to the early statists' depiction of the state as an autonomous entity in developing countries, several scholars have shifted their attention from state strength to state-business relations to explain the success of state policy intervention in newly industrialised countries (NICs). In other words, the existence of an autonomous state alone is not a sufficient condition for the operation of the state's policy-making process. In the words of Linda Weiss (1998: 48), 'What makes the policies so effective is a particular kind of state structure and a particular kind of relationship between the state and industry'.

Three scholars have provided further theoretical support for the state-business relations approach (Evans 1995; Weiss 1995; Chibber 2003). Peter Evans' theory of 'embedded autonomy' represents the first major effort to place state-society relations at the centre of the developmental state model, explaining the effectiveness of the state's policy process to engineer rapid economic growth. While agreeing with early developmental state scholars that state autonomy is important to the ability of the East Asian state to formulate and implement growth-promoting policies without interference from societal interests, Evans (1995) argues that a particular form of the state-business relationship, one in which the state can maintain a dominant role, is also important to effective policy-making during the development process. Evans (1995: 59) stresses that, in order for the state to be developmental, the autonomous state is necessarily 'embedded in a concrete set of social ties that binds the state to society and provides institutionalised channels for the continual negotiation and renegotiation of goals and policies'. In the words of Evans (1995: 12), 'Only when embeddedness and autonomy are joined together can a state be called developmental'.

Linda Weiss further elaborated on Evans' concept of 'embedded autonomy'. Similar to Evans, Weiss (1995: 612) explains that 'East Asian bureaucracies have on the whole been effective coordinators because they have used their insulation from special-interest constituencies to develop more encompassing networks'. As a result, the developmental state 'converts its autonomy into increasing coordinating capacity by entering into cooperative relationships with the private sector in order to enhance the effectiveness of its economic and industrial policies'. Weiss' (1995) idea of 'governed interdependence' emphasises both the importance of the state's leadership in the development process, and the cooperation between the state and the private sector. She argues that such 'governed interdependence' requires three institutional ingredients: transformative goals, a pilot agency, and institutionalised government-business cooperation. As she later writes (Weiss 2003: 247), 'In the absence of the first two criteria, the state lacks an insulated coordinating intelligence and is vulnerable to capture by special interests. In the absence of the third, the state also lacks the embedded (quasi-corporatist) quality of effective policy design and implementation, and is vulnerable to information blockage and policy failure'.

The importance of a form of state-led state-business cooperation for the state's effective policy intervention is even more explicit in the work of Vivek Chibber. Comparing India with South Korea, Chibber (2003) believes that effective government intervention in the economy relies on a country's success in 'installation of the developmental state'. Like Evans and Weiss, Chibber (2003) believes that state strength alone is not a sufficient condition for the success of an effective state policy process, noting that, 'having the autonomy to put the institutions in place was not sufficient for success; for this (state-business relations), the facts internal to the state, on which much of the literature has focused, were of great importance...The antecedent autonomy garnered by the alliance with business was necessary for the state-level processes to be effective'. To Chibber, 'Critical conflicts for building state capacity occur not within the state but between the state actors, particularly the capitalist class' (Chibber 2003: 9). Thus, what made South Korea different from India was the ability of the Korean state to harness a leading segment of the business class in its developmental agenda.

In sum, the essence of the developmental state is a type of state-business alliance in which the state can play a leadership role in formulating national economic strategies and incorporating the business class into an overall development plan. Why, then, does the effectiveness of such state-business alliance s for state economic policy-making inevitably decrease over time? The following section reviews what we already know about the transformation of the developmental state and how this study can advance existing theoretical discussions on the subject.

Existing Studies on Social Forces and the Transformation of the Developmental State

Before I advance my own arguments, it is necessary to review how existing literature explains the emergence of various socioeconomic actors that shape the developmental state, and accounts for variations in the transformation of the developmental state. I contend that studies on the transformation of the developmental state have focused on either one specific period of time or a specific single country, and therefore have overlooked variations across the East Asian region.

Single-Case Studies of the Transformation of the Developmental State in South Korea and Taiwan

Several scholars have attributed the transformation of the developmental state to the evolution of the relationship between the state and businesses in the development process (Moon 1994; E.-M. Kim 1997; Y.-T. Kim 1999, 2005; Cherry 2005). Two studies, focusing on the shifting balance of power between the state and chaebols (big businesses) in South Korea, have already suggested that the decline of the developmental state occurred in the 1980s (Moon 1994; E.-M. Kim 1997). Both studies argue that, with the advent of a more open economy and political system, businesses in Korea have become more assertive politically in order to advance their interests. Yun Tae Kim (1999) focuses more explicitly on the evolution of state-business relations, arguing that the processes of democratic transition and financial liberalisation significantly eroded the power of the state and enhanced the political influence of businesses, which, in turn, led to the decline of the developmental state in Korea. Looking to this structural reform, two recent studies focusing on the evolution of the state-business relations in the post-1997 financial crisis period further confirmed the transformation of the developmental state in South Korea by highlighting the continuing antagonism between the new government and the chaebol owners in the state policy process (Cherry 2005; Y.-T. Kim 2005).

These studies provide detailed descriptions of the evolution of the relationship between the state and the chaebols in South Korea in the 1980s and 1990s. Clearly, the rise of chaebol owners' policy influence provided scholars with strong empirical evidence for suggesting that the decline of the developmental state was a result of the ending of state-dominated state-business relations.

Yet the evolution of this state-business relationship during the process of economic development and democratic transition reflects only one part of the transformation of the East Asian developmental state. A number of studies have examined the institutional changes occurring to the developmental state as a result of social pressure from two major social actors—business elites and organised labour (E.-M. Kim 1993; Minns 2001; Pereira 2008; Tan 2008, 2009; Lim 2009, 2010). However, they have all focused on a single case and have not offered theoretical guidance to explain variations in the transformation of the developmental state across the region.

Eun Mee Kim (1993) examined the decline of the developmental state in the case of South Korea, focusing on its transition from a comprehensive to a limited state, due to internal contradictions within the developmental state as well as external pressures. She argues that if the goals of the developmental state were finite—with successful economic development, i.e. successful attainment of its primary goal—the developmental state is likely to face pressure to curtail its functions and decrease its size. State policies for industry and labour repression promoted strong chaebols and intensive labour activism in South Korea. With the rise of these two groups of social actors, business elites and organised labour, the Korean state became constrained in directing overall economic development. As Kim (1993: 239) writes, 'The task of the comprehensive developmental state in the transition process is to choose between the divergent economic orientations put forward by capitalists and labourers, or to find a way to accommodate the demands of both groups'.

For Kim, both neoliberal economic reform and political democratisation contributed to the rise of business elites and organised labour in South Korea. Kim argues that on the one hand, the demand of labourers and capitalists for market-orientated reform (i.e. reprioritising industrial policies, economic liberalisation and internationalisation) directly led to the weakening of the state's control of the economy. She reasons that, 'Although the demand of capitalists and labour differed significantly, they both wanted the state to alter its old method of managing and controlling the economy (Kim 1993: 238)'. On the other hand, democratisation further complicated the process, because 'the breakdown of an authoritarian regime and the ensuing democratic consolidation led the state to seriously consider the demands of all of the various groups in society. The developmental state is thus put in a quandary, mediating between capitalists' demand for a protectionist government and labour's demand for a welfare state' (Kim 1993: 242).

John Minns (2001) offers another empirical examination of the decline of the developmental state in South Korea. He argues that the decline of the Korean developmental state was the result of the rise of various class forces, whose demands and intrusion into politics undermined the autonomy of the state. Similar to Eun Mee Kim, Minns points out that the increasingly assertive working class and capitalists had challenged the Korean developmental state since the 1980s, but he further highlights a second kind of social force emerging from development—the democratisation movement. In the words of Minns (2001: 1035), 'Throughout the late 1970s and until the democracy declaration of 1987, an uneasy alliance had been developing between the middle-class opposition and the growing working-class movement'. Together, these two types of social forces resulted in the decline of state autonomy and the 1997 financial crisis. Minns (2001: 1038) dismisses international factors concerning pressure from the US as an adequate explanation for the rapid decline of the developmental state model in South Korea, focusing instead on the significance of three socioeconomic actors—labourers, capitalists and the middle class—in shaping the developmental state since the 1980s:

> First, there is the problem of timing. The retreat of the state began under Chun in the early 1980s—during Reagan's "New Cold War"—a time when the US State Department still placed great importance on defending the military frontier between the two Koreas. Second, this formation fails to give sufficient importance to the domestic interests which have their own reasons for challenging the power of a relatively autonomous developmental state. In different ways, workers, sections of the middle classes and the bourgeoisie did so. Each had their own, quite distinct, reasons for wanting an end to the type of state that had operated in the 1960s and 1970s. US and other international pressure may well have played a part in tearing down whatever was left of the kind of state power over which Park presided. But the job had already been largely carried out by South Korean themselves.

Studies by Alexander C. Tan and Haeran Lim explore the impact of democratisation on the state's capability to govern the economic reform processes in South Korea and Taiwan. Examining institutional changes to the state's policy-making in the 2000s, Tan (2008: 161) argues, 'The political democratisation process has also forced the democratisation of the economic decision-making process. The opening of the economic decision-making sector empowered interest groups and other relevant social actors. Consequently, the increase in the number of actors has led to the reduction in the policy choice set of the government'. While Lim echoes Tan's assertion that democratisation weakens the autonomy and efficiency of technocratic bureaucrats, he also suggests that democratisation led to two other institutional consequences: firstly, democratisation strengthened the political power of big businesses as regular elections increased election costs, which reshaped the connections between the government—and political parties—and corporations; secondly, democratisation increased the oversight power of legislative branches of the government over the bureaucracy, which resulted in political constraints (Lim 2009, 2010).

These studies provide theoretical guidance to understand the transformation of the developmental state. While neoliberal liberalisation facilitates the transformation of the developmental state by strengthening the power of capitalist class, political democratisation weakened the political foundation of the developmental state (Kim 1993; Minns 2001). Drawing from examples of economic reform in South Korea and Taiwan, scholars have provided detailed analysis on how democratisation processes have resulted in political constraints on the state policy process (Tan 2008;

Lim 2009, 2010). But why did the same effect as occurred in Taiwan in the 2000s not occur in the 1990s, despite the country's 1986 democratic transition? Compared with the South Korean and Taiwanese cases, why did the same processes not occur in the case of Singapore?

Studies Focused on the Variations in the East Asian State's Transformation

The current literature on the transformation of the developmental state has tended to focus on single case studies, most notably on South Korea, where the rise of chaebols gave rise to both strong business elites and a working class that undermined the effectiveness of the traditional state-business alliance in the development process.[4] Little attention has been paid to the variation of the developmental state's transformation throughout East Asia. South Korea and Taiwan, for example, have both undergone democratic transition and economic liberalisation since the 1980s; but the developmental state in South Korea had a rapid transformation after 1987, while the developmental state in Taiwan was slower to transform. What, then, can account for this variance?

Several scholars have noticed such differences between the two cases (Clark and Jung 2002; Heo and Tan 2003). To explain why the two states had such divergent developmental processes, Clark and Jung (2002) explored the rationale behind their performance during the 1997 Asian financial crisis. They find that the states had disparate development strategies. The South Korean state gave rise to strong business actors (i.e. the chaebols), while the Taiwanese state consciously nurtured small businesses. This difference set Taiwan apart from South Korea during the Asian financial crisis of 1997. Whereas the emergence of the chaebols significantly altered the state-business relations in South Korea, Taiwan's lack of strong, giant firms allowed the state to retain its dominance over the private sector (Clark and Jung 2002). These variations led to wildly different performances in 1997. As Cal Clark and Changhoon Jung write, while South Korea fared poorly during the crisis, 'Taiwan's political

[4] A newly published article entitled 'State-Led Development Reconsidered: The Political Economy of State Transformation in East Asia since the 1990s by Henry Yeung (2017) offers a comparative overview of the transformation of the developmental state resulting from the rise of socioeconomic forces. Although Yeung's study notes the internal divergence within the three cases (South Korea, Taiwan and Singapore), he provides no explanation for the sources of these empirical divergences in developmental East Asia.

economy made it less vulnerable to the Asian financial crisis and allowed the state act decisively in the response to the challenge' (Clark and Jung 2002: 36).

The most theoretically developed scholarly efforts to account for variations in the transformation of the developmental state come from Uk Heo and Alexander C. Tan. Adopting an interest-group perspective, Heo and Tan (2003) compared South Korea and Taiwan's state policy-making. They argue that these policy choices resulted in either a concentrated or dispersed industrial structure, which in turn, produced concentrated or dispersed economic interest groups. The strength of these interest groups to shape state policy-making has impacted the transformation of the developmental state. Heo and Tan point out that the South Korean government's decision to promote the chaebols led to the development of concentrated economic interest groups, which greatly weakened the institutional capacity of the state. In contrast, the Taiwanese state's choice to nurture SMEs led to the development of dispersed economic interest groups which produced a relatively low level of policy constraints on the state's policy-making process.

Heo and Tan's study directs me to link the transformation outcome of the developmental state with the pressure of various of interest groups and the state's policy choices. However, the studies bring up many questions. Firstly, can the degree of capital concentration alone be sufficient to explain the variation? If so, how can we explain the low policy constraints on the state policy process in Singapore, where the economy has been dominated by large-sized multinational companies (MNCs) and government-linked companies (GLCs)?

While Korean and Taiwanese specialists have attempted to explain the decline of the developmental state, Alexius A. Pereira (2008) has proposed a class model to explain its resilience in the region. Utilising a class-relation perspective, Pereira argues that the rise of the capitalist class and working class can challenge the state's dominance in society, thereby forcing the developmental state to retreat from the developmental process. In the case of Singapore, he argues that the resilience of the developmental state was a result of the continued weakness of the domestic capitalist class and the state's successful incorporation of labour in the development process. In his opinion, the developmental state 'need not necessarily devolve, if they can continue to provide economic growth as well as to carefully "manage" class relations in society' (Pereira 2008: 1198). Pereira's study therefore indicates that the state-business and state-labour relationships are key to understand the resilience of the developmental state. He does attempt to address the 'exceptionalism' of the Singaporean developmental state in his conclusion, noting briefly that it is different from other cases of East Asian developmental states in two ways: the presence of transnational capital and controlled organised labour; and the lack of an affluent and autonomous middle class.[5]

The discussion thus far suggests that the existing literature offers insufficient theoretical guidelines to understand the variation in the transformation of the developmental state in East Asia; the East Asian puzzle has not been fully resolved. The search is still open for a theory to account for the variations across the cases of authoritarian developmental states in the region.

The Theory: Economic Interests, Democratic Transition and Policy Constraints

My theory will advance the existing framework offered by Heo and Tan (2003) to account for the outcome of the state's transformation process. Like Heo and Tan, I trace the variation in the state's transformation to the historical period in which the state emerged. My theory will also make two theoretical advancements. First, I will demonstrate how two types of capital ownership—FDI and SOE—can lead to the emergence of a type of non-constraining economic interest groups that does not produce constraints on the state's policy-making. Second, in addition to business and organised labour, the middle class also plays an important role in transforming the developmental state by forcing East Asian ruling elites to change the political environment in which the state's policy-making occurs. In this section, I will develop a theory to account for the developmental state's transformation process.

The Rise of the Developmental State and the Formation of the Industrial Structure of a Country

Studies have traced the formation of the developmental state model to the political survival of East Asian regimes. As Manuel Castells (1992)

[5] These two points were also emphasised by him during a private conversation in July 2015.

argues, the East Asian developmental state, with the exception of Japan, was born out of the need for survival in a period of political uncertainty in these countries. According to Castells (1992), both internal and external political pressure are crucial for understanding the emergence of the developmental state model in East Asia. Internally, East Asian regimes lacked popular political support and had extremely weak social bases. Externally, the political regimes faced existential challenges from sources abroad.[6] The combination of internal and external threats, according to Castells (1992: 59), motivated these political regimes to 'shape their states around the developmental principle of legitimacy on the basis of specific political projects that had, in each case, specific political subjects, all of which were created in rupture with the societies they were about to control'.

How exactly did this combination compel East Asian ruling elites to create the developmental state model? Richard F. Doner et al. (2005) have argued that economic institutions for state policy-making emerged from the challenges of East Asian ruling elites to deliver side payments to restive popular sectors. In this sense, ruling elites' strategy for political survival has been characterised by the state's promotion of rapid economic development through aggressive policy intervention to achieve performance-based legitimacy. To explain why the adoption of this strategy was inevitable, Doner et al. (2005) argue that East Asian ruling elites face so-called systematic vulnerability when 'the provision of such payments is rendered difficult by security threats, which siphon revenues into the defence sector, and by resource limitations, which impose hard budget constraints'. Thus, the only way that the ruling elites can achieve political survival is by 'continuously expanding the national pie through sustained growth, yet without pursuing a cheap-labour, "race to the bottom" strategy that could alienate coalition members' (Doner et al. 2005: 331).

Based on these works, we can now conclude that the adoption of a combination of political control and economic promotion is a typical strategy of East Asian ruling elites to achieve regime survival. This survival

[6] The three developmental state cases—South Korea, Singapore and Taiwan—all faced challenges from external sources. In Taiwan, the KMT regime was confronted by the military threat of Communist China. In South Korea, there was a consistent threat from the North Korean regime. In Singapore, following its separation from Malaysia, the political regime was surrounded by hostile Southeast Asian neighbours.

strategy requires the creation of two types of political institutions: authoritarian institutions that can impose political control in a country and an economic policy-making agency that can direct overall national economic development (Castells 1992). Both institutional components are crucial for the political survival of the ruling elites. The creation of a series of coercive institutions within an authoritarian system allows the ruling elites to maintain control if they enjoy limited popular support from society. Such political coercion alone, however, is insufficient for power consolidation of the ruling elites beyond a short period of time. Long-term consolidation depends on elites' ability to generate economic growth in order to meet the material expectation of a society that has been politically repressed. In the words of Doner et al. (2005: 331), 'The key to the NICs' robust economic institutions lie in how popular sectors have been compensated for their political marginalisation'.

These two types of political institutions form the institutional basis of the developmental state. The core policy-making agency plays an important role in spearheading the development process and making sure that the country is moving to achieve its economic goals. Leading a highly competent and disciplined economic bureaucracy staffed by the best managerial talents available, a policy-making agency is capable of directing the national economic development programme of a country (Wade 1990; Amsden 1989; Johnson 1982, 1987). The Council for Economic Planning and Development (CEPD) in Taiwan and the Economic Planning Board (EPB) in South Korea were examples of such an agency (Wade 1990; Johnson 1982, 1987). The authoritarian corporatist types of political institutions result in a kind of state autonomy that allows the bureaucracy to have sufficient protection and authority to take initiative in policy-making and operate effectively (Johnson 1987; Wade 1990). This plays an important role in creating the situation in Chalmers Johnson's (1982) view that the politicians 'reign' while the bureaucrats 'rule'. As a result, these highly-capable economic bureaucrats are able to resist pressure for rent-seeking from the private sector and take long-term perspectives on the development process (Onis 1991).

How can a strong state convince local industrialists to form a state-directed state-business alliance for economic development? Alexander Gerschenkron's notion of late development provides the starting point to understand how a state-dominated state-business alliance can be formed once the state-led development process is launched. According to Gerschenkron (1962), centralisation of economic resources carried out by the state is a prerequisite for overcoming economic backwardness through initiating state-driven catch-up growth. The control of finance is a typical practice in the developmental state (Woo 1991). The ability of the ruling elites to exercise selectivity in allocating financial resources lets the state easily gain an upper hand during interactions with business elites.

In East Asia, the Taiwanese state pursued an SME-focused growth strategy that led to low DPCC in the country, while the South Korean state increased DPCC through the promotion of chaebols, and the Singaporean state preferred the use of SOE and FDI instead. This begs the question: Why did these states, despite their similar statist institutional arrangements, adopt such divergent policy choices during the development process? The answer will require an understanding of the political motivations behind these choices.

The ruling elites' policy choices originate from the domestic threat facing them—the lack of popular support and legitimacy. Heo and Tan (2003) argue that, in a developmental state, the policy preferences of the ruling elites are shaped in an institutional context that is closely affected by a polity's specific historical experience. The policy goals of the East Asian ruling elites have often been associated with these regimes' need to generate domestic political legitimacy (Tan 2001; Chu 1999a). The creation of statist institutional arrangements to ensure the state's policy-making process provides the ruling elites with useful tools to accomplish their various objectives, including non-developmental and purely political ones (Kohli 1999: 133). For this reason, state policies generated within the state institutional context are closely tied to the political preference of the ruling elites to consolidate their political power, expand social support and assure political survival.

Now I turn to how the state's policy choices affect the industrial structure in terms of DPCC, FDI, SOE. Through the allocation of financial resources, state policy can shape the percentage of DPCC and SOEs in an economy (Fields 1995). These policies influence the degree of DPCC by either restricting or promoting the role of private enterprises this resource allocation, which either leads to dense capital concentration among a few private enterprises, or, if there is a lack of financial support from the state, can cause widespread capital dispersion across the economy. A major principle of the developmental state is that it commits to the development of the private sector (Onis 1991). Therefore, SOEs can supplement private enterprises but cannot replace them, indicating a negative association between DPCC and SOEs because the allocation of financial resource to SOEs would naturally restrict the growth of domestic private capital. As for FDI, the third type of foreign private capital, its availability can substitute the country's need to develop domestic private capital. In other words, the state's promotion of FDI would inevitably crowd out the presence of domestic private capital in an economy.

The Transformation of the Political Foundation of the State: Elite Decisions and Democratic Transition

Economic Development and Democratic Mobilisation

A major part of the transformation of the developmental state is the process of the country's democratic transition. The rise of two pro-democratic social classes accompanied by structural socioeconomic transformation is a driving force of this political process. The first is the middle class; Seymour Martin Lipset argued that economic development cultivates a sizeable middle class that holds democratic values and supports democracy. According to Lipset (1959), such positive linkage between development and democracy is a result of two structural processes. Firstly, economic development associated with increases in wealth, industrialisation, urbanisation and education facilitate the diffusion of democratic values among the sizeable urban middle class. Secondly, wealth creation gives rise to a sizeable middle class who would 'develop longer time perspectives and more complex and gradualist views of politics' (Lipset 1959: 78). Barrington Moore (1966) argued that members of the middle class (bourgeoisie) are pro-democratic due to their great desire to protect their material interests from the state. Diamond (2008) also stress the democratic aspiration of the economically well-off and politically sophisticated new middle class, who acts as an internal agent for democratisation in rapidly industrialising countries.

The second class is the working class. Rueschemeyer, Stephens and Stephens (1992) examine how the development process animates the class consciousness of the working class to collectively challenge the existing political structure of a country. Emphasising the role of the working class in democratisation, Rueschemeyer, et al. (1992: 59) argue that 'the relative size and the density of organisation of the working class—of employed manual labour outside of agriculture are of critical importance for the advance of democracy'. As they further explain, capitalist development 'enlarges the urban working class at the expense of agricultural labourers and small farmers; it thus shifts members of the subordinate classes from an environment extremely unfavourable for collective action to one much more favourable, from geographical isolation and immobility to high concentration of people with similar class interests and far-flung communications' (Rueschemeyer et al. 1992: 58). Rueschemeyer et al. (1992) attribute the consistent interest of the working class in demanding democratic change to their historical subordination in society and the fact that this class was more insulated from the hegemony of dominant classes than the rural lower classes.

In contrast with the perception of the working class as consistent democrats, some studies have suggested that the middle class are contingent democrats in the development process. Suggesting the contingent nature of the middle class, Moore (1966) pointed out that the middle class, emerging from the development process, only pushes for democratic transition to advance its own perceived class interests. Similarly, Rueschemeyer et al. (1992) argue that the middle class is not always a potential democratic coalition partner of the working class in the process of economic and political development, noting that the middle class can take the lead in the struggle for democracy, with an often still small working class playing a secondary role. As they write, 'Even professionals and entrepreneurs may play a significant role, provided that they see their interests sufficiently protected and anticipate gains from a more inclusive democratisation' (Rueschemeyer et al. 1992: 60). However, if they start feeling threatened by popular pressure under a democratic regime, the middle class will turn to support an authoritarian alternative.

Given the above literature review, we can also conclude that the middle class and the working class represent very different kinds of social actors in the process of economic development and democratic transition. On the one hand, the working class are consistent democrats due to their subordinated roles in capitalist political economies (Rueschemeyer et al. 1992). On the other hand, the middle class are contingent democrats who push for democratic transition in order to achieve their own political inclusion, but will oppose democratic transition and support the authoritarian state if their perceived class interests are undermined by popular political pressure. (Moore 1966; Rueschemeyer et al. 1992).

How can the emergence of the two social classes turn into a democratisation movement? While economic development gives rise to powerful social classes, what motivates a movement for the establishment of a liberal democracy during the development process is the idea of liberalism itself. Ruth B. Collier (1999: 34) argues that an early pattern of democratisation consisted of liberal projects that 'were typically pursued by middle-sector groups'. As Collier (1999: 34) reasons, 'Excluded from political participation, these groups adopted a liberal agenda in their fight to gain their own political inclusion and to oppose the hegemony and dominance of the political privileged traditional elite and/or corporate groups'. The work of Gregory M. Luebbert (1987, 1991) also indicates how the middle class and the working class can be mobilised by liberal elites around the ideas of liberal democracy. As Luebbert (1987: 453) explains, 'In these societies, the bourgeoisie gained a dominant position, through the vehicle of liberal parties, before workers mobilised autonomously. In societies that were becoming pluralist, working class unions and parties gained access to the state through collaboration with the liberal community'. Clearly, the idea of liberal democracy advocated by liberal elites makes democratic transition highly attractive to both the bourgeoisie interests and labour interests. Consequently, with the leadership of liberal elites, democratic coalitions supported by either, the middle class alone or a cross-class alliance between the working class and the middle class become possible.

However, the liberal community is not always united in rapidly industrialising societies. In societies where the liberal movement is divided, a Lib-Lab strategy becomes highly unlikely. Luebbert (1991) notes that the division within the liberal community is a result of preindustrial cleavages (e.g. conflicts of national territory, religion, the centre versus periphery, the city various the country, and divisiveness of national communities) at the time of mass mobilisation. In his words, 'These divisions within the liberal community generally reflected the incompleteness of nation-state formation before industrialisation' (Luebbert 1987: 458). As liberal interests are unable to lead the democratisation movement, labour interests have to fight for their own class inclusion in a political economy. Luebbert therefore argues that, in the face of limited opportunities to gain influence through alliance with bourgeois interests, arguments for class-based worker organisations are made more compelling. Consequently, 'Liberalism was empirically refuted by the political and labour-market experiences of workers (Luebbert 1987: 459)'. According to him, the outcome is a high level of class consciousness, radicalisation and polarisation in these societies. That is to say, disgruntled workers are likely to resort to political mobilisation through more radicalised channels.

This literature imparts three important lessons. Firstly, economic development animates both the middle class and the working class for democratic transition. Secondly, while the middle class are contingent democrats, the working class are consistent democrats. Thirdly, a strong liberal community can mobilise both bourgeoisie interests and labour interests in democratic transition based on the idea of liberal democracy; however, the liberal community is not always united. When we turn our attention to the state-led development in East Asia, we find significant variations in the formation of democratic mobilisation patterns between the middle class and the working class. To explain the emergence of different patterns of democratic mobilisation during state-led development, I formulate my first hypothesis:

Hypothesis 1 The state-led development process can give rise to four patterns of democratic mobilisation: (1) middle class-led democratic mobilisation; (2) mobilisation of a cross-class alliance; (3) working class-led democratic mobilisation; and (4) the absence of democratic mobilisation.

The hypothesis contains four patterns of democratisation mobilisation of social classes. In the first two scenarios, as economic development empowers the social classes, liberal elites receive an enormous amount of bottom-up support and energy from a rapidly industrialising society. Firstly, when liberal elites can mobilise both the middle class and the working class around the idea of achieving a liberal democracy, the middle class and the working class form a democratic coalition against an authoritarian state. Secondly, when the mobilisation of the working class is hindered by structural factors which cause the dispersion of domestic labour forces, only the middle class are mobilised by liberal elites to push for greater democratic rights. In the third scenario, the liberal community remains divided due to certain preindustrial cleavages. In this case, while the working class become highly radicalised in pursuit of their own class inclusion, the middle class as contingent democrats are likely to take a pro-authoritarian position and side with the existing regime in order to protect their own material interests from labour pressure. Finally, the last scenario is one in which the liberal elites cannot mobilise either of the social classes. Economic development therefore does not always automatically shift the balance of power between the state and society towards society.[7] In this last case, the authoritarian state remains

[7] This possibility does not indicate that economic development fails to empower society. The point is that economic development does not automatically lead to democratic

the dominant power despite rapid socioeconomic transformation. Consequently, both the middle class and the working class remain inactive in demanding greater democratic rights due to the high risk of participating in democratisation movements.

Elite Adaptation, Regime Transition Outcomes and Institutional Constraints

This section explains how these different patterns of democratic mobilisation lead to one of two outcomes for regime transition: democratic transition and non-democratic transition. Central to this process are the strategic decisions made by East Asian ruling elites. Mancur Olson (1993) argues that when authoritarian rulers can no longer retain a dominant position in a country, democratic transition becomes a political strategy of the ruling elites to prolong their political power through power sharing. To explain why the process of democratic transition occurs in some cases but not others, we must understand the strategic calculations of East Asian ruling elites in response to the various patterns of democratic mobilisation. How do the four different patterns of democratisation pressure highlighted above prompt ruling elites to make adaptive choices to achieve maximum political power? Table 1.1 highlights three strategic decisions of East Asian ruling elites: democratic concession, authoritarian repression, and authoritarian co-optation.

Table 1.1 Democratic mobilisation patterns and elite choices

		The middle class	
		Yes	*No*
The working class	Yes	Ruling elites' decision: initiate democratic transition	Ruling elites' decision: Authoritarian repression
	No	Ruling elites' decision: initiate democratic transition	Ruling elites' decision: Authoritarian co-optation

changes. Authoritarian rulers are certainly not passive actors in the process of economic development and democratisation. It is possible that authoritarian rulers can weaken and even break the linkage between socioeconomic development and democratisation by controlling a set of activities in a society. This point appears in the work of Bruce Bueno de Mesquita and George W. Downs (2005).

Based on these potential strategic decisions, I formulate my second hypothesis:

Hypothesis 2 Four patterns of democratic mobilisation prompt the ruling elites to make three strategic decisions: (1) democratic concession; (2) authoritarian repression; and (3) authoritarian cooperation. These strategic decisions lead to three regime transition outcomes, respectively: (1) transition to democracy; (2) reproduction of a repressive authoritarian government; and (3) transformation towards a responsive authoritarian government.

The left-hand side of the table indicates that when a significant number of the middle class are mobilised by the opposition elites, the strategic decision of the ruling elites is democratic concession regardless of the attitude and participation of the working class. As their old legitimacy formula no longer enables them to control the country, ruling elites are highly incentivised to adapt to the new political environment by initiating democratic concession. The result is the emergence of a liberal democratic system.

The right-hand side indicates that when the working class is highly mobilised for democratic transition while the middle class supports the authoritarian rule, the ruling elites will choose authoritarian repression, i.e. repressive measures to restore public order and maintain social stability. When neither of the social classes is willing to challenge the political status quo, the ruling elites choose authoritarian co-optation. The primary target of the co-optation strategy is the affluent and educated middle class, who are likely to become increasingly assertive towards the authoritarian regime. Consequently, the political system of the country transforms towards a more responsive type of authoritarian system.

A crucial process within democratic transition is the introduction of elections. The work of Carles Boix (1999) provides useful insights to understand the strategic calculation of the ruling elites to introduce democratic elections. Boix (1999) argues that the ruling elites change electoral rules to maximise their political representation in parliament in the face of electoral threat. This strategy is pursued in accordance with the following rule: 'As long as the electoral arena in which they compete is stable and the electoral system serves them well, the ruling parties have no incentives to modify any electoral norms. A sudden transformation of the electoral market and a corresponding increase in the degree of uncertainty are likely to trigger a change in the electoral regime' (Boix 1999: 621).

The level of democratic reform allowed by the ruling elites is closely related to how much electoral threat the ruling party expects to face in a democratic environment. Boix (1999) argues that the degree to which the ruling parties decide to modify the current electoral rules depends on the extent to which the latter undermine the formers' political viability in the new electoral arena. This, according to Boix (1999), is a function of two main conditions: the strength of the new parties; and the capacity of the old ruling parties to coordinate among themselves to block the growth of new parties.

Boix's insights suggest two possible scenarios for adaptation by authoritarian rulers. First, if the new party commands high levels of electoral support, the old ruling party is highly incentivised to initiate a thorough democratic reform because it acknowledges that its electoral dominance has come to an end. In this case, a series of institutional changes to introduce competitive elections are needed to ensure maximum political representation of the old authoritarian party in the state decision-making process. Second, when the new party does not pose any electoral threat to the ruling elites, the authoritarian structure of the country will remain unchanged. As the authoritarian ruling elites can clearly still benefit from the existing political arrangements, it would be irrational for them to pursue a strategy of democratic transition to prolong their political power.

Boix's work offers historical guidance to explain the pace of democratic transition in developmental Asia.[8] During the elite-negotiation process, East Asian ruling elites are likely to face a certain degree of electoral threat from opposition elites. This is because of two factors. As new opposition parties emerge as credible political rivals, they are generally more liberal and progressive and thus capable of mobilising pro-democratic middle-class voters. Additionally, in the past, authoritarian institutions ensured the political dominance of the ruling elites. With the decision to end authoritarian rule, the ruling elites do not possess any effective tools to contain the growth of opposition parties. East Asian dominant parties

[8] In this study, the area of developmental state covers Northeast Asia (excluding Mongolia) and Singapore. The concept of 'developmental Asia' is introduced in the work of Slater and Wong (2013) which include several newly-industrialised Southeast Asian countries.

are highly adaptable to new political situations associated with their electoral decline (Friedman and Wong 2008). It is therefore highly desirable for Asian ruling elites to adopt some forms of adaption in response to the possibility of losing elections. The introduction of competitive democratic elections—a form of most basic democratic electoral rules—would allow Asian ruling elites to ensure their maximum political representation in the democratic politics of a country. This point leads to my third hypothesis:

Hypothesis 3 :Ruling elites introduce democratic transition in response to an electoral threat posed by opposition elites.

One potential outcome is that the ruling elites delay the introduction of democratic electoral rules if they expect to retain electoral dominance.[9] If they still benefit from the existing political system, they have no incentive to change the rules. The other outcome is that ruling elites opt for a rapid democratic transition if they can no longer command a high level of electoral support. In this case, an immediate introduction of democratic electoral institutions allows them to ensure maximum representation in the state decision-making process.

The nature of the political regime provides the foundation for the state's policy-making process. The strategic decisions of the ruling elites will undoubtedly influence the transformation of the developmental state, as their pursuit of either authoritarian co-optation or authoritarian repression reinforces the authoritarian structure of the state, while their offer of democratic concession s results in the transformation of the political system. The strengthening of the authoritarian structure allows the ruling elites to single-mindedly pursue their old political strategy of performance-based legitimacy. In contrast, the advent of democratic elections provides ruling elites with the motivation to pursue a form of political legitimacy that is built on the principle of democratic competition, representation and accountability. Consequently, their political survival becomes entirely dependent on their ability to achieve electoral success in a free and fair political environment.

[9] With economic legacies created during the rapid period of industrialisation, it is possible that the old authoritarian rulers will retain their electoral dominance despite the rise of a democratisation movement if they manage to undermine the electoral strength of the opposition.

These institutional changes instantly transform the political context in which the state policy process occurs. The outcome of democratic transition can create the political conditions for the emergence of a new set of institutional constraints on the state's policy-making process. This is because democratic transition alters the logic of the state-led development (Wong 2005). In the new political environment, the political consolidation of the ruling elites has to be achieved through a new form of legitimacy that is built on the democratic principles of competition, representation and accountability. This is not to say that performance-based legitimacy becomes irrelevant for the political consolidation of the ruling elites; the ruling elites will still be held accountable for the economic performance of the country. However, single-minded promotion of the economy is no longer sufficient for ensuring their hold on political power.

As the context of state policy-making changes during a democratic transition, ruling elites face *institutional constraints* from the increasing political influence of two groups of social actors. The first group is business elites, who supply political financing to the ruling elites. Ruling elites will rely on their financial support in order to win the next election; thus, the bargaining power of business elites in state policy-making in the developmental process increases (Lim 2009). The second group is the middle and working class es, who make up the majority of voters and will directly determine the political fate of the ruling elites. Consequently, the desire to please voters is likely to push the ruling elites to abandon their long-term policy-making perspective in order to serve their short-term political victory.

The Emergence of Policy Constraints Imposed by Economic Interests

International Trade, Economic Interest Groups and Structural Constraints

The development process also forms powerful interest groups around economic policy-making, who in turn produce a set of structural constraints on the state's policy-making process. The driving force behind their emergence is the functioning of international trade activities within the process of economic development in the fast industrialising countries. Ronald Rogowski (1989) suggests that international trade unevenly affects the material interests of three types of societal actors—business actors, labour actors and land-owning actors—in any given economy. These disparate effects inevitably produce numerous winners and losers within each economy. Rogowski suggests that consequently, societal actors desire to defend and advance their material interests in the development process, motivating the formation of societal coalitions to push trade policies in a direction they deem favourable. As these societal actors share common interests and policy preferences, they will 'devise mechanisms that can surmount the obstacles to collective action' (Rogowski 1989: 5). In short, it is the economic situations of factor owners unevenly affected by trade that incentivise societal actors to form economic interest groups along class lines to shape the state's trade policies in their favour.

Do these economic interest groups intend to shape the economic decision-making process of the state in the development process? According to Rogowski (1989: 5), the trade-driven economic development process politically empowers societal actors who 'enjoy a sudden increase in wealth and income'. Rogowski (1989) explains that, when international trade expands, owners of locally abundant factors in each country assert themselves more, while owners of scarce factors become defensive. To understand who is empowered by the development process, it is important to identify the abundant factor owners in each economy. According to Rogowski (1989), while the level of the economy determines a country's endowment of capital, a country's endowment of two other factors—land and labour—is determined by the land-labour ratio. In the East Asian developmental state, which relies on an adequate supply of labour to sustain labour-intensive manufacturing, labour as a factor endowment is clearly abundant while land is scarce. With this in mind, economic development pursued by the developmental state inevitably results in the political empowerment of two kinds of societal actors—capitalists and workers—which is to say, almost the entire urban industrial sector. At the early stage of development, trade expansion would politically empower labourers who subsequently become assertive in the country. At a later stage of development, both capitalists and workers become politically assertive. Thus, at an advanced level of economic development, we expect to see both capitalists and labourers benefit from the increase in wealth and income brought by trade expansion and therefore seek to expand their political influence in the domestic political process.

Given the above review, I consider international trade as a major factor to understand the emergence of economic interest groups in the fast industrialising countries. With the economy closely connected to global trade activities, the development process inevitably creates winners and losers who are incentivised to form class-based domestic coalitions to defend their material interests. At the same time, export-driven growth and a focus on international trade can eventually result in the political empowerment of both labourers and capitalists in fast-industrialising East Asia. As capitalists and labourers seek to defend their material states, they have greater incentive and capacity to politically challenge the state's policy-making. On the contrary, the land-owning classes, who are concentrated in the agricultural sector, are the only victims of such development process and will become defensive. Given the fact that they are largely dispersed within the economy and co-opted by the state, it is unlikely that they will mobilise limited financial resources to challenge the state's economic decision-making.

This process explains the source of the emergence of structural constraints from business elites and organised labour in developmental East Asia. What remains to be answered is, how can these groups gain access to the state policy process? According to Peter Gourevitch (1986), the effective implementation of all policy decisions requires compliance or even enthusiasm from countless individuals who work, invest or buy. Therefore, politicians' choices are constrained by the need to mobilise or retain support. In the words of Gourevitch (1986: 238), 'Politicians sitting at the centre of state decision making must find support for policies from a number of actors who have varying modes of resistance or assistance at their disposal'. Ruling elites need support from both capitalists and labourers for economic policy-making. For major capitalists, their decisions to advance or withhold private investment serve as a mode to respectively, assist or resist the state. Ultimately, the economic policies of ruling elites must be supported by investment from the private sector. While capitalists' investment decisions directly affect the performance of the country, organised labour draws power from its ability to disrupt economic programmes formulated by the alliance of the state and business in the development process.[10]

The emergence of *structural constraints* occurs when the interests of business elites and organised labour can shape the state's decision-making. Given that policy-making within a developmental state is insulated by the authoritarian political system, the democratic transition can facilitate the

[10] As the state has an absolute monopoly over the use of violence, it can suppress the ability of organised labour to resist state policy decisions. In a democratic context, there is a clear limit on how far the state can go in deploying its security apparatus against organised labour.

entry of business and labour interests into the state's decision-making process. Democratic transition intensifies business interests for lobbying, as no one is guaranteed favourable policies from the state in a pluralist decision-making environment unless they have the ability to capture the state's attention (Kong 2004). More importantly, democratic transition also makes the state's economic policy-making process more accessible to business elites (Kim 1993; Tan 2008). Unlike business elites, though, labourers are excluded from the state policy-making mechanism by the authoritarian structure of the state during the development process (Deyo 1987, 1989). The end of authoritarian rule also allows industrial workers to defend their economic interests through organisation of independent labour unions. The emergence of labour demand consequently imposes a new set of constraints on the state-business alliance.

I have discussed how the state-led economic development process driven by rapid export expansion gives rise to both business and labour interest groups, and how they subsequently produce structural constraints on the state's policy-making process. This explains the emergence of structural constraints produced by business elites and organised labour in East Asia. Now we must tackle another question: Why are the levels of these structural constraints so divergent across the region?

Different Types of Economic Interest Groups, Different Levels of Structural Constraints

This section discusses how the state-led development process gives rise to divergent levels of structural pressure on the state policy process. We can identify different types of economic interest groups, which each have their own capabilities to influence the state's decisions. To understand the variation in these capabilities, we need to pay attention to another consequence of developmental policies—the industrial structure of the country. My hypothesis is as follows:

Hypothesis 4 The composition of the industrial structure of a country (in terms of DPCC, FDI and SOE) affects the level of structural constraints generated by business elites and organised labour.

Table 1.2 presents a summary of these various types of economic interests resulting from the variations in the composition of the country's industrial structure. As a result of economic strategies pursued by the state, there are basically six types of economic interest groups that emerge from the development process: concentrated/dispersed business interest

Table 1.2 Variations in the types of economic interest groups

	DPCC	*FDI*	*SOE*
Business elites	Concentrated/dispersed business interests	*Non-indigenous (foreign) business interests*	*State-linked business interests*
Organised labour	Concentrated/dispersed labour interests	*State-managed labour interests*	State-sector labour interests

Non-Italicised: Constraining economic interests
Italicised: Non-constraining economic interests

groups, concentrated/dispersed labour interest groups, non-indigenous business interest groups, state-managed labour interest groups, state-affiliated/linked business interest groups and state-sector labour interest groups. In this table, I stress the difference between two different kinds of economic interests, namely, constraining interest groups and non-constraining interest groups. As the names suggest, they are differentiated by whether or not they impose constraints on the state's policy-making process.

As business elites and organised labour emerge as economic interest groups, the specific types of group directly affect their capabilities to influence the state's policy-making process. The DPCC rate is a crucial factor in determining the ability of constraining interest groups to influence the state policy process by producing either concentrated or dispersed economic interest groups. As illustrated previously, a high degree of DPCC in the economy results in the emergence of concentrated/dispersed business interests. With a large amount of assets at stake, concentrated business interests have greater bargaining power vis-à-vis the state to push for policy change. On the contrary, a low degree of DPCC results in a high number of small business entities whose owners have neither the capacity nor desire to mobilise their limited financial resources to shape policy-making. Each firm's tiny contribution to success and equally tiny returns further reduce the incentives of individual business actors for group-based actions (Horowitz and Heo 2001; Tan 2001; Heo and Tan 2003).

A similar effect of DPCC can be found in the organisation of labourers. A high degree of DPCC results in the emergence of concentrated/dispersed labour interests. The concentration of industrial labourers makes it easy for labour unions to organise at the enterprise and national levels. If they have the strength to challenge the state-business alliance through mobilisation and industrial actions, organised labour will chase their perceived material interests by challenging the state-business alliance. In contrast, the dispersion of industrial labourers resulting from a low degree of DPCC deters the development of a labour union movement, which leads to lower labour pressure on the state policy process (Horowitz and Heo 2001; Tan 2001; Heo and Tan 2003).

Based on the above discussion, there is a clear relationship between DPCC and structural constraints. The proportion of DPCC corresponds with the levels of structural constraints generated by business elites and organised labour. The higher the level of DPCC, the greater the structural constraints imposed on the state's policy-making process.

The impact of FDI and SOE on structural constraints from business elites and organised labour is largely negative. I will first discuss the emergence of structural constraints from business elites. Both FDI and SOE can cultivate non-constraining business interests. The amount of FDI signifies the presence of foreign investors in the economy. Given that it is relatively easy for foreign investors to move their assets across borders, the state has a greater desire to look after the interests of these non-indigenous business interests by developing mutually beneficial relationships with them. Since the economic desires of foreign investors are well looked after by the state, these investors are not inclined to jeopardise this relationship by engaging in activities to shape state development agendas. For this reason, unlike the collaboration between the state and indigenous private investors, which is likely to run into conflict over respective interests, the cooperation between the state and foreign investors is more likely to last in the development process. Similarly, SOEs also have a negative effect on the emergence of business interests in the economy. A direct consequence of the presence of SOEs is state-appointed business leaders. In most cases, these business leaders are highly trusted confidants of the ruling elites. They are therefore likely to play the role of watchdog of the state in the state policy process. Furthermore, the presence of both non-indigenous/foreign and state-linked economic actors replaces the need for the ruling elites to rely on indigenous capitalists in the private sector. Consequently, indigenous private business interests lack any basic bargaining power to demand policy change.

What about the impact of FDI and SOE on the structural constraints from organised labour? FDI negatively affects these constraints, as rather high levels of FDI facilitate the emergence of a type of non-constraining labour interests—state-managed labour interests. The state's task of attracting FDI requires a favourable environment for investment, which must be achieved by bringing labourers into a sort of corporatist arrangement with the state and capitalists in the development process. Only when the state achieves this incorporation of organised labour can labour interests be carefully managed in accordance with the state's development goals. The amount of SOE leads to the emergence of state-sector labour interests. In the process of economic development, it is important to distinguish labour interests organised in the SOE sector from those in the private sector. Compared to industrial workers in the private sector, they often have a different set of economic concerns given their unique status as workers employed by the state. When SOE workers organise, they are likely to pursue their own material interests which are fundamentally different from that of private-sector workers. Thus, the presence of a large number of SOE workers in the economy can undercut the overall structural constraints from organised labour in a country.

Based on the above discussion, the proportion of FDI and SOE in an economy is negatively associated with the levels of structural constraints generated by business elites and organised labour. The higher the proportion of FDI and SOE, the lower the levels of structural constraints imposed on the state's policy-making process.

The Structure of the Theory

The primary objective of this study is to account for the variations in the transformation of the developmental state. I define the transformation of the developmental state as a process in which a reduction of the state's capability in formulating growth-promoting industrial policies occurs. Such transformation undermines the state's capacity to direct industrial development. I consider that the transformation of the developmental state is evident in institutional changes that occur to the state's policy-making process. Institutional changes can occur in three aspects of the state policy mechanism, that is, the state's strategic vision, state-led state-business cooperation and labour policy subordination. Institutional changes occurring to the state's strategic economic vision concern the reduction in the state's capacity to formulate overall economic programmes for industrial upgrading.[11] Institutional changes occurring to state-business cooperation indicate erosion of the capacity of the state to play a leadership role in its collaboration with the private sector. Institutional changes occurring to policy subordination of organised labour suggest an increase in the bargaining power of organised labour in a development process generally directed by the state-business alliance.

Transformation of the developmental state will therefore occur when at least one of the following three conditions are present: (1) the state's strategic vision is impaired; (2) the state loses the capacity to dominate the cooperation with the private sector; and (3) organised labour is able to obstruct the formulation and implementation of state economic decisions.

How does the transformation of the developmental state occur? The transformation of the state's policy-making mechanism involves the emergence of state policy constraints by three types of social actors—business elites, organised labour and the middle class. An illustration of the transformation of the state policy mechanism is shown in Fig. 1.1. There are two types of state policy constraints: structural constraints (the two straight lines) produced by business elites and organised labour; and institutional constraints (the two curved lines) generated by business elites and the middle class. However, such structural constraints can only occur after democratic transition (the blue dashed line) has taken place in a country. The emergence of these policy constraints results in the remaking of the state's policy mechanism between the state and three groups of social actors: (1) institutional constraints produced by the middle class affect the state's strategic vision; (2) policy influence of business elites is determined by both the institutional and structural constraints from business elites; and (3) policy influence of organised labour is exclusively the result of structural constraints from organised labour.

My basic arguments for explaining the variations in the transformation of the developmental state are presented in this model. My logic begins a

[11] The formulation of coherent overall economic development programmes has been examined by statists (e.g. Wade 1990; Amsden 1989; Haggard 1990). The formulation of state strategic vision in East Asian NICs from the early 1990s onwards has not been the centre of scholarly attention. This study will provide an examination of the formulation of the major national economic agendas of three East Asian states (South Korea, Singapore and Taiwan) since the early 1990s. My empirical chapters will demonstrate both coherent and eroded/impaired state strategic visions in these economies in recent decades.

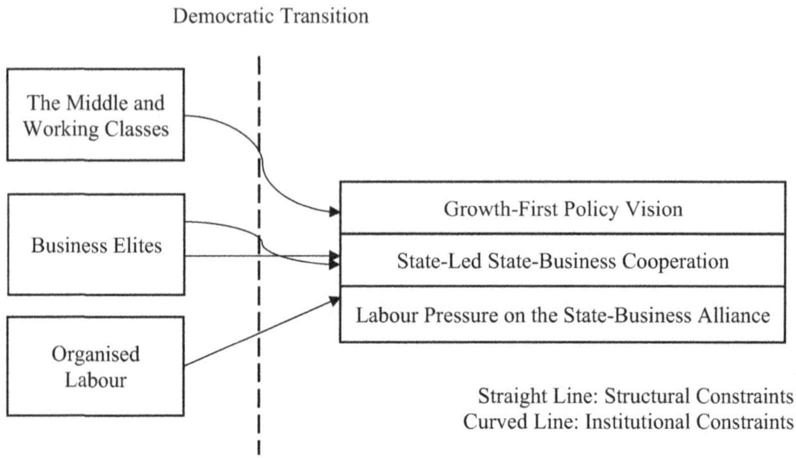

Fig. 1.1 Transformation of the state policy mechanism

dynamic understanding of the developmental state.[12] The very successes and processes promoted by the developmental state lead to two political processes: (1) the emergence of business and labour interests; and (2) the emergence of the middle and working class es. These two socioeconomic and political processes result in the emergence of both economic and political interest groups in the development process (see Fig. 1.2). I include business elites and organised labour into a group called economic interest groups. These social groups can produce policy constraints on state policy-making. I also regard the middle class and the working class as political interest groups.[13] These groups can push the political system of a country to evolve, which in turn transforms the political foundation of the developmental state. The functioning of both political processes—the rise of economic interest groups and the emergence of political interest groups—leads to the transformation of the developmental state.

[12] I will provide detail theoretical justification for the dynamic understanding of the developmental state in Chapter 2.

[13] The two political interest groups (i.e. the middle class and the working class) form nearly an entire society.

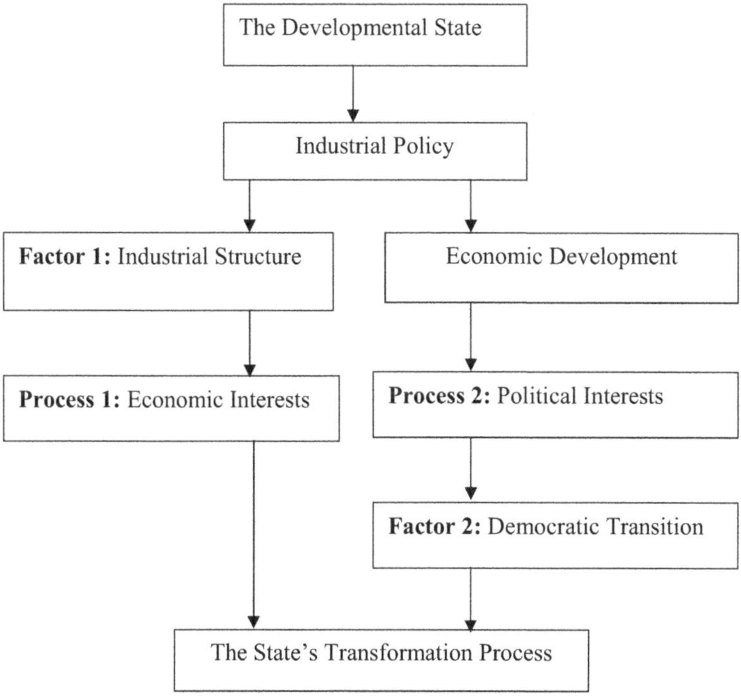

Fig. 1.2 The structure of the main argument in this study

The dynamic understanding of the developmental state is the first step in unravelling the puzzle concerning variations in the transformation of the developmental state. The second crucial step for solving the puzzle is to account for the variations of two factors—industrial structure and democratic transition outcome—which are closely linked with the two political processes (see Fig. 1.2). While industrial structure can influence the emergence of economic interest groups during the development process, democratic transition is a direct consequence of the emergence of political interest groups. The functioning of these two factors produces variations in the state's transformation process. In the previous sections, I have offered an explanation in regard to how different types of economic interest groups are created by the industrial structure of a country (Factor 1) and how different outcomes of democratic transition (Factor 2) are generated by the emergence of different patterns of democratic mobilisation.

Research Design and Case Selection

The detailed empirical chapters of the book illustrate my theory in three cases: South Korea, Taiwan and Singapore. These three cases exhibit significant variations in the states' transformation processes. I indicated previously that variations were exhibited not only across the country cases but also within the cases of South Korea and Taiwan. The cases show three distinctive outcomes of the transformation of the developmental state: the rapid transformation of the developmental state in South Korea; the non-transformation of the developmental state in Singapore; and the two-phase transformation of the development in Taiwan.

The Taiwan case represents a two-phase transformation of the developmental state. In the 1990s, the state still retained most of its developmental capacity and a central role in a few strategic areas such as the financial sector (Tan 2001; Heo and Tan 2003; Clark and Jung 2002). In the post-2000 period, however, evidence seems to suggest that the Taiwanese developmental state could no longer direct the development process (Wu 2007; Lee and Chu 2008; W.-W. Chu 2011). The Singapore case represents a case of non-transformation of the developmental state. Unlike the other East Asian developmental states, the Singaporean developmental state has shown no sign of transformation and appears to be strengthening its position in society by embarking upon several recent economic programmes (Pereira 2008; Yeung 2005). The Korean case, in contrast, demonstrates a case of rapid transformation of the developmental state. The decline of the developmental state was also clear in the early 1980s (E.-M. Kim 1997; Moon 1994). The 1990s witnessed a complete transformation of the developmental state, which was vividly demonstrated by the collapse of the country's financial system in 1997 (Heo and Tan 2003; Minns 2001; Y.-T. Kim 1999). Despite some signs of revival after the financial crisis, the developmental state never fully recovered its lost transformative capacity (Cherry 2005; Y.-T. Kim 2005; Hundt 2014).

The empirical chapters show how the two factors of industrial structure and democratic transition have shaped the states' transformation processes. Each empirical case consists of three components: (1) how the state's industrial structure (in terms of DPCC, FDI, and SOE) has affected the emergence of economic interests; (2) how elite decisions shaped the (non-) democratic transition; and (3) how the interaction of these two processes has led to the transformation of the developmental state.

Empiric #1: The Emergence of Economic-Interests Constraints and the Process of Democratic Transition

The first and second components involve testing my two major theoretical hypotheses concerning the emergence of interest-group pressure and the process of democratic transition. The three empirical cases constitute a test of the effect of the industrial structure of a country on the levels of structural constraints generated by economic interests. In the case of South Korea, the state-led development process resulted in an industrial structure featuring a high level of DPCC. In the case of Taiwan, an industrial structure characterised by a much lower level of DPCC and high level of SOE was formed by the end of the 1970s. These two types of industrial structures are two extreme cases to demonstrate my claim that the percentage of DPCC corresponds with the levels of structural constraints generated by business elites and organised labour.

The South Korean case demonstrates how the emergence of concentrated economic interests leads to a high level of structural constraints, while the Taiwanese case shows how the emergence of dispersed business and labour interests, and state-sector labour interests, contributes to a low level of structural constraints. The Taiwanese case also contains an internal variation. The level of DPCC increased significantly due to a process of privatisation initiated in the late 1980s and accelerated in the 2000s. This transformation of the country's industrial structure shows the emergence of more concentrated business interests following the formation of a higher percentage of DPCC that resulted in a much higher level of structural constraints from business elites.

In contrast to both South Korea and Taiwan, the case of Singapore saw a high accumulation of non-domestic non-private capital in the form of FDI and SOE as a result of the domination of MNCs and GLCs in the economy. The Singaporean case demonstrates why FDI and SOE are the two types of capital ownership that can negatively affect the structural constraints from business elites and organised labour. To show this relationship, I will demonstrate how the emergence of non-indigenous and state-linked business interests, and state-managed labour interest groups led to the weakness of both business elites and organised labour to influence the state's economic policy-making.

The empirical chapters also offer an empirical testing of my hypothesis concerning a country's democratic transition. There are both external and internal variations on the processes of democratic transition across the three cases (see Table 1.2). In South Korea, the first regime transition took place in 1980 in response to growing demands for democracy. The outcome of the political transition was not democratic transition but a reproduction of another military dictatorship. A rapid democratic transition finally occurred in 1987 when the first direct democratic presidential election was held. In comparison, Taiwan's democratic transition took place over a much longer period. Direct presidential elections did not occur until 1996. In Singapore, the political system remains authoritarian and no significant move has been made by the government towards democratic transition.

These varied experiences of democratic transition provide empirical bases for testing my hypotheses. I select the cases of South Korea in 1980, South Korea in 1987, Taiwan in 1986 and Singapore to test the hypothesis concerning different elite decisions in response to different patterns of democratic mobilisation. I compare external variations between South Korea in 1987 and Taiwan in 1986, as well as internal variation between Taiwan in 1986 and Taiwan after 1989, to verify the assertion that an electoral threat posed by opposition elites incentivises East Asian ruling elites to introduce democratic elections.

There are still rival explanations for ruling elites' decision to democratise a country's political system. It is often argued that external geopolitical factors such as pressure from the 1988 Olympics and public pressure from the US government forced South Korean ruling elites to carry out democratic reform (see Fowler 1999). Domestic social cleavage (i.e. regional cleavages) is also believed to have contributed to the ruling elites' strategic decision to democratise the political system (Kwon 2004).

The internal variation within South Korea eliminates social cleavage as a variable to account for elites' decision to initiate democratic transition. Regionalism was a constant factor in South Korea, yet ruling elites made different choices in 1980 and 1987. An argument can also be made that a divergence in external factors such as pressure from the 1988 Olympics and public pressure from the US government between 1980 and 1987 resulted in the discrepancy in strategic choices. The case of China, the largest developmental state in Asia, indicates that external geopolitical factors do not necessarily correlate with East Asian elites' decision to initiate democratic transition. My empirical analysis will identify that the democratic mobilisation of the middle class is the variable determining ruling elites' decision to end authoritarian rule.

Alternative explanations for elites' decisions to introduce democratic elections include both external and internal factors. These explanations seem effective in understanding variations between South Korea and Taiwan, specifically that the US military presence in South Korea might have put the Korean ruling elites under greater pressure to introduce democratic elections. It could also be argued that the scheduled 1988 Olympics produced more constraints for Korean ruling elites to delay the introduction of democratic elections. Furthermore, domestic regional cleavages may have incentivised the Korean ruling elites to push forward with the country's democratisation process. Yet none of these factors can explain Taiwan's internal variation. In the following section, I will demonstrate how Taiwanese ruling elites' interest to introduce democratic elections corresponded with the levels of electoral threat s they faced.

Empiric #2: Explaining the Transformation of the Developmental State

The other major part of my empirical analysis covers changes to the state's policy-making. I will show that the transformation of the developmental state is a result of the interaction of the emergence of interest-group pressure and the process of democratic transition. Table 1.3 describes how the causal mechanism works in each of the three cases. I consider that the transformation of the developmental state occurs when societal interests shape the state's policy choices. In determining whether the state policy process is influenced by societal interests, I look for evidence in the outcomes of the state's policy-making that can suggest if these policies were reformulated to appeal to any certain societal. Institutional changes can occur in three aspects of the state policy mechanism, that is, the state's strategic vision, state-led state-business cooperation and labour policy subordination.

I will further explain these three aspects of the transformation of the developmental state. Institutional changes occurring to the state strategic vision concern the reduction in the state's capacity to formulate coherent economic programmes for industrial upgrading. Institutional changes occurring to state-business cooperation indicate erosion of the capacity

Table 1.3 The process of the state's transformation in three comparative cases

	The emergence of interest-group pressure	*The process of democratic transition*	*The state's transformation process*
South Korea	Ruling elites' policy choice: promoting domestic capital concentration DPCC: High – > concentrated economic interests – > high policy constraints	1980: A working-class-led democratisation movement – > ruling elites' decision: authoritarian repression 1987: A cross-class alliance – > ruling elites' decision: democratic transition A high level of an electoral threat—ruling elites' decision: immediate introduction of democratic elections	Rapid transformation after 1987
Singapore	Ruling elites' policy choice: substituting domestic private capital FDI and SOE: High – > Non-Constraining economic interests – > no policy constraints	An absence of democratic mobilisation – > ruling elites' decision: authoritarian co-optation	No sign of the state's transformation
Taiwan	Ruling elites' policy choice: restricting domestic capital concentration DPCC: Low – > dispersed economic interests– > low policy constraints	1986: a middle-class-led democratisation movement – > ruling elites' decision: democratic transition Before 1989: low level of an electoral threat – > ruling elites' decision: delay the introduction of democratic elections After 1989: Growing level of an electoral threat – > ruling elites' decision: gradual introduction of democratic elections in the early 1990s	Minor transformation in the 1990s and major transformation after 2000

of the state to play a leadership role in its collaboration with the private sector. Institutional changes occurring to policy subordination of organised labour suggest an increase in the policy status of organised labour in the development process directed by the state-business alliance. Thus, transformation of the developmental state will occur when at least one or all of the three conditions are present in the development process: (1) the state's strategic vision is impaired; (2) the state loses the capacity to dominate the cooperation with the private sector; and (3) organised labour is able to obstruct the formulation and implementation of state economic decisions.

Organisation of the Book

Chapter 2 explains the transformation of the developmental state in South Korea. The chapter first examines the formation of a highly concentrated industrial structure shaped by the political calculations of the Korean ruling elites. It then shows the process of democratic transition in South Korea. Two processes are examined: (1) the democratisation movement pushed by the working class without the support of the middle class, which led to a repressive military regime in 1980; and (2) the formation of a cross-class alliance that led to rapid democratic transition in the late 1980s. In this section, I test the hypotheses about ruling elites' decision to end authoritarian rule in response to the democratic mobilisation of the middle class, as well as ruling elites' decision to introduce democratic transition in response to an electoral threat. I then examine the transformation of the developmental state in three respects. First, democratic transition undermined the state's ability to prioritise growth-first economic agendas. Second, the high rate of DPCC can give rise to the formation of concentrated economic interest groups that have the capacity and strength to shape the state's policy-making process. This set of structural constraints, coupled with institutional constraints from business elites, led to a rapid decline of the state's leadership role vis-à-vis business elites. Similarly, the high rate of DPCC also gave rise to concentrated labour interests that were capable of producing policy constraints on the state's economic policy-making.

Chapter 3 concerns the non-transformation of the Singaporean developmental state. The chapter first traces the formation of an FDI-SOE dominated industrial structure to the Singaporean ruling elites' political struggles in the 1960s. I then examine Singapore's non-democratic transition. I will show that the Singaporean ruling party pursued a strategy of authoritarian co-optation in response to the absence of a democratisation movement. The remainder of the chapter examines how the state retained its strategic positions in all three aspects of economic policy-making. Firstly, with the continuation of the authoritarian system of the country, the Singaporean ruling elites formulated overall economic strategies to ensure economic performance. Second, the country's developmental programme, which had relied heavily on the use of FDI and SOE, led to the emergence of two types of non-constraining business interest groups, i.e. non-indigenous, and state-linked business interests, which allowed the state-dominated state-business cooperation to continue. Third, the country's economic development also resulted in the emergence of a type of non-constraining labour interest groups: state-controlled labour interests. I will demonstrate that, contrary to labour interests in Taiwan and South Korea, the economic interests of the Singaporean organised labour have been strategically managed by the state throughout the development process.

Chapter 4 examines transformation of the developmental state in Taiwan. The chapter first reviews how the Taiwanese ruling elites' preference for preventing private capital concentration led to the country's initial industrial structure. I also examine how the democratisation movement, driven largely by the middle class, gradually pushed the ruling elites to introduce democratic electoral institutions between the late 1980s and mid-1990s. In this section, the two strategic decisions of East Asian ruling elites—to initiate democratic transition and to introduce democratic elections—will be tested in the case of Taiwan. The last three sections examine the state's transformation. I will show that divergences in the overall level of policy constraints occurred between the 1990s and the post-2000 period. In the 1990s, policy constraints from business elites remained low as a result of the emergence of dispersed business interests and the ruling elites' financial independence. Similarly, both DPCC and SOE deterred the structural constraints generated by organised labour. In the other aspect, the erosion of growth-first economic vision occurred in the 1990s following the country's democratic transition. While policy constraints from organised labour remained unchanged, the rise of concentrated business interests and the ruling elites' growing financial dependence on businesses resulted in strong policy constraints from business elites, and was accompanied by the state's formulation of even more politicised economic visions after the 2000 regime turnover.

Chapter 5 stresses the two theoretical contributions to the study of the transformation of the developmental state. First, different types of business and labour interest groups can emerge in a state-led development process. In particular, I categorise a type of economic interest group, 'non-constraining groups', that do not produce policy constraints on the state's economic decision-making process. Second, apart from business elites and organised labour who reshape the developmental state by directly challenging the state's economic policy-making, the middle class is a third actor that contributes to the state's transformation process by forcing ruling elites to transform the political foundation of a state. I also provide an assessment of the other East Asian developmental state which emerged in more recent decades (the 1980s and early 1990s)—China.

References

Amsden, A. H. (1989). *Asia's Next Giant: South Korea and Late Industrialisation*. Oxford: Oxford University Press.

Appelbaum, R. P., & Henderson, J. (1992). Situating the State in the East Asian Development Process. In R. P. Appelbaum & J. Henderson (Eds.), *State and Development in the Asian Pacific Rim*. Newbury Park: Sage.

Beeson, M. (2004). The Rise and Fall (?) of the Developmental State: The Vicissitudes and Implications of East Asian Interventionism. In L. Low (Ed.), *Developmental States: Relevancy, Redundancy or Reconfiguration?* (pp. 29–40). New York: Nova Science Publishers, Inc.

Boix, C. (1999). Setting the Rules of the Game: The Choice of Electoral System in Advanced Democracies. *The American Political Science Review, 93*(3), 609–624.

Bueno de Mesquita, B., & Downs, G. W. (2005). Development and Democracy. *Foreign Affairs* (online). Available at: https://www.foreignaffairs.com/articles/2005-09-01/development-and-democracy. Accessed 22 June 2017.

Castells, M. (1992). Four Asian Tigers with a Dragon Head: A Comparative Analysis of the State, Economy, and Society in the Asian Pacific Rim. In R. P. Appelbaum & J. Henderson (Eds.), *State and Development in the Asian Pacific Rim* (pp. 33–70). Newbury Park: Sage.

Cherry, J. (2005). 'Big Deal' or Big Disappointment? The Continuing Evolution of the South Korean Developmental State. *The Pacific Review, 18*(3), 327–354.

Chibber, V. (2003). *Locked in Place: State-Building and Late Industrialisation in India*. Princeton and Oxford: Princeton University Press.

Chu, W.-W. (2011). Democratisation and Economic Development: The Unsuccessful Transformation of Taiwan's Developmental State (in Chinese). *Taiwan: A Radical Quarterly in Social Studies, 84*, 243–288.
Chu, Y.-H. (1994). The Realignment of Business-Government Relations and Regime Transition in Taiwan. In A. MacIntyre (Ed.), *Business and Government in Industrialising Asia* (pp. 113–141). Ithaca and London: Cornell University Press.
Chu, Y.-H. (1999). A Born-Again Dominant Party? The Transformation of the Kuomintang and Taiwan's Regime Transition. In H. Giliomee & C. E. W. Simkins (Eds.), *The Awkward Embrace: One-Party Dominance and Democracy* (pp. 61–95). Cape Town: Tafelberg.
Chu, Y.-P. (2006). The Political Economy of Taiwan's Industrialisation: The 'Developmental State' and Its Mutinous Mutation. In Y.-P. Chu & H. Hill (Eds.), *The East Asian High-Tech Drive* (pp. 119–181). Cheltenham: Edward Elgar.
Clark, C., & Chan, S. (2004). What Can One Learn from the Asian Flu? Implications for the Developmental State. In L. Low (Ed.), *Developmental States: Relevancy, Redundancy or Reconfiguration?* (pp. 41–56). New York: Nova Science.
Clark, C., & Jung, C. (2002). The Implications of the East Asian Flu for Developmental State Theory: The Case of South Korea and Taiwan. *Asian Affairs, 29*(1), 16–42.
Collier, R. B. (1999). *Paths Towards Democracy: The Working Class and Elites in Western Europe and South America*. Cambridge: Cambridge University Press.
Cumings, B. (1999). The Asian Crisis, Democracy, and the End of 'Late' Development. In T. J. Pempel (Ed.), *The Politics of the Asian Economic Crisis* (pp. 17–44). London and Ithaca: Cornell University Press.
Deyo, F. C. (1987). State and Labour: Modes of Political Exclusion. In F. C. Deyo (Ed.), *East Asian Development in The Political Economy of the New Asian Industrialism* (pp. 182–202). Ithaca: Cornel University Press.
Deyo, F. C. (1989). *Beneath the Miracle: Labour Subordination in the New Asian Industrialism*. Berkeley: University of California Press.
Diamond, L. (2008). *The Spirit of Democracy: The Struggle to Build Free Societies around the World*. New York: Times Book.
Doner, R. F. (1992). Limits of State Strength: Toward an Institutionalist View of Economic Development. *World Politics, 44*(3), 398–431.
Doner, R. F., Ritchie, B. K., Slater, D. (2005). Systemic Vulnerability and the Origins of Developmental States: Northeast and Southeast Asia in Comparative Perspective. *International Organisation, 59*(2), 327–361.
Evans, P. (1995). *Embedded Autonomy: State and Industrial Transformation*. Princeton: Princeton University Press.

Fields, K. J. (1995). *Enterprise and the State in Korea and Taiwan*. Ithaca: Cornell University Press.

Friedman, E., & Wong, J. (2008). Learning to Lose: Dominant Parties, Dominant Party Systems, and Their Transitions. In E. Friedman & J. Wong (Eds.), *Political Transitions in Dominant Party Systems: Learning to Lose* (pp. 1–11). London and New York: Routledge.

Fowler, J. (1999). The United States and South Korean Democratisation. *Political Science Quarterly, 114,* 265–288.

Gerschenkron, A. (1962). *Economic Backwardness in Historical Perspective*. Cambridge: Belknap Press of Harvard University Press.

Gourevitch, P. (1986). *Politics in Hard Times: Comparative Reponses to International Economic Crises*. Ithaca: Cornell University Press.

Haggard, S. (1990). *Pathways from the Periphery: The Politics of Growth in the Newly Industrialising Countries*. Ithaca: Cornell University Press.

Haggard, S. (2018). *Developmental States*. Cambridge: Cambridge University Press.

Heo, U., & Tan, A. C. (2003). Political Choices and Economic Outcomes: A Perspective on the Differential Impact of the Financial Crisis on South Korea and Taiwan. *Comparative Political Studies, 36*(6), 679–698.

Horowitz, S., & Heo, U. (2001). Explaining Precrisis Policies and Postcrisis Responses: Coalitions and Institutions in East Asia, Latin America, and Eastern Europe. In S. Horowitz & U. Heo (Eds.), *The Political Economy of International Financial Crisis: Interest Groups, Ideologies and Institutions* (pp. 3–13). Landam: Rowman & Littlefield.

Huff, W. G. (1995). The Developmental State, Government, and Singapore's Economic Development Since 1960. *World Development, 23*(8), 1421–11438.

Hundt, D. (2014). Economic Crisis in Korea and the Degraded Developmental State. *Australian Journal of International Affairs, 68*(5), 499–514.

Johnson, C. (1982). *MITI and the Japanese Miracle: The Growth of Industrial Policy, 1925–1975*. Stanford: Stanford University Press.

Johnson, C. (1987). Political Institutions and Economic Performance. In F. C. Deyo (Eds.), *The Political Economy of the New Asian Industrialism* (pp. 136–164). Princeton: Princeton University Press.

Kang, D. C. (2002a). *Crony Capitalism: Corruption and Developments in South Korea and the Philippines*. Cambridge: Cambridge University Press.

Kang, D. C. (2002b). Bad Loans to Good Friends: Money Politics and the Developmental State in South Korea. *International Organisation, 56*(1), 177–207.

Kim, E. M. (1993). Contradictions and Limits of a Developmental State: With Illustrations from the South Korean Case. *Social Problems, 40*(2), 228–249.

Kim, E. M. (1997). *Big Business, Strong State: Collusion and Conflict in South Korean Development, 1960–1990*. Albany: State University of New York Press.

Kim, Y. T. (1999). Neoliberalism and the Decline of the Developmental State. *Journal of Contemporary Asia, 29*(4), 441.
Kim, Y. T. (2005). DJnomics and the Transformation of the Developmental State. *Journal of Contemporary Asia, 35*(4), 471–484.
Kim, S.-Y. (2018). Wither Developmentalism After Democratisation? In T.-J. Cheng & Y.-H. Chu (Eds.), *Routledge Handbook on Democratisation in East Asia* (pp. 457–470). New York: Routledge.
Kohli, A. (1999). Where Do High-Growth Political Economies Come From? The Japanese Linkage of Korea's "Developmental State". In M. Woo-Cumings (Ed.), *The Developmental State* (pp. 93–136). Ithaca: Cornell University Press.
Kong, T. Y. (2004). Patterns of Government-Business Relations in South Korea and the Impact of the Recent Crisis. In E. Amann & H. J. Chang (Eds.), *Brazil and South Korea: Economic Crisis and Restructuring*. London: Institute of Latin American Studies, University of London.
Kwon, K. (2004). Regionalism in South Korea: Its Origins and Role in Her Democratization. *Politics and Society, 32*, 545–574.
Lee, P.-S., & Chu, Y.-H. (2008). The New Political Economy After Regime Turnover in Taiwan: An Assessment of the First Chen Shui-bian Administration. In S. Goldstein & J. Chang (Eds.), *Presidential Politics in Taiwan: The Administration of Chen Shui-bian* (pp. 143–166). Norwalk: EastBridge.
Lim, H. (2009). Democratisation and the Transformation Process in East Asian Developmental States: Financial Reform in Korea and Taiwan. *Asian Perspective, 33*(1), 75–110.
Lim, H. (2010). The Transformation of the Developmental State and Economic Reform in Korea. *Journal of Contemporary Asia, 40*(2), 188–210.
Lipset, S. M. (1959). Some Social Requisites of Democracy: Economic Development and Political Legitimacy. *The American Political Science Review, 53*(1), 69–105.
Luebbert, G. M. (1987). Social Foundations of Political Order in Interwar Europe. *World Politics, 39*(4), 449–478.
Luebbert, G. M. (1991). *Liberalism, Fascism, or Social Democracy: Social Classes and the Political Origins of Regimes in Interwar Europe*. New York and Oxford: Oxford University Press.
Minns, J. (2001). Of Miracles and Models: The Rise and Decline of the Developmental State in South Korea. *Third World Quarterly, 22*(6), 1025–1043.
Moon, C.-I. (1994). Changing Patterns of Business-Government Relations in South Korea. In A. Macintyre (Ed.), *Business and Government in Industrialising Asia* (pp. 142–166). Crows Nest, NSW, Australia: Allen & Unwin.
Moon, C., & Prasad, B. (1998). Network, Politics, and Institutions. In S. Chan, C. Clark, & D. Lam (Eds.), *Beyond the Developmental State: East Asia's Political Economies Reconsidered* (pp. 9–24). New York: St. Martin's Press.

Moore, B. (1966). *Social Origins of Dictatorship and Democracy: Lord and Peasant in the Making of the Modern World*. Boston: Beacon Press.
Ng, I. Y. H. (2011). Workfare in Singapore. In C. K. Chan & K. Ngok (Eds.), *Welfare Reform in East Asia: Towards Workfare?* (pp. 131–148). London: Routledge.
Olson, M. (1993). Dictatorship, Democracy, and Development. *The American Political Science Review, 87*(3), 567–576.
Onis, Z. (1991). The Logic of the Developmental State. *Comparative Politics, 24*, 109–121.
Pereira, A. (2008). Whither the Developmental State? Explaining Singapore's Continued Developmentalism. *Third World Quarterly, 29*(6), 1189–1203.
Rogowski, R. (1989). *Commerce and Coalitions: How Trade Affects Domestic Political Alignments*. Princeton, NJ: Princeton University Press.
Rueschemeyer, D., Stephens, E. H., & Stephens, J. D. (1992). *Capitalist Development and Democracy*. Chicago: University of Chicago Press.
Slater, D., & Wong, J. (2013). The Strength to Concede: Ruling Parties and Democratisation in Developmental State. *Perspectives on Politics, 11*(3), 717–733.
Stubbs, R. (2009). What Ever Happened to the East Asian Developmental State? The Unfolding Debate. *The Pacific Review, 22*(1), 1–22.
Tan, A. C. (2001). Taiwan: Sustained State Autonomy and a Step Back from Liberalization. In S. Horowitz & U. Heo (Eds.), *The Political Economy of International Financial Crisis: Interest Groups, Ideologies and Institutions* (pp. 165–176). Lanham: Rowman & Littlefield.
Tan, A. C. (2008). From State Entrepreneurs to Political Entrepreneurs: Democratisation and the Politics of Financial Liberalisation. In P. Paolino & J. Meernik (Eds.), *Democratisation in Taiwan: Challenges in Transformation* (pp. 153–166). Burlington, VT: Ashgate.
Tan, A. C. (2009). The Politics of Financial Reform in Taiwan: Actors, Institutions and the Changing State. *Asian Affairs: an American Review, 36*(4), 201–212.
The World Bank. (1993). *The East Asian Miracle: Economic Growth and Public Policy*. New York: Oxford University Press.
Thurbon, E. (2020). The Future of Financial Activism in Taiwan? The Utility of a Mindset-Centered Analysis of Developmental States and Their Evolution. *New Political Economy, 25*(3), 320–336.
Wade, R. (1990). *Governing the Market: Economic Theory and the Role of Government in East Asian Industrialization*. Princeton: Princeton University Press.
Weiss, L. (1995). Governed Interdependence: Rethinking the Government-Business Relationship in East Asia. *The Pacific Review, 8*(4), 586–616.

Weiss, L. (1998). *The Myth of the Powerless State: Governing the Economy in a Global Era*. Cambridge: Polity Press.
Weiss, L. (2000). Developmental States in Transition: Adapting, Dismantling, Innovating, Not 'Normalising'. *The Pacific Review, 13*(1), 21–55.
Weiss, L. (2003). Guiding Globalisation in East Asia: New Roles for Old Developmental State. In L. Weiss (Ed.), *States in the Global Economy: Bringing Domestic Institutions Back In* (pp. 245–270). Cambridge: Cambridge University Press.
Wong, J. (2004). The Adaptive Developmental State in East Asia. *Journal of East Asian Studies, 4*(2004), 345–362.
Wong, J. (2005). Re-making the Developmental State in Taiwan: The Challenges of Biotechnology. *International Political Science Review, 26*(2), 169–191.
Wong, J. (2011). *Betting on Biotech: Innovation and Limits of Asia's Developmental State*. Ithaca: Cornell University Press.
Woo, J. (1991). *Race to the Swift: State and Finance in Korean Industrialisation*. New York: Columbia University Press.
Woo-Cumings, M. (1999). *The Developmental State*. Ithaca: Cornell University Press.
Wu, Y.-S. (2007). Taiwan's Developmental State: After the Economic and Political Turmoil. *Asian Survey, 47*(6), 977–1001.
Yeung, H. W. (2005). Institutional Capacity and Singapore's Developmental State: Managing Economic (In)Security in the Global Economy. In H. E. Nesadurai (Ed.), *Globalisation and Economic Security in East Asia: Governance and Institutions*. London: Routledge.
Yeung, H. W. (2017). State-Led Development Reconsidered: The Political Economy of State Transformation in East Asia Since 1990s. *Cambridge Journal of Regions, Economy and Society, 10*(1), 83–98.

CHAPTER 2

The Rapid Transformation of the Developmental State in South Korea

The chapter demonstrates how an industrial structure dominated by DPCC and democratic transition resulted in a rapid transformation of the South Korean developmental state, as a result of strong structural and institutional constraints created through two parallel processes. Firstly, the high level of DPCC of the country created structural constraints from both business elites and organised labour by producing concentrated economic interest groups. Secondly, South Korea's rapid democratic transition process gave rise to institutional constraints from business elites and the middle class. As a result, the state's policy-making process was increasingly constrained by various societal interests.

This chapter consists of five sections. The first section will explain the formation of South Korea's industrial structure. I will locate the source of the country's high level of DPCC as the military's intrusion into politics in the early 1960s, and then explain how the ruling elites' policy choices solidified the industrial structure. In the second section, I will examine the process of South Korea's democratic transition, in particular verifying three theoretical propositions concerning ruling elites' decisions to push for (non-) democratic transition: that a working-class-led democratisation movement compelled the ruling elites to resort to a strategy of authoritarian repression in 1980; that a cross-class alliance pushed the authoritarian rulers to pursue a strategy of democratic concession in 1987; and lastly, that the country's rapid democratic transition was a strategic choice of the ruling elites in the face of a strong electoral threat.

T. He, *The Political Economy of Developmental States in East Asia*,
https://doi.org/10.1007/978-3-030-59357-5_2

The third, fourth and fifth sections will explain how the industrial structure and democratic transition have affected the transformation of the South Korean developmental state. The third section will examine whether the state's capacity to formulate strategic visions was undermined after the late 1980s, with detailed analysis of the formulation of national development agendas under seven administrations between 1980 and 2016. In the fourth section, I will explain the emergence of high levels of policy constraints generated by business elites within the development process. I argue that while the high level of DPCC led to strong structural constraints from business elites by producing concentrated business interest groups, the rapid democratic transition also resulted in a high level of institutional constraints from these same business elites. I will analyse the similarly high level of policy constraints imposed by organised labour on the state's policy-making process in the fifth section, proving that the country's industrial structure is mainly responsible for producing such an outcome; the high level of DPCC led to the emergence of concentrated labour interest groups, which resulted in strong structural constraints from organised labour on the operation of the state-business alliance following the country's democratic transition.

How Elite Survival Shaped South Korea's Industrial Structure

The Rise to Power of a Military Regime

The external threat from North Korea certainly played an important role in compelling South Korean rulers to create a developmental state. However, the political origins of the elite choice to promote DPCC come from internal political difficulties during the 1960s and 1970s, in particular the military's intrusion into politics beginning in 1961. The period between April 1960 and May 1961 was marked by popular demand among South Koreans for total reform to break away from the corrupt and inefficient Syngman Rhee regime, and the desire for national reconstruction to modernise the nation (H.-A. Kim 2004: 64). The demand for strong leadership provided a strategic basis for Major General Park Chung-hee and his junior officers to seize power through a military coup on 16 May 1961. What followed after the coup was the formation of the Korean ruling elites' political strategy for regime survival. As Castells (1992: 61) notes, the military officers who seized power seem to have been closer to nationalist military regimes than to the mainstream Latin American pro-oligarchic military coups. In other words, the coup was generally seen as inevitable and necessary to bring about major change in Korean society. However, the nationalist actions of the coup leaders did not translate into political legitimacy for the military regime to consolidate political power. As Cole and Lyman (1971: 35) observe, although the military had reasonably good relations with the populace, they were nevertheless 'not accepted in Korean culture as an honoured group nor as an accepted source for the ruling class'.

The power consolidation of the Park regime involved extensive actions to impose political control in the country. To this end, the regime launched a huge state re-building project aimed at creating a strong and effective state, creating the Supreme Council for National Reconstruction (SCNR) to direct the reform measures that Park referred to as a 'surgical operation'. The military government made the SCNR into the state's most powerful agency, which controlled the three branches of government and dissolved the National Assembly. In order to further concentrate political power, Park banned all political parties and other non-governmental interest groups. He also banned all political activities and over 4000 politicians were prohibited from political activities for six years. To purge the bad elements of the government, Park and his associates dismissed over 40,000 members of the bureaucracy and even established a Revolutionary Tribunal that tried thousands of government officials for corruption. A large number of criminal gangs were arrested and paraded down the street. The government also put the press, which had been largely unrestricted from 1960 to 1961, under direct state control (Kim 2004; Cole and Lyman 1971).

The core of the Park regime's state structure was authoritarian in nature. One important authoritarian institution to ensuring the regime's political control was the Korean Central Intelligence Agency (KCIA), established in June 1961. The military leaders aimed to develop it into a sophisticated organisation to not only collect intelligence on external threats to national security, but also to eliminate all obstacles in the execution of the regime's revolutionary tasks (Han 2011; Kim 2011). Within just three years, Park expanded it from an initial 3000 employees to 370,000 employees (Johnson 1987: 157). As Seth (2010: 380) describes, 'Its tentacles reached into almost every school, business, and political or social organisation. It even extended overseas, where the KCIA kidnapped dissident Koreans to bring them back home for punishment and bribed foreign officials to shape policies favourable to the ROK'. This institution provided a political basis for the Korean state's economic interventions in the market. According to Kim (2011: 86), the KCIA was instrumental in establishing the powers of the Park government's key economic institutions; thus, it is 'the architect of the South Korean developmental state'.

Despite the transition to a civilian government in the 1970s, little change took place to Park's authoritarian structure. The KCIA remained in place as a main instrument of political control, which facilitated the continuation of the state's domination in the country (Kim 2011; Johnson 1987; Oh 1999). Park further increased his control through a constitutional change that strengthened the power of the executive branch of the government in 1963. The passage of the Political Purification Act also created disunity in the opposition by withholding politicians from participation in the elections, among other coercive measures (Cole and Lyman 1971: 71). Consequently, the legislature under Park remained a weak body dominated by the Democratic Republican Party (DRP), a party made up of former military officers, meaning the military maintained a strong presence in the civilian government. Cole and Lyman (1971: 69) point out that seven of the original 17 ministers and nine of the total 31 officials were former military officers. As a result, the political arrangement of the civilian government remained largely authoritarian-corporatist.

Political control alone was not enough for the ruling elites' survival. From the outset, economic development constituted the other crucial part of the coup leaders' strategy for generating political legitimacy. As Ezra Vogel (1991: 51) puts it, Park 'needed economic progress to defend his political base against those who regarded his seizure of power as illegitimate'. This point is clear following the military coup in July 1961. Shortly after the establishment of the KCIA in 1961, the coup leaders established the Economic Planning Board (EPB) to direct overall economic development.[1] However, the creation of this state economic policy-making agency did not mark the beginning of a true emphasis on growth-first principles. When the first Five-Year Economic Development

[1] The economic planning function of the EPB was absorbed into the Ministry of Finance and Economy in 1994 to form a super-ministry for directing overall economic development. The Ministry of Finance and Economy and the Ministry of Planning and Budget merged into the Ministry of Strategy and Finance in 2008.

Plan (FYEDP) was released in January 1962, it was criticised domestically for being too optimistic and unfeasible (Wolf 1962; Oh 1999: 52). What went wrong prior to 1963? Cole and Lyman (1971: 84) note that in the immediate period following the military coup, leaders were intent on projecting the image of a nationalist state undergoing nationwide reform, and could not focus as much on formulating growth-promoting policies:

> The leaders of the 1961 coup had viewed economics largely as a poorly directed part of the national structure which could, as much else in Korean life, by set quickly and dramatically on the right path. Moreover, economics was seen as one means of several towards the end of an overall political-economic entity sketched vaguely, in terms of 'purer politics', greater national independence and vigour, and improved international stature. The economic policies of the Military Government reflected these attitudes. They were often bold and designed to produce sweeping results.

Only when the transition to a civilian government occurred in 1963 did the revolutionary elements of the military government diminish, allowing for a single-minded focus on economic growth. As Cole and Lyman (1971: 85–86) observe, 'Instead of being a piece of a larger nationalistic programme of somewhat vague dimensions, as had been the case with the military government, concrete economic performance became the touchstone of political performance and economic progress'. The state's commitment to growth led to two important changes that formed the basis for better economic planning in the years to come: (1) a stabilisation programme was adopted in 1963 involving budget reductions and credit outlays, forcing a more realistic scale-back from the military government's earlier economic goals; and (2) the Joint US-Korean Economic Cooperation Committee was established to seek closer cooperation with the US on economic policy formulation (Cole and Lyman 1971: 86).

In the early 1970s, the political foundation of the Korean developmental state was reinforced as the Park regime tried to ensure political survival. By then, the original institutional arrangement designed by Park to impose political control became increasingly insufficient for the ruling elites to maintain their power monopoly. In the 1971 presidential and national assembly elections, the opposition New Democratic Party (NDP) rallied around its presidential candidate, Kim Dae-jung, in a strong challenge to the ruling party (Im 1987, 2011; Clifford 1994). In simple words, the defeat of the ruling DRP in a presidential election looked like a very real possibility. Emboldened by the opposition victory, anti-authoritarian forces including college students, the press, the judiciary, and university professors increased their demand for political autonomy (Im 1987).

As the authoritarian institutions designed in the 1960s could no longer assure the dominance of the ruling party, the ruling elites launched a second round of state institutional building. In October 1972, Park declared martial law and dissolved the National Assembly, while banning political parties and closing all colleges and universities. The following month, Park institutionalised his shift to utter authoritarianism with a national referendum that ratified the new Yushin Constitution, a notoriously repressive document that allowed dissolution of the National Assembly and appointment of one-third of its members. The election of the President was made indirect. With the ability to stage state-controlled presidential elections, Park no longer had to worry about losing elections. The new constitution essentially made Park president for life (Oh 1999: 58; Clifford 1994: 76–77; Heo and Roehrig 2010: 23).

At this point, South Korea was at the height of the state-led development process. As the Park regime rekindled their attempt to impose political control, it also accelerated industrialisation to ensure economic performance of the country. In the early 1970s, the state formulated concrete short-term and long-term economic goals. To stabilise the economy in the short-term, the Park Regime issued the Emergency Economic Decree and launched a major industrial upgrading project—heavy and chemical industrialisation (HCI) (Jones and Sakong 1980: 106–108). With a series of bureaucratic re-organisations, Park enhanced the power of the executive branch to push for HCI (B.-K. Kim 2011: 221–230; Woo 1991: 129).

Promoting Domestic Private Capital Concentration in the Economy

The above discussion explained how the coup leaders' desire for political survival gave rise to the developmental state. The state's economic policy-making consequently shaped the percentage of DPCC in South Korea. The high level of DPCC by the late 1970s was a result of two rounds of deliberate promotion.

The first round began with the launch of the industrialisation period following the military coup. In the 1960s, support from the country's largest group of entrepreneurs—the chaebol—were essential as the ruling elites geared up to accelerate export-led growth. At the time, the chaebol owners were put under arrest following the issuance of a guideline to eliminate 'illicit accumulation of wealth' during the Rhee period; this was an initial promise of the military coup (Jones and Sakong 1980: 280–281). The Park regime did not intend to punish these businessmen, rather they targeted them for two reasons. Firstly, given their military background, the coup leaders, including Park, did not know what to do about the economy. Without economic expertise, the regime's justification of the coup through economic growth was a remote dream. Secondly, originating during the Japanese colonial period, chaebols had succeeded in penetrating the economy by the end of the Rhee period. They possessed most of the country's managerial experience, economic expertise, personnel, and physical facilities, which were essential for initiating the industrialisation process (Kim and Park 2011; E. M. Kim 1988; K.-D. Kim 1976; Fields 1995: 51–52).

In short, the new military rulers saw only one option to jumpstart the economy—turning to leading entrepreneurial talents for assistance. Neither the state sector nor the SMEs were better equipped than the chaebols to assist Park in his national development programme.[2] For this reason, the ultimate objective of the Park government during the Illicit Wealth Accumulation Charges (1961–1962) was to seek the chaebols' compliance and assistance in generating growth. The issue of 'illicit wealth accumulation' (particularly the amount of fines that would need to be paid) was in fact used by the ruling elites as a leverage to force the chaebols' full-hearted participation in Five-Year Economic Development Plan (FYEDP) (Kim and Park 2011).

In August 1961, Park summoned ten major business leaders to strike a deal. As Jung-en Woo (1991: 84) reports, 'In exchange for exempting businessmen from criminal prosecution and respecting their properties whether ill or well gotten, businessmen 'paid' fines levied on them by establishing industrial firms and then donating shares to the government'. This compromise laid the foundation for cooperation between the government and the chaebols in the development process, and initiated the government's strategy of relying on chaebols to lead the country's export growth. As Woo (1991: 84) writes, 'In retrospect, this deal had the quality of an historical compromise; in any case, it occasioned the

[2] The state sector was largely corrupted and inefficient due to its close ties with the ousted Rhee regime.

launching of 'Korea Inc.' Henceforth, state and big business would share the same destiny: prosper or perish'. This strategy was deemed particularly critical in mid-1962, when Park ruled out the possibility of developing SOEs to speed up the development process through the state-controlled Korea Industrial Development Company (KIDC) because of US objections (Kim and Park 2011: 271).

As the chaebols became the main engine of the state-led development process, the promotion of export growth meant a de facto promotion of the chaebols. The initial period of export promotion and chaebol expansion was facilitated by the favourable international situation at the time; the long post-war boom in advanced Western economies and Japan provided expanding markets. The Vietnam War provided further economic opportunities in the transportation and construction industries. To maximise exports, the Park government directed generous financial resources to the chaebols, primarily state-guaranteed foreign loans with a guaranteed repayment of 90%. In this way, the government state socialised the financial risk, allowing the chaebols to finance their business expansion and diversification aggressively. To further increase exports, between 1965 and 1970, while the South Korean domestic banks' interest rates ranged from 24 to 26%, the rates on export-policy loans, many of which were provided to the foreign loan-financed chaebols, stood in the range of 6.0–6.5% (Lee 2002; Kim and Park 2011; Woo 1991; S.-J. Chang 2003).

By the end of the 1960s, the first round of chaebol promotion had already shaped the country's industrial structure. The government's aggressive financing of chaebol expansion resulted in a significant increase in the percentage of the domestic capital concentration in the economy. As Kim and Park (2011: 283) report, 'Industrial concentration had been high even before Park's big push, with 12.5% of business firms accounting for 39.8% of South Korea's total value-added and 36.6% of its total production in 1960. By 1968, however, large firms, accounting for 12.4% of South Korea's total number of business enterprises, were responsible for 65.2% of the total value-added and 64.8% of the total volume of production'. As the chaebols dominated the economy, SMEs became marginalised within the development process. In 1963, SMEs produced 58.5% of the total output in manufacturing; by 1971, their share had plummeted to 27.7% (Chiu 1992: 102). During the financial turbulence of the late 1960s, even the government had begun to show concern about the rapid expansion of the chaebols relative to the rest of the economy (Fields 1995: 53).

The chaebol-led development strategy was irreversible by the 1970s. Two factors heightened the urgency to promote the chaebols, both of which stemmed from the Park regime's desire to retain political power. Firstly, facing increasing opposition in the 1970s, the Park regime stepped up its efforts to generate rapid economic growth in order to obscure its political shortcomings. Secondly, given the increased weight of the chaebols in the nation's economy, the role of the regime in export promotion became even more closely related to the promotion of the chaebols (Kim and Park 2011; Fields 1995; Kim 1988). The regime was thus, in the words of Ku-hyun Jung (1988: 72), 'really not in a position to regulate the business groups who were the workhorses in the achievement of its economic goals'. Consequently, Park's strategy of chaebol cooperation continued in the 1970s, for example, with the announcement of the Emergency Decree of Economic Stability and Growth (EDESG) in August 1972. Although the EDESG intended to improve the financial situation of all businesses by freezing loans on the curb market, the greatest beneficiaries were the chaebols, which held 64% of the private curb-market loans. The result was that the chaebols' financial base was greatly strengthened, and their ability to exploit further business opportunities during the state's push for HCI was also significantly enhanced (Kim and Park 2011; Fields 1995; Kim 1988).

The result of the industrial upgrading of the 1970s was therefore a second round of chaebol promotion engineered by the state for maximisation of exports—the institutionalisation of a system of general trading companies (GTCs). The state granted licences to 13 GTCs, 12 of which belonged to large chaebols and only one of which was established to coordinate the export activities of SMEs. The creation of the GTCs made it even easier for the chaebols to gain access to various financial benefits such as cash subsidies tied to export volume and preferential access to foreign exchange. As a consequence, the chaebols, which already enjoyed outsize advantages in size and scope, received an additional financial boost to expand business operations. By 1979, half of the nation's exports were handled by chaebol-controlled GTCs. The government was single-minded in promoting a few chaebol-affiliated trading companies at the expense of thousands of small trading companies, which were forced out of business due to a lack of financial support (Fields 1995; Woo 1991; Kim and Park 2011).

With the state's deliberate policy support, the phenomenal growth of the chaebols consequently reinforced the country's DPCC. Table 2.1

Table 2.1 Combined sales of top ten chaebols as percentage of Gross National Product (GNP), 1974–1984

Year	*Percentage*
1974	15.1
1975	17.1
1976	19.8
1977	26.0
1978	30.1
1979	32.8
1980	48.1
1981	55.7
1982	57.6
1983	62.4
1984	67.4

Source Amsden (1989: 116)

shows a steady increase of the percentage of the combined sales of the largest ten chaebols to South Korea's total GNP from the mid-1970s to the mid-1980s. These sales accounted for 15.1% of Korea's GNP in 1974; in 1980, this percentage was 48.1%, and by 1984 it reached 67.4%. In comparison, small firms played relatively insignificant roles in domestic production. The total sale of the top 50 Korean large firms accounted for 93.8% of the country's GNP, compared to 31.7% in Taiwan (Heo and Tan 2003: 689).

Elite Decisions, South Korea's Authoritarian Reinforcement and Speedy Democratic Transition

South Korea's pathway to democracy was marked by two divergent regime transition outcomes: authoritarian enforcement in 1980 and speedy democratic transition in 1987. The reproduction of a military dictatorship in 1980 serves to illustrate a scenario in which ruling elites pursue a strategy of authoritarian crackdown when challenged by a working class-led democratic movement. South Korea's later democratic transition in 1987 was marked by the end of authoritarian rule and an immediate introduction of democratic elections, two processes that happened quickly over a period of several months. The speed of this democratic transition will serve to illustrate two of my arguments. First, a cross-class alliance formed between the working class and the middle class can force East Asian ruling elites to end authoritarian rule by initiating a democratic transition. Second, when facing a high level of electoral threat, East Asian ruling elites are greatly incentivised to introduce democratic elections.

Reproducing a Military Dictatorship in 1980

The case of South Korea in 1980 represents a situation in which East Asian ruling elites are confronted by a democratisation mobilisation of the working class. In South Korea, the democratisation movement centred on socioeconomic injustice. By the early 1970s, the state-led development had resulted in a significant socioeconomic disparity. The issue became linked with the discourse of democratic reform, as this inequality was not simply the inevitable result of capitalist development, but rather a product of political institutions that favoured a small group of elites while excluding the majority of citizens from the fruits of economic growth (Choi 1993). To challenge the regime, Korean opposition elites tied their liberal political agenda to a demand for socioeconomic justice that emerged after the 1979 Y.H. Company incident (Sohn 1989). This demand provided fertile ground for the development of a grass-roots democratisation movement—the Minjung movement (Koo 1993).

The working class and the middle class began to mobilise during the 1970s. The rise of the working class was aided by two social forces. The first was the university students who formed a labour-student alliance and championed labour rights following the tragic death of Chon Tae-il. The second was progressive Christian groups who provided space for the students and labourers to meet, organised night schools to empower labourers, and offered political protection for those involved in the labour movement (Lee 2007: 218–222). During the 1970s, the working class showed a strong willingness to challenge the authoritarian state, for example, in Pangnim Textile Company's overtime payment dispute, the Peace Market labour struggle, and the repression of the trade union at Tongil Textile Company (Sohn 1989: 132–140). In the national assembly election in 1978, the middle class displayed significant anti-government sentiment; for the first time, the main opposition party won more popular votes than the ruling party (Nam 1989: 144). As it gained more resources and strength from the development process, the Minjung movement provided it with 'an outlet for their growing dissatisfaction' with the authoritarian system (Dalton and Cotton 1996: 279).

The working class was quick to mobilise, but the success of a democratic transition was dependent on the ability of the opposition elites to bring the middle class into a cross-class democratic coalition. This coalition was not formed in 1980 because of internal conflict between the main opposition elites, Kim Young-sam and Kim Dae-jung. They had been rivals since the NDP convention in 1970, and each enjoyed their regional loyalties, which could be traced back to the three-kingdoms era and had been exacerbated by Park's imbalanced regional development strategy. There was significant ideological difference between Kim Yong-sam's 'moderate centre line' and Kim Dae-jung's 'left-of-centre' view (Cotton 1989). In 1976, this intraparty conflict was addressed by the adoption of a collective leadership model and the creation of a six-member Supreme Council consisting of various faction leaders (Nam 1989: 103). The collective leadership model, however, was abandoned in 1979, and the party remained deeply divided. Kim Yong-sam won the 1979 party election by a small margin, mostly because he enjoyed the support of Kim Dae-jung, whose regional base overlapped with Kim Young-sam's opponent (Sohn 1989: 156). After Park's death, however, as the opposition was expected to win the forthcoming election by a wide margin, open conflict escalated between the two Kims. Nam (1989: 196) describes the situation: 'The competition between the two Kims erupted into violent clashes between the followers of the men in March 1980 at various local party conventions held to choose branch leaderships. As the delegates of the two Kims confronted and clashed, regional animosities were aroused'.

The Korean case shows how the lack of a strong liberal community can lead to a democratisation movement led by the working class. The labour's class interest began to be articulated vigorously as early as October 1979 when a massive uprising had broken out in Pusan and Masan. By them, the liberal political agenda had already been seriously challenged by the establishment of a radical interpretation of social phenomena, particularly among university students. As Sohn (1989: 166) writes, 'The arguments of the students tended increasingly to contrast the interests of workers and farmers with those of a government they saw as serving only a privileged minority... This structural approach, coupled with a conception of social justice focused particularly on working people, dominated the student movement'. Such radicalisation of labour reached a new level after Park's death. Seeing the power vacuum as a rare opportunity for political liberalisation, militant students stepped up their campaign for socioeconomic justice. Beginning in March 1980, the students held on-campus demonstrations that quickly spread to the streets and lost control. As Nam (1989: 219) notes, 'Even some of the die-hard dissidents urged the students to go slow, while still agreeing with aims to liberalise campus surroundings and the country's political structure'.

Another distinct example of labour radicalisation was in April 1980, when industrial actions launched by miners and steel mill workers led to large-scale riots. These disaffected Korean workers mobilised as a group for their own political inclusion not locally organised interest groups (Lee 1981; Nam 1989). Yet as the working class become more radicalised, the middle class was unlikely to mobilise for democratic transitions. Seeing that the opposition elites were preoccupied with party realignments, while the students and workers were rioting, the middle class was increasingly concerned about social instability. As Sung-Joo Han and Oknim Chung (1993: 206) observe,

> Even though riots broke out in certain cities such as Kwangju when martial law was extended throughout the nation in May 1980, citizens began to show as much concern about the social instability and disorder accompanying the democratisation process as about its delay. Such concern became more poignant as student demonstrations intensified and after large-scale riots by miners and steel mill workers broke out in April.

The case of South Korea in 1980 confirms my hypothesis concerning East Asian ruling elites' decision to pursue a strategy of authoritarian repression in response to a democratisation movement spearheaded by the working class. General Chun Doo Hwan, the de facto authoritarian ruler after Park's death, had no incentive to concede to democracy. Instead he turned to a strategy of repression, starting from 17 May 1980, repressive measures were taken to quash social unrest and tightening political control, including the arrest of student leaders and opposition leaders, the imposition of full martial law, and the issuance of new Martial Law Decree No. 10, which restricted all political activities by closing universities, banning political gatherings and censoring publications and broadcasts. Chun was willing to do anything to restore social order; army paratroopers trained for combat with North Korea were deployed to brutally suppress a massive uprising in the southern city of Kwangju, where Chun's repression strategy was being challenged. To project an image of themselves as social reformers, the military also ordered the arrest of Park's close allies (C.-S. Lee 1981). As a result of this strategy of authoritarian repression, social and political order was restored in South Korea by the end of May.

To prolong the country's authoritarian structure, Chun introduced a new constitution in October 1980 that ruled out the possibility for a direct presidential election; this resulted in the dissolution of all political parties and of the National Assembly. Chun subsequently formed the Legislative Council for National Security to perform the legislative function of the government, effectively putting South Korea under a 'constitutional dictatorship' (C.-S. Lee 1981; Nam 1989). Chun passed a Political Climate Renovation Law that purged 567 important opposition politicians and intellectuals, banning them from playing any role in politics until 1988 (Nam 1989). The regime also cracked down on remaining student activism (C.-S. Lee 1981). The ban on political parties was lifted in November 1980 to allow for the formation of government-controlled parties to provide citizens with a false sense of political participation in the upcoming election (Nam 1989: 244).

Pursuing a strategy of authoritarian repression in response to the social unrest in May 1980 allowed Chun's regime to achieve a near monopoly of power in both the executive and legislative branches of the government. In February 1981, there was little doubt about Chun's ability to achieve a sweeping victory in the presidential election, as all he needed was a simple majority of the 5278 electoral college deputies. The legislative election in March was also an easy win for the ruling party. With severe limitations on campaign activities, a political ban on key opposition leaders, and new controls on the press, Chun's Democratic Justice Party (DJP) received 69.4% of the votes in the March legislative elections (Nam 1989; Suh 1982).

The failed democratic transition of South Korea in 1980 demonstrates how a democratisation movement led by the working class emerged in the process of state-led economic development. In this case, divisions within the liberal community and the subsequent radicalisation of the working class pushed the middle class to side with the authoritarian regime. Additionally, it confirms my argument that a democratisation movement pushed by only the working class, without a cross-class alliance, prompts East Asian ruling elites to pursue a strategy of authoritarian repression. which allows the elites to consolidate political power.

A Speedy Transition to Democracy in 1987

South Korea's speedy democratic transition in 1987 was a result of two strategic decisions by the ruling elites. The first was in response to the formation a cross-class democratic alliance, and the second was made in the context of a high level of electoral threat.

There was some, albeit limited, political liberalisation in the early period of Chun's rule. Starting in December 1983, university professors who had been dismissed from their jobs because of anti-government activities in the late 1970s were allowed to return. Students were permitted to go back to universities and military police were withdrawn from the campus. About three hundred political prisoners or 'public peace breakers' were pardoned, and the ban on political activities was lifted on 202 former politicians in February 1984 (S. Kim 2000: 80). However, the Chun regime's decision to liberalise the political system was not motivated by an intention to transform the legitimacy formula but to strengthen authoritarian power. Domestically, Chun was confident that the existing authoritarian institutions were more than sufficient to control society and allow him to pursue performance-based legitimacy. Not only would state-controlled political liberalisation improve the terrifying image of the regime, but it could also contribute to further fragmentation and fractionalisation of the opposition. Externally, Chun was keen to boost the regime's legitimacy by hosting two international sports events—the Asian Games in 1986 and the Olympics in 1988. He believed that a certain degree of political contestation and participation was essential to achieve these goals (S. Kim 2000: 80; Hsiao and Koo 1997). So when exactly did the regime decide to end authoritarian rule and begin democratisation?

The ruling elites' decision to transform the regime's legitimacy formula through democratic transition only came in 1987, when a powerful cross-class democratic alliance was formed, owing to the emergence of a strong and unified opposition party. In January 1985, some of the former opposition politicians that had been relieved from the ban on political activities established the New Korea Democratic Party (NKDP) in preparation for the forthcoming election. By then, both major opposition elites—Kim Young-sam and Kim Dae-jung—had announced that they would abandon personal ambitions to collectively challenge the power monopoly of the ruling elite (M. Lee 1990: 25). This newly formed opposition had the strong backing of a powerful political interest group—the middle class. In the National Assembly election of February 1985, the NKDP enjoyed an impressive 29.26% of the vote. Meanwhile, the DJP's share of the popular vote declined to 35.3%, down from 35.6% in 1981, and it lost three seats it had won in 1981 (Nam 1989: 301).

Intraparty squabbles did break out because of the regime's attempt to divide the NKDP. However, this was a temporary division between a minor group of opportunists—Lee Min-woo, Lee Chul-seong, Lee Taeck-hy—and the two united de facto party leaders—Kim Yong-sam and Kim Dae-jung (M. Lee 1990: 23–32). As a result, a stronger and more unified opposition liberal party emerged in March 1987, as the two Kims broke away from the NKDP and formed a hard-line opposition party, the Reunification Democratic Party (RDP), taking with them 66 of the 90 NKDP lawmakers (S. Kim 2000).

Throughout this process, the Minjung movement further intensified and gained new momentum. In March 1985, the movement's radical and moderate factions united to form the People's Movement Coalition for Democracy and Reunification (PMCDR) (S. Kim 2000; M. Lee 1990). A clear sign of the PMCDR's commitment to the establishment of a liberal democratic system was the creation of the Committee for Attaining Democratic Constitution under the PMCDR in November 1985. Under this common objective, throughout 1986, the Minjung movement and NKDP pushed for democratic transition through constitutional revision. As Sunhyuk Kim (2000: 87) notes, social pressure emerged in three distinct forms: a series of public statements and declarations from Minjung activists that chastised the authoritarian regime; a signature collection campaign by the NKDP; and a number of mass rallies organised jointly by the Minjung movement and NKDP. Simultaneously, the middle class was particularly angered by the killing of Bak Jong-cheol and Lee Han-yeol which vividly demonstrated the immoral, illegitimate, violent and repressive nature of the authoritarian regime (Hsiao and Koo 1997). As a result, unlike in 1980, the middle class realised they were better off without an authoritarian ruler and were thus incentivised to join the democratic coalition in early 1987. In the subsequent 20 days-long '6.10 struggle' in June 1987, millions of citizens all over the country demonstrated in a cross-class alliance to demand democracy and challenge the regime (Han 1988; Oh 1999: 91–93; Nam 1989: 308–309).

The formation of a cross-class alliance was thus the decisive factor that forced the regime to initiate democratic transition. That authoritarian repression was no longer sufficient to retain power became apparent when the conflict between the state and society reached a stand-off in the summer of 1987; even the military was 'unhappy with the prospects of yet again taking a direct role in politics, a role that would undoubtedly have led to severe domestic and international censure' (Cotton 1989: 253). At the height of the '6.10 struggle', Gaston Sigur, the US assistant secretary of state for Asian affairs, arrived in South Korea to warn Chun that the US would not participate in any military intervention. The US had realised that Chun's regime was doomed to fail against the mobilisation of the middle class. Sigur remarked, 'The government wasn't dealing with a handful of left-wing students. They may have been out front, but it was plain you had strong middle-class support for the demonstrations' (Gibney 1992: 87).

The effect of the democratic mobilisation of the middle class was particularly evident as presidential candidate Roh Tae-woo pursued a strategy of democratic concession in 1987. Roh's democratisation declaration on 29 June marked the regime's adoption of a new legitimacy formula, as he later stated in his inaugural address that 'the era when human rights and freedom were neglected in the name of economic growth and security has now ended' (Gibney 1992: 87).

In short, the formation of a cross-class alliance prompted the ruling elites' decision to initiate democratic transition. What must still be explained is why a full democratic transition was implemented so quickly; the entire process of removing authoritarian institutions and installing new democratic electoral rules was completed by political elites over a span of just four months. Why were the ruling elites in such a hurry to introduce democratic elections? In the following analysis, I attribute the Korean ruling elites' preference for a speedy democratic transition to the high level of electoral threat facing them at the time. The 1985 legislative election has already indicated that the ruling party could not dominate elections; under Chun, the DJP faced a tough challenge from the opposition. The difference between the DJP's share of the vote share and that of the NKDP was a mere 5.9%. Meanwhile, the other opposition parties reached a combined share of 35.5.

The intensive electoral threat facing the ruling elites was also clear in a secret survey conducted by the pro-government Kyunghyang Daily in 1985, which suggested that nearly 53% of the respondents did not support the Chun regime (M. Lee 1990: 21) (Table 2.2).

The South Korean case suggests a strong linkage between the level of electoral threat and East Asian ruling elites' enthusiasm to introduce

Table 2.2 The vote share of political elites in the 1985 South Korea Legislative Election

Party	*Vote share (%)*
Democratic Justice Party	35.2
New Korea and Democratic Party	29.3
Democratic Korea Party	19.7
Korean National Party	9.2
Others	6.6

Source Nohlen et al. (2001)

democratic elections. Facing an enormous electoral threat from the opposition party, the ruling elites had no reason to delay the introduction of democratic electoral rules that were essential to maximise their political power. The option to carry out an immediate full democratic transition became even more attractive when the elites realised that democratic competition would increase their chance of winning the first presidential election by renewing the conflicts between opposition elites (Saxer 2003; Heo and Roehrig 2010: 40). Consequently, the authoritarian regime was highly incentivised to carry out an immediate full transition to democracy in 1987.

Roh had already made it clear in his 29 June declaration that he was willing to concede to practically all the demands of the opposition party. By October, the National Assembly had adopted sweeping revisions to the constitution, which were soon ratified by a national referendum. These changes included the removal of authoritarian institutions that restricted various civil and political rights such as freedom of the press, campus autonomy, the banning of arrests without a warrant, and the lifting of restraints on artistic creativity. This removal paved the way for the installation of democratic electoral institutions. The first direct presidential election, which Roh won, was held on 16 December 1987, and the National Assembly election was held in early 1988 (Bedeski 1994; Henderson 1988; Oh 1999).

In sum, South Korea's 1987 democratic transition supports my hypothesis concerning two strategic decisions of the ruling elites. The first is the decision to initiate democratic transition in response to a cross-class alliance; the ruling elites were willing to concede to democracy and transform their legitimacy formula once the middle class and the working class had joined forces. The second is the decision to introduce democratic elections in response to an electoral threat; a high level of electoral threat from the opposition motivated the Korean ruling elites to push for rapid constitutional changes to usher in democratic elections between June and October 1987. As I will later contrast, in the absence of an electoral threat in Taiwan, the ruling elites lacked any incentive to introduce democratic elections.

The Formulation of the State's Strategic Visions in South Korea

South Korea Under Abortive Reform: From a Growth-First Vision to Policy Inconsistency

The period of rapid industrialisation driven by the state-chaebol alliance had resulted in structural imbalance and economic inequality, as well as social discontent. This section will assess the inability of the authoritarian state and later two democratically-elected governments to implement chaebol reform between the early 1980s and mid-1990s. I explain how the state's failure was rooted in various political contexts. Before the democratic transition in 1987, the state's reform agenda was overshadowed by a growth-first economic vision. After the democratic transition, the reform agenda was hindered by the state's inability to balance structural reform and economic growth as a result of the emergence of significant institutional constraints.

I will first examine the formulation of the state strategic vision under Chun's authoritarian regime between 1980 and 1987. This period witnessed a policy shift towards a more balanced development model due to economic and political factors. Economically, Park's push for HCI had destabilised the economy. Economists from both the state apparatus and international organisations regarded neoliberal reform to introduce some elements of market-led development as a cure for the economic crisis of 1980. Chun also personally believed that, thrown into the rough waters of the international market without deliberate state support, the chaebols would be forced to change their monopolistic ways.

Politically, neoliberal reform proved a viable tactic for the Chun to defuse public anger at Park's harsh repression, particularly after the bloody Kwangju uprising in 1980. In other words, a shift to a more market-orientated development vision could differentiate Chun from the unpopular Park regime that had coddled the privileged chaebol sector. The necessity for structural reform led to the placement of neoliberal economists within the state apparatus as the principal architects of state policy. The Fifth Five-Year Economic Plan (1982–1986) kicked off the first round of neoliberal reform in the 1980s (Moon 1994; Kong 2000; Kim 1999; Haggard and Moon 1990).

The state's neoliberal policy shift was a limited one, however. With the growth-first policy vision remaining unchanged, the state-chaebol alliance remained central to Chun's strategy. Despite the Fifth Five-Year Plan's promised shift to a market-led development model, the state continued its interventionist approach to reconstruct the chaebol sector (Moon 1994). To maintain the viability of the chaebol sector, there were clear limits on how much reform the ruling elites would allow in financial liberalisation. Also at odds with the state's purported liberalisation agenda was the injection of $2.1 billion into the financial system to bolster the chaebols from 1985 to 1987 (Hundt 2008: 78). This financial support to chaebols was meant to ensure the development of new export sectors, but at the same time the state could not rigorously apply de-concentration measures to eliminate the market distortions caused by chaebol economic domination. The 1981 Monopoly Regulation and Fair Trade Act entrusted regulatory power to the EPB—the pilot agency to promote growth—and gave it wide discretion over implementation (B.-K. Kim 2003: 60). In the later period of the Chun regime, the state's effort to reform the chaebols became even weaker because the government 'fully appreciated the extent of the interdependence between state and conglomerate and the costs to both sides of any rupturing of the relationship' (Kong 2000: 148).

The Chun government's partial reform illustrates what Tat Yan Kong (2000) refers to as 'chaebol non-reform'. Kong argues that the will of the state to forcibly restructure the chaebols tended to weaken once the urgency of the financial crisis had passed, and once the degree of short-term economic pain that would result from structural reform became evident. A contradiction between maintaining growth and conducting structural reform had clearly emerged, and the state was unwilling to give up its growth-first principle. Maintaining the effectiveness of the government-chaebol alliance was the top priority of the politically insecure Chun regime in the 1980s.

Democratic transition had a significant impact on the formulation of the state's strategic vision. The growth-first vision was replaced by majorly inconsistent policy-making after the 1987 political liberalisation. On the one hand, the state's economic reform vision became the most effective way for ruling elites to strengthen their political profile. On the other hand, the dangers associated with such reform (e.g. slower growth, unemployment) weighed heavily on the minds of the ruling elites. Consequently, the first two democratically-elected administrations of Roh Tae-woo and Kim Young-sam suffered from a lack of consistent economic policy-making.

What emerged from the 1987 political opening was not a strategic vision to upgrade the economy, but rather a populist reform agenda. Two developments shaped this outcome. Firstly, the favourable external economic climate of the late 1980s guaranteed the country's satisfactory economic performance; blessed by the 'three lows'—low interest rates, low oil prices and a low (weak) *won*, Roh was simply not concerned about economic development (Lee 2002: 53; Kong 2000). Instead, as he was insecure in regard to political legitimacy, Roh attempted to buy popularity through the implementation of populist development policies (Kong 2000; Oh 1999: 112). Secondly, to fulfil the DJP's electoral promise of emphasising greater 'equity' rather than 'efficiency', Roh's administration now had even more reason to reform the privileged chaebol sector and transform the state-chaebol alliance. To make good on this promise, one concrete step that Roh took was to promote his head economic secretary to the level of minister, allowing the latter to execute restrictive policies on the chaebols (Lee 2002: 57).

The state's lack of coherent economic vision became visible after 1989, as the country shifted to crisis management mode.[3] The slowdown of growth in 1989 and the return to trade deficits in 1990 turned the attention of the ruling elites back to economic performance. As the ruling elites moved to stimulate growth, the impulse for chaebol reform was over-ridden by the public's desire for recovery, as it was assumed that only the chaebols could spearhead such recovery. With the appointment of a conservative economic team, Roh launched a new round of interventionist policies to strengthen the state-chaebol alliance (Lee 2002; Kong 2000; B.-K. Kim 2003).

After the change of leadership in 1993, the state's capability to form a viable economic strategy continued to erode. There is no doubt that Kim Young-sam, Roh's successor, wished to develop a higher international profile and to differentiate himself as a new civilian leader from the

[3] A long-term five-year economic development plan was formulated by the Roh government in 1992. However, the new plan was not implemented because it had to be revised by the new government after the presidential election in 1992.

generals who had ruled before him. Two key means of achieving these objectives were gaining membership of the Organisation for Economic Co-operation and Development (OECD)—something that would require considerable structural reform—and the creation of a 'new economy' (Gills 1996; Kong 2000). More importantly, labelling his economic management as 'Y-S NOMICS', Kim was eager to impress the middle class with economic growth to achieve greater popularity. As Iain Pirie (2007: 94) writes, 'although the "poor" economic performance of the economy in 1993 was largely a result of the government's own short-lived but serious attempt to force the chaebols to rationalise their activities, this does not alter the fact that the administration clearly felt that "something" ought to be done to boost the economy'. Kim's commitment to economic development was made crystal clear in a 100-day plan and subsequent five-year economic plan (Cha 1994; Kong 2000: 146–147). The final imperative of the liberalisation plan was the new administration's mandate to put an end to *jungkyung yuchack* (state-chaebol relations) through a comprehensive programme of globalisation, known as the *segyehwa* drive, which introduced greater market discipline within the domestic economy while encouraging domestic firms to face global competition (Lee and Han 2006; Kong 2000; Hundt 2008).

Yet Kim's structural reform agenda was half-hearted. The emergence of a growth-orientated neoliberal vision exacerbated the problem of 'chaebol non-reform' by further deterring the state's willingness to reform the chaebol-state alliance. The *jungkyung yuchack* proved difficult to relinquish. Barry Gills points out that Kim's 'initial anti-chaebol (big deal) measures and attempts to dismantle vested interests and root out corrupt practices made part of the middle class uneasy, reviving a conservative backlash against reform. More fundamentally, Kim Young-sam concluded that he could not conduct his economic policy without the cooperation of the chaebols, and thus turned away from the idea of a decisive break in the government-chaebol reliance' (cited in Dent 2000: 281). The goal of industrial upgrading ultimately had to be carried out by the state-business alliance. Gills (1996) also notes the tension between the Kim's twin *segyehwa* policy objectives, concluding, 'the imperative of supporting chaebol global strategies proved stronger than that of economic liberalisation, and that replacing statist, neo-mercantilist forms with 'competitive capitalism' in Korea's political economy was generally unworkable' (cited in Dent 2000: 283). According to Dent (2000), the *segyehwa* policy was formulated to shift the chaebols' strategies from internal internationalisation (export-based) of the Korean economy towards external internationalisation (FDI-based).

More Coherent Economic Visions After 1997: From Structural Reform to Shared Growth

The Korean state regained some coherence in the formulation of overall economic visions after 1997, which I attribute to the end of the inherent contradiction between structural reform and economic growth after the Asian financial crisis. Institutional constraints consequently pushed the Korean state to focus its economic agenda on two distinctive priorities of the country: structural reform between 1998 and 2007 to overcome the financial crisis, and economic revival to drive economic growth from 2008 to 2017. The remainder of this section examines the formation of economic visions under the four democratically-elected administrations from 1998 to 2017.

The 1997 financial crisis intensified the urgency for structural reform. Such reform had the strong support of the middle class, as demonstrated by a surge of social movements from civil society (e.g. the minority shareholder movement) to reform the chaebol-dominated economic system in the post-1997 period (Kalinowski 2008; S. J. Lee 2008). As the movements gained momentum, maintaining growth and deepening reform were no longer in opposition. The result was the end of 'chaebol non-reform'. Consequently, what emerged as state strategy during the Kim Dae-jung administration and the Roh Moo-hyun administration between 1998 and 2007 was a thorough neoliberal structural reform.

One major part of this reform-first economic vision was to push forward the long-overdue reform of the government-chaebol alliance. By the time Kim Dae-jung took office in February 1998, a comprehensive neoliberal reform programme had already been formulated by the government and the International Monetary Fund (IMF) (in conjunction with the World Bank) to majorly overhaul the state-led development model (Kong 2000; Shin and Chang 2003; Ha and Lee 2007; Mo 2008). Although the IMF programme 'was expected to deepen the economic and social pain' (Kong 2000: 216), Kim's political legitimacy was clearly contingent on his ability to carry out this externally-imposed reform programme. The state's determination to implement the corporate reform programme was vividly demonstrated in the handling of the Daewoo

Group's bankruptcy in the second half of 1999. Hitherto, the state had been reluctant to allow chaebols of Daewoo's scale to collapse due to the potential social and economic fallout. In contrast, Kim was adamant in pursuing a strategy of corporate restructuring and thus refused to rescue Daewoo when it failed to comply with the conditions of the government's programme (Mo and Moon 2003; Hundt 2008; Shin and Chang 2003). The state's reform agenda was further fuelled by the leadership of Roh, who was elected on the basis being an outsider politician and an anti-establishment voice (Lee 2008). One example is his establishment of task force to oversee a three-year plan for market reform (Roh 2003).

While structural reforms to dismantle the government-chaebol alliance were underway, serious attempts were also made to move the Korean economy towards a new market-orientated paradigm of economic growth. To further strengthen the government's political standing in the eyes of the public, some concrete steps also had to be taken to enhance the competitiveness of the economy and meet public desire for economic revitalisation. This strategic calculation provided a rationale for the government to push a new round of globalisation drive in the aftermath of the 1997 financial crisis. Ambitious initiatives were launched during both the Kim and Roh administrations, aimed at making South Korea into a regional economic hub for the Northeast Asia region (K.-K. Lee 2004; Lee and Hobday 2003). Another major state effort to accelerate the globalisation drive was the government's Free Trade Agreements (FTA) strategy. By then, trade and liberalisation through FTA came to be realised as an integral part of South Korea's long-term economic vitality (Sohn 2001; Liou 2008). The financial crisis also served as a wake-up call as to the importance of supplementary trade mechanisms at the sub-multilateral level in safeguarding South Korea's economic security (Park and Koo 2007). The most ambitious project of the government's push for the FTA strategy was the pursuit of an FTA with the US (Lim 2006; Choi 2009). By setting the wheels of the Korea-US FTA in motion, the Roh administration advanced South Korea into the next stage of a market-orientated growth model.

A shift in policy-making focus from reform to growth after 2008 transformed the state's strategic vision as it rekindled developmental visions. However, this growth-first strategy was fundamentally different from those of the authoritarian period. They were produced not by the Korean ruling elites' single-minded desire for performance legitimacy but rather the institutional constraints from the middle class within a democratic system.

The impetus for the return of state developmentalism appeared after 2008. Towards the end of Roh's rule, the middle class was increasingly dissatisfied with the neoliberal restructuring project that Kim and Roh had pursued. As H. Y. Kwon (2010) observes, 'Many South Koreans became disappointed by the decade-long rule of liberal presidents, who promised much but failed to deliver on either robust economic growth or increased quality of life'. While support for structural reform was fading, the desire of the middle class for a revival of the state developmental model was growing. The post-1997 period saw the rise of an intriguing social phenomenon of 'Park Chung-hee nostalgia' (Moon 2009). This developmental nostalgia was particularly notable in the years immediately preceding the 2008 and 2012 presidential elections, when two conservative candidates who campaigned on the basis of reviving state developmentalism enjoyed sweeping victories (W.-T. Kang 2010; W.-J. Kang 2018). In the context of renewed social support for developmentalism, the ruling elites shifted back to the state-led policy paradigm to strengthen their political standing. Indeed, by offering themselves as a 'new Park' for the middle class, the two conservative presidents—Lee Myung-bak (2008–2013) and Park Geun-hye (2013–2017) did not hesitate to rely on an interventionist approach for economic promotion. Consequently, there was a statist push for 'Green Growth' launched by the Lee government in the wake of the global financial crisis of 2008, and a 'creative economy' plan formulated by the Park Geun-hye administration to promote a state-led innovation (Kim and Thurbon 2015; Connell 2013).

The return to state developmentalism was not accompanied by a renewal of the chaebol strategy. Despite the new rulers' aspiration to revive Park's statist model, they had no intention to emulate Park's chaebol strategy to achieve rapid growth in democratic Korea. Rather, they based their decisions on the preferences of the middle class, who associated the chaebol strategy with the economy's structural imbalance. After the 1997 crisis, the power of the chaebols had been strengthened through government-led corporate restructuring, while SMEs had suffered greatly (Mo and Moon 2003; Gregory et al. 2002). To most economic observers, the weakening of the SME sector had contributed to the decade of 'jobless growth' from 1997 to 2007. This structural imbalance continued to fuel anti-chaebol sentiment among the middle class.

In response, the Lee administration targeted the chaebols to improve its standing with the public and to reverse the lame duck status of the outgoing president (H.-S. Lee 2012). Despite the initial attempt of the state, anti-chaebol sentiment further escalated throughout the Park administration.[4]

Realising the policy preference of the middle class, the ruling elites began to reduce the economy's reliance on the chaebols in 2010. Following a major loss for the DJP in a by-election, the ruling party decided to focus on serving the interests of the middle class to boost their popularity (Jung 2011); the result was a policy of 'shared growth' (Jeon 2012). Under this principle of promoting the co-existence of SMEs and chaebols, a series of government policies were formulated to contain the overcrowding effect that latter had had on the former during the second half of the Lee administration (Mukoyama 2013). Along with the previously established Fair Trade Commission (FTC), a semi-governmental organisation—the Presidential Commission on Shared Growth—was set up to enforce the chaebol-containing policies. A dispute dubbed the 'tofu war' broke out as the commission waged an uphill battle to loosen the iron grip of the chaebols on the economy (Oliver 2011). Park Geun-hye's administration furthered the policy shift away from reliance on chaebols as a driver of economic growth and emphasised the importance of 'chaebol-SME co-prosperity' as soon as Park came into power (Seo 2013). The government even went further to meet the expectations of the middle class by with the 'creative economy plan', by which the government provided funding and infrastructure to aid grass-roots innovation and boost the SME-dominated service sector (Connell 2013; Mundy 2015).

Policy Constraints from Business Elites in South Korea

The Rise of Concentrated Business Interests

In South Korea, business elites have produced enormous policy constraints on the state's policy-making process since the early 1980s. The two variables of industrial structure and democratic transition have

[4] The most dramatic event to illustrate the level of anti-chaebol sentiment was perhaps the massive public outcry after an infamous nut rage incident involved the heiress of the Hanjin group (see Deciantis and Lansberg 2015).

produced a high level of constraints on the state's policy-making process. The first important factor to explain these constraints from business elites was the country's high percentage of DPCC, which gave rise to concentrated business interest groups.

In South Korea, the concentrated business interest groups consisted of major business leaders, i.e. the chaebol owners. The rise of chaebol interests was clear in the Federation of Korean Industries' (FKI) call for greater autonomy in the early 1980s. In its 1981 annual report, the FKI announced its desire for greater economic decision-making power in the state policy process, stating, 'We must actively seek and adopt the opinions and expertise coming from various corners of our society, and in particular from the business elites...Thus, we will be able to improve the total efficiency of our economic and social activities' (Kim 1997: 198). Chaebol interests were also visible at an individual enterprise level. As Jong-Chan Rhee (1994: 213) observes, 'During the latter half of Chun's presidential terms...owners of the largest business groups often directly contacted the top of the government, while hired top managers of business groups met with the minister- or vice-minister-level bureaucrats in order to represent big business interests and to demand individual conglomerates' interests.

The strong capability of these concentrated business interests to influence the state's economic decision-making was solidified in the 1980s. Chun's policy of reducing the concentration of the chaebols (i.e. the fair Trade and Anti-Monopoly Act) failed because of the chaebols' open defiance, as they increased their horizontal integration by acquiring new firms. Although the chaebols were forced to sell off some of their real estate, they had acquired land holdings worth 20 times the value of the land they had released (Kim 1997: 195; Kim 1993; Moon 1994: 152). During the reorganisation of the HCI, the chaebols even reversed the state's initial policy decision not to support Daewoo; not wanting to jeopardise its relationship with other chaebols, the state compromised by creating a SOE to produce electrical generators (Kim 1997: 193–194; Kim 1993).

The structural power of the chaebols to challenge the state was significant given the state's preference for the promotion of the private sector and the privatisation of the public sector. The state did not lose all of its control over business elites; the government's success in forcing the bankruptcy of Kukje, the seventh-largest, demonstrated that the state could still exercise its authority in determining the fate of big businesses. However, the ability of even more powerful chaebols to control the process of distributing Kukje's assets nevertheless suggests the significant structural capacity of the chaebols vis-à-vis the state (Kim 1997: 200–203; Hundt 2008: 80).

The strong influence of concentrated business interests on the state was even more impressive in terms of the chaebols' success to strengthen their financial power during economic liberalisation. Although the government's expectation was that neoliberal reform would curb the economic power of the chaebols, the reform process provided the chaebols with new opportunities to enhance their financial strength. Chaebols were able to acquire shares of government-controlled commercial banks during the privatisation process; in the mid-1980s, the top ten chaebols were believed to have collectively secured 22–57% ownership in five commercial banks (Zeile 1996: 261). The ownership of non-banking financial institutions (NBFIs), which were developed specifically to bypass the nationalised banking system, allowed the chaebols to achieve financial independence from the state (E. M. Kim 1997: 189). The ownership of the Korean stock and bond markets also grew rapidly in the second half of the 1980s (Lee et al. 2002: 23). As these alternative financing channels came to replace banks as a major source of funds, corporate financing of the chaebols changed from a reliance on bank loans to NBFIs loans and direct financing (Lee et al. 2002: 23).

The above discussion has indicated that by the 1980s, a high level of DPCC had led to the emergence of concentrated interests and therefore strong structural constraints from business elites. The chaebols successfully resisted the government's attempt to curb their economic power and quickly achieved financial independence during the process of financial liberalisation. Their structural constraints were further heightened in South Korea's democratic period. The following sections will analyse how the business elites' strong structural constraints on the state, combined with institutional constraints, led to a rapid decline of the state-led state-business cooperation in democratic South Korea.

Democratic Transition and the End of State-Led State-Business Cooperation

The opening of the country's political system greatly enhanced the structural constraints produced by Korean business elites. Following the 1987 democratic transition, the FKI, essentially a chaebol club, called for greater market autonomy. The FKI's 1988 New Year announcement, traditionally reserved for supporting state policies, focused on the importance of a free market for future economic growth and the establishment of a creative entrepreneurial spirit; media considered this a 'bombshell announcement' (Kim 1988). The FKI's call for less government interference in the economy increased in the 1990s and culminated in a 1995 policy report, in which the chaebols advocated for a radical retrenchment of the state and the reduction of government bureaucracy by 90% (Chang and Evans 2005). On an individual level, politically empowered by the opening of the political system, several chaebol owners and high-ranking managers ran for National Assembly seats in the late 1980s and early 1990s in order to directly participate in the state's decision-making process (Lee 2002; Kim 1997). Perhaps the most significant example of assertiveness was reflected in the decision by Chung Ju-yong, the founder of Hyundai, to form his own party and run against the government's candidate in the 1992 election. His provocative campaign promise was to 'get government out of business' (cited in Evans 1995: 229).[5]

In addition to the increasing structural constraints generated by concentrated business interests, the democratic transition also produced institutional constraints from business elites. As political parties in South Korea were more dependent on their leaders than on any ideology or formal organisational structure, politicians faced a high demand for political funds to reward their followers, to activate party organisations and to mobilise voters to win electoral competitions. David C. Kang (2002: 161) used the term *oribal* (duck feet) to describe the situation; 'on the surface decorum is maintained while below the surface the parties scramble like mad to raise funds'. In addition to running a party, the ruling elites also needed funds for the increasingly capital-intensive elections. As Aurel Croissant (2002: 258) analyses the increased role of money in politics since democratisation, 'Money matters in electoral competition... The more a candidate spends, the better his chance of winning'. The source of the increasing demand for political funding came from the business community, particularly the chaebols. The result was a drastic increase in quasi-taxes between the government and big businesses from 1994 to 1998 under the Kim Young-sam administration (Kang 2002: 163; Eckert 1993: 109).

[5] Chung was later convicted for electoral and financial malpractices. However, he was later pardoned by the new president in 1993 for his apparent influence over the economy (Hundt 2008: 85).

As the ruling elites turned to the chaebols for political funding, state-business relations continued to evolve.[6] It was clear by then that, with financial leverage over the ruling elites, the chaebols had gained an upper hand in the state policy process. The FKI's October 1988 announcement warned the ruling party that the FKI intended to use its formidable concentration of wealth politically, through the election process, to push the government to relinquish more control of the economy to the private sector (Eckert 1993: 109). Towards the end of Kim Young-sam's rule, the kind of state-business relations that had once ensured the insulation of the state from societal interests was completely lost, and a new relationship closely associated with 'crony capitalism' emerged (Kang 2002). Individual chaebols could essentially buy direct access to state policy-making. As Ha-Joon Chang (1998: 1557) observes, 'Under the Kim Young-sam government, for the first time in the post-1960s Korean history, we heard the names of some particular chaebols, such as Samsung, talked about as being 'close to the regime'. Previously, the chaebols as a group were treated preferentially, but rarely was any one or few of them regarded as being closer to the government than the others'.

The emergence of both structural and institutional constraints from business elites led to the rapid decline of the state's leadership role in directing state-business cooperation after 1987. The Roh administration's chaebol reconstruction effort, mainly to force the chaebols to sell off their non-productive real estate holdings and enhance their competitiveness by selecting three core industries in which to specialise, largely failed (Fields 1995: 59; Moon 1994). The early 1990s saw a drastic decline of the state's strategic position vis-à-vis business elites. As a result, industrial policy began to reflect the private interests of the chaebols rather than national interests. The Kim government's decision to support the market entry of 'a medium-sized chaebol with a dubious track-record in manufacturing' was 'not taken as a part of coherent industrial policy' (Chang et al. 1998: 740). As the investigation into the bankruptcy of the Hanbo group later revealed, behind the government support of Hanbo lay high-profile corruption involving close aides and even the son of President Kim (Chang 1998; Chang et al. 1998).

[6] To many statists, the transformation of the state-dominated state-business relationship led to a problem of 'moral hazard', which many deemed responsible for the 1997 financial crisis (e.g. Chang 2000).

The state's neoliberal economic restructuring was also hijacked by chaebol interests. After gaining financial independence through NBFIs and direct financing, the chaebols began to push a liberalisation of restrictions on foreign borrowing to gain new sources of funding. In the late 1980s, the government still had control over foreign borrowing, but five or six years later there were virtually no restrictions left. The opening of capital accounts, particularly short-term loans, outpaced the introduction of effective instruments of corporate governance. Towards the mid-1990s, as the state essentially lost control over chaebols, the latter became unsupervised and indulged in the accumulation of foreign debts. This behaviour paved the way for the 1997 financial crisis (Chang 1998; Chang et al. 1998; Wang 2012: 115–124; Kalinowski and Cho 2009).

Chaebol Interests and the State in the Post-crisis Period

The strong policy constraints from the chaebols significantly declined after the 1997 financial crisis. The reduction of structural constraints was the result of the chaebols' temporary weakness; not only did the economic crisis financially weaken previously privileged corporate and financial actors, but it also removed the political status of the chaebols as builders of the economy (Wang 2012: 126).[7] Consequently, the chaebols could not maintain the same level of influence over state policy-making. The ruling elites could also escape from institutional constraints created by their need for political. Sweeping the December 1997 presidential election in the midst of the financial crisis, Kim Dae-jung was incentivised to dismantle the ties between previous governments and the chaebols in order to advance both his ideology and the interests of his primary constituents. In an interview shortly after his election, Kim criticised the financial crisis as a result of a 'collusive intimacy between business and government' (cited in Cumings 1999: 38). As the former ruling party was widely criticised for having mismanaged the economy, favouring chaebol interests was now a politically risky strategy.

The reduced policy constraints from the chaebols resulted in a temporary renewal of state-led state-business cooperation in South Korea. Despite the unwillingness of the chaebols to fully cooperate with the government, Kim's interventionist approach succeeded in trimming down

[7] Chaebols were regarded as being primarily responsible for the crisis and were subject to public criticism for the hardships that Korea experienced after 1997.

the excessive capacity of the chaebols and increasing their competitiveness through six swaps that were completed by the end of December 1999 (Mo and Moon 2003; Cherry 2006; Weiss 2003; Pirie 2007). Although scholars disagree on the degree of success or failure of the Big Deal programme, the fact that major industry realignment did occur demonstrated the state's increased power compared to previous failed attempts to rein in the chaebols. The state's renewed policy-making capacity was even clearer during Kim's neoliberal restructuring of the financial sector. Unlike the previous rounds of financial liberalisation that served the interests of the chaebols, the financial liberalisation in the immediate post-crisis period was designed to tackle the power of the chaebols. A key strategy of the government was to allow increasing foreign entry into Korean markets, especially in the banking sector, to tackle 'crony capitalism' and rampant corruption, and eventually to discipline the investment behaviour of the chaebols. To hinder reckless expansion by the chaebols, the government also tightened regulatory measures in the financial sector (Kalinowski and Cho 2009; Wang 2012: 125–133).

The temporary reduction in the policy constraints from the business elites as an unexpected consequence of the financial crisis was short-lived. Korean business elites remained highly concentrated despite the structural programme to reform the chaebol sector.[8] In 2017, sales revenue earned by the top 10 chaebols accounted for 67.8% of the country's GDP. Chaebol assets equalled nearly 11% of the country's GDP, with Samsung's assets alone accounting for 42% (Premack 2017: 4). South Korea's high level of DPCC is perhaps most evident in the fact that the five largest chaebols (i.e. Samsung, Hyundai, SK, LG, and Lotte) accounted for more than half of the country's stock index in the 2010s (Pae 2017). With the chaebols' huge economic contributions, it was just a matter of time before they regained their title as the 'saviours of the national economy'. They had already regained some standing during Roh Moo-hyun's presidency in 2003–2008, 'due to their ability to earn the foreign currency that was needed to repay foreign debt and recover from the financial crisis' (Kalinowski 2009: 296). Consequently, the state and business elites were already 'on a collision course' when the Roh administration pushed further against chaebol interests (Shim 2003). Towards the end of Roh's term, as he pushed a pro-growth state vision, the bargaining power of the

[8] Although the total number of chaebols reduced, their size increased after the crisis.

chaebols was indisputable; many chaebol leaders who had been convicted for wrongdoings were spared prison terms either by judges who recognised their significance to the national economy or by ruling elites who sought to lift national spirits (Choe 2008; Cheng 2015). The chaebol's significant bargaining power was indisputable in the 2010s, when scholars raised the question of 'whether top chaebol leaders are too big to indict, regardless of their behaviour' (Haggard and Rhee 2017).

Institutional and structural constraints from business elites had also returned by the early 2000s. The investigation of a political scandal involving President Park Geun-hye and her confidant in 2016 offered a glimpse of the continuation of money politics in the state policy process. The FKI, which previously acted to connect the state and business elites, was now considered an avenue used by the government to extract funds from the conglomerates, and was on the verge of disbanding (Yeo 2016). As policy constraints from business elites re-emerged, the state's leadership in state-business cooperation once again diminished. The financial reform pursued after the Kim Dae-jung administration was no longer free from chaebol influence (Wang 2012). As the state moved to promote industrial upgrading after 2008, chaebol interests dominated the policy agenda. The 'green growth' strategy of the Lee Myung-bak administration did not support infant industries but rather amounted to a government subsidy for sunset industries, such as an oversized construction sector dominated by chaebols (Kalinowski 2009). Similarly, Park Geun-hye's 'creative economy' plan also demonstrated the limit of the state's industrial policy against the rise of chaebol interests. Despite the government's intention to reduce reliance on the chaebols by promoting high-tech SMEs, the newly-established regional innovation centres were all put under the control of the chaebols (Mundy 2015). While it is debateable whether the business culture of the chaebols makes them best placed to nurture the sort of creative and dynamic start-ups able to compete with those in Silicon Valley, it is almost certain that the creation of such innovation tightened the chaebols' grip on the economy and therefore undermine the state's development goals.

Policy Constraints from Organised Labour in South Korea

The Rise of Concentrated Labour Interests

The policy constraints imposed by organised labour on the state were as strong as those from business elites. One reason was the high percentage of DPCC, which gave rise to concentrated labour interest groups that were capable of challenging the state. In South Korea, the domestic labour actors who provided the organisational base of concentrated labour interests groups are industrial workers employed in chaebol-owned firms. Even before South Korea's democratic transition, there were signs of an emergence of concentrated interests during two periods of temporary political relaxation within the military dictatorship. During the first decade of export-oriented industrialisation (EOI), the number of female workers employed in light industries grew rapidly and were mainly concentrated in the Seoul-Inchon area (Koo 1993, 2001). By the early 1970s, this concentration created the initial conditions for the formation of concentrated labour interest groups. As a result, a first wave of chaebol worker unionisation occurred, with several attempts to set up new independent unions or capture the control of company unions at large textile companies (Koo 2001: 73).

The temporary relaxation of authoritarian rule following the death of Park Chung-hee provided a political environment for chaebol workers to assert their economic demands. With the intensified desire of the chaebols to advance their economic interests, labour unrest erupted to dismantle the company-controlled unions in the period between 1979 and 1980 (Koo 1993: 142). However, the emergence of labour interests was constrained by country's authoritarian system. As Koo (1993: 149) puts it, 'Over the next three years, organised labour found no legitimate space in which to operate, and the labour movement was forced into a state of apparent quiescence'. As a consequence of Chun's anti-labour policy, there was a dramatic drop in both the number of unions and the number of union members (Koo 1993: 148).

Although the first wave of unionisation ended abruptly when the military intervened in May 1980, it had already proven the organisational advantage that a high level of DPCC has for labour interest groups. This advantage became even clearer in the early 1980s, as favourable conditions for the organisation of chaebol workers were developed. The promotion of the HCI resulted in an extremely high concentration of male workers in the domestic private sector, in two forms. Firstly, there was an increasing concentration of industrial workers in large-scale private enterprises. In 1985, almost two-thirds of Korean workers were employed in large-scale enterprises. The majority of them were employed in the HCI sector. Secondly, there was a significant geographical concentration of industrial workers. As the government encouraged the development of strategic industries in certain areas, about half of all manufacturing workers resided in the Seoul-Kyungin area and another 40% in the Youngnam area in the southeast cities of Pusan and Taegu. Within these densely populated areas, workers were concentrated in newly built industrial zones (Koo 1990, 2001; Yu 1993).

More importantly, Chun's political liberalisation provided essential political space for the demonstration of labour interests. The rapid export-led growth re-activated the desire of these industrial workers to defend their economic interests within the development process. As Koo (1993: 151) observes, 'the character of the labour conflicts had changed noticeably by the mid-1980s, [and] the focus of workers' struggles was no longer on isolated economic issues but on organising new independent unions'. The eruption of labour interests resulted in the creation of 200 independent labour unions, between which industrial workers attempted to develop regional solidarity (Koo 1993: 150).

With such a clear organisational advantage, it was hardly surprising that the 1987 democratic transition led to a rapid emergence of concentrated labour interests in South Korea. Following the removal of authoritarian institutions, in the summer of 1987 there was a full-scale eruption of collective efforts by chaebol workers, known as 'the Great Workers' Struggle'. This massive labour outburst was led by HCI workers in the southern coastal cities of Ulsan, Masan and Changwon (Koo 1993, 2001; D.-O. Chang 2009). Having experienced two waves of unionisations in the 1970s and mid-1980s, the chaebol workers were more than ready to mobilise in the new political environment.

According to Koo (2001: 196), at the end of 1989, the unionisation rate in companies with 300 or more workers was 60%, whereas the rate in small companies with between 50 and 99 employees and in medium companies with between 100 and 299 workers was 9.5% and 26%, respectively. In a short period, the chaebol-based unions quickly developed themselves to parallel the organisation of the chaebol (Koo 1993, 2001; Chang 2009). Given their membership base, the chaebol unions had strong structural power to advance the economic interests of their members. One clear indication was the significant transformation of labour relations. After the late 1980s, although the state returned to a more cohesive stance against organised labour, neither private capital nor the state was able to return labour relations to how they were during the summer of 1987. Collective bargaining, which had been largely ignored or regarded as a merely formal procedure between old company unions and chaebol owners, now became a necessary procedure for the state-business alliance to implement managerial decisions. The result was that chaebol owners could no longer exercise the maximised managerial authority 'to make unilateral decisions about wage and employment conditions' and now had to reach agreements with trade unions through collective bargaining (Koo 2001: 233).

The great capability of concentrated labour interests to influence the state was demonstrated by a huge wage hike in 1987. As the state took a hands-off approach to labour unrest in 1987 and 1988, workers obtained wage increases of over 20% in many large factories by forcing the management to make concessions (Koo 2001: 189). Consequently, the rise of labourers' demands for greater economic benefits resulted in the quick loss of South Korea's comparative advantage over a range of products in the global export market by the end of the 1980s and early 1990s (Minns 2001).

In the aftermath of the 1997 crisis, it was even more evident that concentrated labour interests possessed adequate organisational strength to push for their own interests. In annual wage negotiations, for example, chaebol-based unions used collective bargaining to push the adjustment of wage levels. As Lee (2011: 199) observes, chaebol unions were able to 'exert their mobilisation strength to maximise company-level gains beyond the recommended guidelines set by the government'. The existence of concentrated labour interests capable of securing material interests led to two important developments in democratic South Korea. First, compared to Taiwan's SME-dominated domestic sector, South Korea witnessed a much more dramatic increase (about 3.4 times) of real wage. Second, industrial workers employed in large firms experienced higher and quicker wage increases than workers employed in the SME sector (Lee 2011). Given the superior capability of chaebol-based unions to demand wage increases, chaebol workers have largely resisted attempts to move from enterprise-based unionism to industrial unionism, as industry-wide bargaining would potentially undermine their improved wages and working conditions (Yoon 2010).[9]

The strength of concentrated labour interests was also demonstrated by the capability of chaebol workers to secure their economic interests during the full-scale neoliberal restructuring in the 2000s. Despite the government's push for labour market flexibility, organised chaebol labourers were able to enhance their job security as 'regular workers' to protect themselves against labour market uncertainties. One of the most extraordinary company-level gains was priority employment opportunities for the children of retiring workers with more than 25 years of service (H.-A. Kim 2013). The strong capability of chaebol-based unions set them apart from the rest of the Korean labour forces. While the industrial workers belonging to powerful chaebol unions elevated their economic status and became 'labour aristocracy' (H.-A. Kim 2013), SME workers that were not protected by unions lost out during the period of economic restructuring.[10] By the mid-2000s, there was a dual market divided between the privileged regular chaebol workers and underprivileged irregular workers mainly located in the SME sector emerged in South Korea (Chan 2006).[11]

In sum, the high level of DPCC led to the emergence of concentrated labour interest groups with organisational advantages even before the 1987 democratic transition. The transition made it possible for these industrial workers to form strong chaebol unions with the necessary structural power to acquire their perceived interests. The next section will examine how the emergence of concentrated labour interests has resulted in a high level of policy constraints on the state-business alliance since the 1987 political opening.

[9] Although most big unions have joined industrial unions, they have all retained independent decision-making bodies and a large share of union budgets.

[10] According to Koo (2007), in 2007, 70% of union members were employed at large firms hiring with more than 300 employees.

[11] The unbalanced development did eventually give rise to the desire of irregular workers to advance their economic interests. However, in contrast to the chaebol workers, without the organisational advantage to organise large and stable labour unions, irregular workers had to risk their lives by resorting to extreme forms of labour resistance such as 'sky protests' in order to make their economic demands heard by the government (see Y.-K. Lee 2015).

The Unstainable Tripartite Arrangements

As a result of the emergence of concentrated labour interest groups after the 1987 democratic transition, organised labour was capable of challenging the economic agendas of the state-business alliance. One clear indication of their strong policy constraints has been the ineffectiveness of tripartite arrangements between the state, labour and business leaders since the late 1980s.[12] With the presence of powerful chaebol unions, organised labour in Korea—the Korean Confederation of Trade Unions (KCTU) and the Federation of Korean Trade Unions (FKTU)—has retained strong bargaining power within the state's policy-making process. Consequently, as I will show, the government's attempt to bring labour to the negotiation table with the state-business alliance has continually failed.

In the late 1980s, as the state moved to enhance the competitiveness of the economy in order to mitigate the sharp wage hike following the 'Great Workers' Struggle', policy constraints from organised labour first emerged during labour market reform. The economic reform process was difficult, as the state attempted to minimise the discontent of organised labour while maintaining a strong alliance with business leaders. The creation of the first tripartite arrangement was ineffective, as negotiations failed to submit any meaningful reform proposal due to the unwillingness of organised labour to compromise (B.-K. Kim 2003).

Challenged by organised labour, the state could no longer carry out coherent developmental policies. The urgency for reform eventually forced the ruling elites to bypass the tripartite mechanism and push through reform bills through the legislative process, triggering an unprecedented general strike (Koo 2001). The bill also suffered from serious policy inconsistencies. As Byung-Kook Kim (2003: 72) assessed the 1996 labour market reform bill as 'essentially compromise bills [that] suffered from internal contradictions, doing too little to deal effectively with the structural flaws of Korea's fragmented system of company unionism, but too much for both capital and labour to remain politically unruffled'.

The 1997 financial crisis provided the catalyst for reform of the labour market, as policy constraints from labour interests were suddenly reduced.

[12] See Kong (2004b) for a discussion of the government's efforts to create tripartite arrangements between the late 1980s and late 1990s.

Allowing for reform of the labour market, as a major part of the IMF reform programme, became crucial for the state-business alliance and organised labour alike, the latter worrying that the imminent collapse of the national economy would jeopardise their core interests of job security and employment. For the first time, the state-business alliance and organised labour shared a common interest: overcoming the financial crisis. The strategic compromise of organised labour consequently led to the formation of an effective tripartite institution—the Tripartite Commission for Fair Burden-Sharing (TAFBS)—in January 1998. Unlike previous negotiations, the creation of the TAFBC symbolised a temporary state-business-labour alliance to jointly overcome the crisis. As Kong (2000: 220) writes, 'While not removing the underlying differences, the financial crisis restored some sense of shared interest between state, organised labour and business'. As an alliance of the state, organised labour was also compensated for accepting economic hardship during the period of neoliberal restructuring. In exchange for lay-offs and labour market flexibility, labour enjoyed a significant gain when the government agreed to extend the social safety-net and to provide schemes for those affected by the reform. Organised labour also gained greater political rights and extended their membership base to the public sector (Kong 2000: 222).

The reduction of labour constraints did not last very long. The social pact between Korean organised labour and the state-business alliance in terms of economic restructuring came to an end in early 1999. The sustainability of the social pact required some genuine transformation of business practices and real sacrifice on the part of the business. However, to organised labour, the growing income inequality and mass lay-offs in the post-crisis period suggested that organised labour had shouldered much more of the burden than businesses had (Kong 2000: 234). With the immediate economic threat removed, organised labour was unwilling to make further compromises at the expense of undermining their economic interests. As Han et al. (2010: 298) write, 'Labour made it clear that more of the burden for restructuring the economy needed to be placed on the chaebols, which had spent recklessly over the years and were regarded by many as the chief of the economic crisis'. With the departure of the KCTU and FKTU from the social pact, the activities of organised labour moved from the negotiation table to the streets. The months of March, April and May of 1999 witnessed major labour strikes (Han et al. 2010; Kong 2000).

The subsequent return of labour constraints on the state policy process was significant. In mid-1999, to lure organised labour back to the negotiation table and avoid the danger of an escalation of labour strikes, the government risked harming its relationship with business elites by making concessions such as the shortening of legal working hours from 44 to 40 hours and requiring businesses to pay the salaries of full-time union officials (Kong 2000: 236; Han et al. 2010). When the state shifted back to a pro-business orientation, the Roh Moo-hyun government reached a deal with the moderate FKTU to further promote labour market flexibility in exchange for some limited labour gains in 2006. Needless to say, the deal triggered strong opposition from the radical KCTU (2006). Despite the government's attempt to reactivate the tripartite negotiations in April 2007 with the renaming of the Korean Tripartite Commission (KTC) to the Economic Social Development Commission (ESDC) in April 2007, the efficiency of this social dialogue mechanism is questionable. With the presence of both strong business and labour interests, deadlocks occurred over several issues, including the permission of multiple unions at the company level and the prohibition of payment for full-time union officials by companies (Han et al. 2010). The tripartite talks between the labour, management and government eventually failed as the government unilaterally pushed for a new round of labour market reform to enhance economic competitiveness and drive up youth employment (Jhoo 2016; Mukoyama 2015). Unlike in 1998, organised labour was no longer willing to make compromises to allow the state-business alliance to achieve its developmental goals through further labour market reform.

This section has assessed the strong connection between the level of DPCC and the structural constraints produced by organised labour. In the case of South Korea, the rise of concentrated labour interests (chaebol-based unions) has produced strong constraints on the state-business alliance in the democratic era. Consequently, with the sole exception of the post-crisis period, the state's attempts to incorporate organised labour into the policy-making process through the establishment of tripartite arrangements since the early 1990s have been largely ineffective.

Summary of the Chapter

In this chapter, I demonstrated how South Korea's industrial structure and democratic have played important roles in rapidly shaping the transformation of the developmental state. I showed how the industrial structure, characterised by a high proportion of DPCC, was shaped by Park Chung-hee partnership with the chaebols to promote growth in the aftermath of a military coup. I also showed that the two regime-transition outcomes—the reproduction of a military dictatorship in 1980 and the rapid transition to democracy in 1987—were both adaptive choices made by the ruling elites. In 1980, when the ruling elites were confronted by a democratic movement led by the working class, their intention to repress labour radicalisation in order to regain the control of the country motivated the establishment of another repressive authoritarian government. In 1987, South Korea's speedy transition to liberal democracy was shaped by the strategic considerations of the ruling elites to transform the old legitimacy formula in response to the formation of a cross-class alliance for democratisation, and to maximise their political representation as they faced a high level of electoral threat.

Both the industrial structure and democratic transition contributed to the rapid transformation of the developmental state by shaping the levels of structural and institutional constraints produced by societal actors on the state's policy-making process. The high level of DPCC produced strong structural constraints from both business elites and organised labour, as concentrated business interest groups (i.e. chaebol owners) and concentrated labour interest groups (i.e. chaebol-based unions) emerged. Given their importance to the economy, the chaebol owners had great capacity to shape the state policy process. As the chaebols achieved financial independence and were empowered by democratic transition, the state-led state-business alliance transformed in the early 1990s. In addition to the powerful chaebols, the emergence of chaebol unions produced further constraints on the state. After democratic transition, these strong labour unions quickly emerged due to the concentration of industrial workers. Given their large membership base, chaebol-based unions were particularly effective in achieving their economic interests within the development process. Consequently, the government's attempt to incorporate organised labour into the developmental alliance through tripartite arrangements has been largely unsuccessful.

South Korea's rapid democratic transition also resulted in institutional constraints from the middle class and business elites. I analysed how institutional constraints from the middle class emerged after the democratic transition. Between 1988 and 1997, the formulation of the state's strategic vision was inconsistent as it tried to balance economic performance and structural reform. This inconsistency lasted until the 1997 financial crisis, as structural reform became a priority of the two liberal governments between 1998 and 2007. After 2008, the state pushed a vision of shared-growth to meet the expectations of the middle class for equitable growth. Furthermore, the institutional constraints from business elites were also present immediately after the 1987 democratic transition. As the ruling elites became financially dependent on business elites for political funding, a new kind of state-business relations closely associated with 'crony capitalism' emerged and persisted in democratic South Korea.

References

Amsden, A. H. (1989). *Asia's Next Giant: South Korea and Late Industrialisation*. Oxford: Oxford University Press.

Bedeski, R. E. (1994). *The Transformation of South Korea: Reform and Reconstitution in the Sixth Republic Under Roh Tae Woo, 1987–1992*. London and New York: Routledge.

Castells, M. (1992). Four Asian Tigers with a Dragon Head: A Comparative Analysis of the State, Economy, and Society in the Asian Pacific Rim. In R. P. Appelbaum & J. Henderson (Eds.), *State and Development in the Asian Pacific Rim* (pp. 33–70). Newbury Park: Sage.

Cha, D.-S. (1994). Korea's New Economy Plan and Recent Economic Reform. *Journal of Asian Economics*, *5*(4), 515–523.

Chan, K. H. R. (2006). *Labour Market Reforms and Polarisation in Korea* (CAPS Working Paper Series). Centre for Asian Pacific Studies, Hong Kong: Lingnan University.

Chang, D.-O. (2009). *Capitalist Development in Korea: Labour, Capital and the Myth of the Developmental State*. Oxford and New York: Routledge.

Chang, H.-J. (1998). South Korea: The Misunderstood Crisis. In K. S. Jomo (Ed.), *Tigers in Trouble: Financial Governance, Liberalisation and Crises in East Asia* (pp. 222–231). London: ZED Books.

Chang, H.-J. (2000). The Hazard of Moral Hazard: Untangling the Asian Crisis. *World Development*, *28*(4), 775–788.

Chang, H. J., & Evans, P. (2005). The Role of Institutions in Economic Change. In S. de Paula & G. Dymski (Eds.), *Reimagining Growth: Institutions, Development, and Society* (pp. 99–129). London and New York: ZED Books.
Chang, H.-J., Park, H.-J., & Yoo, C. G. (1998). Interpreting the Korean Crisis: Financial Liberalisation, Industrial Policy, and Corporate Governance. *Cambridge Journal of Economics, 22*(6), 735–746.
Chang, S.-J. (2003). *Financial Crisis and Transformation of Korean Business Groups: The Rise and Fall of Chaebols*. Cambridge: Cambridge University Press.
Cheng, J. (2015). South Korea's President Park Geun-hye Pardons Chey Tae-won and Thousands of Others. *The Wall Street Journal* (online). Available at: https://www.wsj.com/articles/south-koreas-president-park-geun-hye-pardons-chey-tae-won-and-thousands-of-others-1439438683. Accessed on 10 February 2017.
Cherry, J. (2006). 'Big Deal' or Big Disappointment? The Continuing Evolution of the South Korean Developmental State. *The Pacific Review, 18*(3), 327–354.
Chiu, S. W.-K. (1992). *The State and the Financing of Industrialisation in East Asia: Historical Origins of Comparative Divergences*. PhD thesis, Princeton University.
Choe, S.-H. (2008). Former Samsung Chief Is Convicted. *The New York Times* (online). Available at: http://www.nytimes.com/2008/07/17/business/worldbusiness/17samsung.html. Accessed on 2 February 2017.
Choi, J.-J. (1993). Political Cleavages in South Korea, Political Cleavages in South Korea. In H. Koo (Ed.), *State and Society in Contemporary Korea* (pp. 13–50). Ithaca and London: Cornell University Press.
Choi, W.-M. (2009). Aggressive Regionalism in Korea-US FTA: The Present and Future of Korea's FTA Policy. *Journal of International Economic Law, 12*(3), 595–615.
Clifford, M. L. (1994). *Troubled Tiger: Businessmen, Bureaucrats, and Generals in South Korea*. Armonk, NY: M.E. Sharpe.
Cole, D. C., & Lyman, P. N. (1971). *Korean Development: The Interplay of Politics and Economics*. Cambridge: Harvard University Press.
Connell, S. (2013). *Building a Creative Economy in South Korea: Analysing the Plans and Possibilities for New Economic Growth* (Academic Papers). Washington, DC: Korea Economic Institute of America.
Cotton, J. (1989). From Authoritarianism to Democracy in South Korea. *Political Studies, 37*(2), 244–259.
Croissant, A. (2002). Electoral Politics in South Korea. In A. Croissant (Ed.), *Electoral Politics in Southeast and East Asia* (pp. 233–276). Singapore: Friedrich-Ebert-Stiftung, Office for Regional Cooperation in Southeast Asia.

Cumings, B. (1999). The Asian Crisis, Democracy, and the End of 'Late' Development. In T. J. Pempel (Ed.), *The Politics of the Asian Economic Crisis* (pp. 17–44). London and Ithaca: Cornell University Press.

Dalton, B., & Cotton, J. (1996). New Social Movements and the Changing Nature of Political Opposition in South Korea. In G. Rodan (Ed.), *Political Oppositions in Industrialising Asia*. London and New York: Routledge.

Deciantis, D., & Lansberg, I. (2015). *A Little Nut Rage Is Good* (online). Available at: https://www.theatlantic.com/international/archive/2015/03/a-little-nut-rage-is-good/387787/. Accessed on 3 March 2017.

Dent, C. M. (2000). What Difference a Crisis? Continuity and Change in South Korea's Foreign Economic Policy. *Journal of the Asia Pacific Economy, 5*(3), 275–302.

Eckert, C. J. (1993). The South Korean Bourgeoisie: A Class in Search of Hegemony. In H. Koo (Ed.), *State and Society in Contemporary Korea* (pp. 95–130). Ithaca and London: Cornell University Press.

Evans, P. (1995). *Embedded Autonomy: State and Industrial Transformation*. Princeton: Princeton University Press.

Fields, K. J. (1995). *Enterprise and the State in Korea and Taiwan*. Ithaca: Cornell University Press.

Gibney, F. (1992). *Korea's Quiet Revolution: From Garrison State to Democracy*. New York: Walker and Co.

Gills, B. K. (1996). Economic Liberalisation and Reform in South Korea in the 1990s: A 'Coming of Age' or a Case of 'Graduation Blues'? *Third World Quarterly, 17*(4), 667–688.

Gregory, G., Harvie, C., & Lee, H. H. (2002). *Korean SMEs in the Wake of the Financial Crisis: Strategies, Constraints, and Performance in a Global Economy* (Economics Working Paper 02-12). Wollongong: University of Wollongong.

Ha, Y.-C., & Lee, W. H. (2007). The Politics of Economic Reform in South Korea: Crony Capitalism After Ten Years. *Asian Survey, 47*(6), 894–914.

Haggard, S., & Moon, C.-I. (1990). Institutions and Economic Policy: Theory and a Korean Case Study. *World Politics, 42*(2), 210–237.

Haggard, S., & Rhee, I. (2017). *Too Big to Indict? The Samsung Case* (online). Available at: https://piie.com/blogs/north-korea-witness-transformation/too-big-indict-samsung-case?utm_source=dlvr.it&utm_medium=twitter. Accessed on 19 January 2017.

Han, S.-J. (1988). South Korea in 1987: The Politics of Democratisation. *Asian Survey, 28*(1), 52–61.

Han, S.-J., & Chung, O. (1993). South Korea: Economic Management and Democratisation. In J. W. Morley & T. P. Bernstein (Eds.), *Driven by Growth: Political Change in the Asia-Pacific Region* (pp. 197–223), Armonk: M.E. Sharpe.

Han, Y.-S. (2011). The May Sixteenth Military Coup. In B.-K. Kim & E. F. Vogel (Eds.), *The Park Chung Hee Era: The Transformation of South Korea* (pp. 35–57). London and Cambridge: Harvard University Press.

Han, C., Jang, J., & Kim, S. (2010). Social Dialogue and Industrial Relations in South Korea: Has the Tripartite Commission Been Successful? *Asian Pacific Viewpoint, 51*(3), 288–303.

Henderson, G. (1988). Constitutional Changes from the First to the Sixth Republics: 1948 to 1987. In I. J. Kim & Y. W. Kihl (Eds.), *Political Change in South Korea* (pp. 22–43). New York: The Korean PWPA.

Heo, U., & Tan, A. C. (2003). Political Choices and Economic Outcomes: A Perspective on the Differential Impact of the Financial Crisis on South Korea and Taiwan. *Comparative Political Studies, 36*(6), 679–698.

Heo, U., & Roehrig, T. (2010). *South Korea Since 1980*. New York: Cambridge University Press.

Hsiao, H. M., & Koo, H. (1997). The Middle Classes and Democratisation. In L. Diamond, M. F. Plattner, Y. Chu, & H. Tien (Eds.), *Consolidating the Third Wave Democracies: Themes and Perspectives* (pp. 312–333). Baltimore and London: The Johns Hopkins University Press.

Hundt, D. (2008). *Korea's Developmental Alliance: State, Capital and the Politics of Rapid Development*. London: Routledge.

Im, H. B. (1987). The Rise of Bureaucratic Authoritarianism in South Korea. *World Politics, 39*(2), 231–257.

Im, H. B. (2011). The Origins of the Yushin Regime: Machiavelli Unveiled. In B.-K. Kim & E. F. Vogel (Eds.), *The Park Chung Hee Era: The Transformation of South Korea*. Cambridge: Harvard University Press.

Jeon, S. (2012). *Using Competition Policy to Promote 'Shared Growth' in Korea* (online). Available at: https://www.competitionpolicyinternational.com/assets/Free/cpiasiajeon.pdf. Accessed on 10 March 2017.

Jhoo, D.-C. (2016). *Labour Group Withdraws from Tripartite Talks* (online). Available at: http://www.koreatimes.co.kr/www/news/nation/2016/11/116_195785.html. Accessed on 16 March 2017.

Johnson, C. (1987). Political Institutions and Economic Performance. In F. C. Deyo (Eds.), *The Political Economy of the New Asian Industrialism* (pp. 136–164). Princeton: Princeton University Press.

Jones, L. P., & Sakong, I. (1980). *Government, Business, and Entrepreneurship in Economic Development: The Korean Case*. Cambridge and London: Harvard University Press.

Jung, K.-H. (1988). Business-Government Relations in the Growth of Korean Business Groups. *Korean Social Science Journal, 14*(April), 77–82.

Jung, S.-K. (2011). *MBnomics to Focus More on Consumers After By-Election Loss* (online). Available at: http://www.koreatimes.co.kr/www/news/nation/2011/05/123_86628.html. Accessed on 6 March 2017.

Kalinowski, T. (2008). State-Civil Society Synergy and Cooperation: The Case of the Minority Shareholder Movement in Korea. *Korea Observer, 39*(3), 339–367.

Kalinowski, T. (2009). The Politics of Market Reforms: Korea's Path from Chaebol Republic to Market Democracy and Back. *Contemporary Politics, 15*(3), 287–304.

Kalinowski, T., & Cho, H. (2009). The Political Economy of Financial Liberalisation in South Korea: State, Big Business, and Foreign Investors. *Asian Survey, 49*(2), 221–242.

Kang, D. C. (2002). *Crony Capitalism: Corruption and Developments in South Korea and the Philippines*. Cambridge: Cambridge University Press.

Kang, W.-J. (2018). The Past is Long-Lasting: Park Chung Hee Nostalgia and Voter Choice in the 2012 Korean Presidential Election. *Journal of Asian and African Studies, 53*(2), 233–249.

Kang, W.-T. (2010). Missing the Dictator in a New Democracy: Analysing the Park Chung Hee Syndrome in South Korea. *Political and Military Sociology: an Annual Review, 38*(2010), 6.

KCTU. (2006). *KCTU Counter-Report on the South Korean Government's Report to the UN Human Rights Committee, Korean Confederation of Trade Unions* (online). Available at: http://kctu.org/index.php?mid=documents&page=3&document_srl=13349. Accessed on 3 March 2017.

Kim, B.-K. (2003). The Politics of Chaebol Reform, 1980–1997. In S. Haggard, W. Lim, & E. Kim (Eds.), *Economic Crisis and Corporate Restructuring in Korea: Reforming the Chaebol* (pp. 53–78). Cambridge: Cambridge University Press.

Kim, E. M. (1988). From Dominance to Symbiosis: State and Chaebol in Korea. *Pacific Focus, 3*(Fall), 105–121.

Kim, E. M. (1993). Contradictions and Limits of a Developmental State: With Illustrations from the South Korean Case. *Social Problems, 40*(2), 228–249.

Kim, E. M. (1997). *Big Business, Strong State: Collusion and Conflict in South Korean Development, 1960–1990*. Albany: State University of New York Press.

Kim, E. M., & Park, G.-S. (2011). The Chaebol. In B.-K. Kim & E. F. Vogel (Eds.), *The Park Chung Hee Era: The Transformation of South Korea* (pp. 265–294). Cambridge: Harvard University Press.

Kim, H.-A. (2004). *Korea's Development Under Park Chung Hee: Rapid Industrialisation, 1961–1979*. London: RoutledgeCurzon.

Kim, H.-A. (2011). State Building: The Military Junta's Path to Modernity through Administrative Reform. In B.-K. Kim & E. F. Vogel (Eds.), *The Park Chung Hee Era: The Transformation of South Korea* (pp. 85–112). London and Cambridge: Harvard University Press.

Kim, H.-A. (2013). Industrial Warriors: South Korea's First Generation of Industrial Workers in Post-Developmental Korea. *Asian Studies Review, 37*(4), 577–595.

Kim, K.-D. (1976). Political Factors in the Formation of the Entrepreneurial Elite in South Korea. *Asian Survey, 16*(May), 465–477.

Kim, Y. T. (1999). Neoliberalism and the Decline of the Developmental State. *Journal of Contemporary Asia, 29*(4), 441.

Kim, S. (2000). *The Politics of Democratisation in Korea: The Role of Civil Society*. Pittsburgh: University of Pittsburgh Press.

Kim, S.-Y., & Thurbon, E. (2015). Developmental Environmentalism: Explaining South Korea's Ambitious Pursuit of Green Growth. *Politics & Sociology, 43*(2), 213–240.

Kong, T. Y. (2000). *The Politics of Economic Reform in South Korea: A Fragile Miracle*. London and New York: Routledge.

Kong, T. Y. (2004). Neo-Liberalisation and Incorporation in Advanced Newly Industrialised Countries: A View from South Korea. *Political Studies, 52*(1), 19–42.

Koo, H. (1990). From Farm to Factory: Proletarianisation in Korea. *American Sociological Review, 55*(5), 669–681.

Koo, H. (1993). The State, Minjung, and the Working Class in South Korea. In H. Koo (Ed.), *State and Society in Contemporary Korea*. New York: Cornell University Press.

Koo, H. (2001). *Korean Workers: The Culture and Politics of Class Formation*. Ithaca: Cornell University Press.

Koo, H. (2007, July 9). Labour Movement in Korea Losing Steam. *The Korea Herald* (online source). Available at: http://attach3.bdwm.net/attach/boards/Marxist/M.1318357668.A/koo%20hagen_korean%20labor-%20korea%20herald.pdf. Accessed: 11 December 2014.

Kwon, H. Y. (2010). Economic Perceptions and Electoral Choice in South Korea: The Case of the 2007 Presidential Election. *The Pacific Review, 23*(2), 183–201.

Lee, C.-S. (1981). South Korea in 1980: The Emergence of a New Authoritarian Order. *Asian Survey, 21*(1), 125–143.

Lee, K.-K. (2004). Korea, Northeast Asian Economic Hub Country?: A Critical Study on the New Government Strategy. *Ritsumeikan International Affairs, 2*, 1–25.

Lee, M. (1990). *The Odyssey of Korean Democracy: Korean Politics, 1987–1990*. New York: Praeger.

Lee, N. (2007). *The Making of Minjung: Democracy and the Politics of Representation in South Korea*. Ithaca and London: Cornell University Press.

Lee, S. J. (2008). The Politics of Chaebol Reform in Korea: Social Cleavage and New Financial Rules. *Journal of Contemporary Asia, 38*(3), 439–452.

Lee, Y.-H. (2002). *State, Society and Big Business in South Korea*. London and New York: Routledge.
Lee, Y.-K. (2011). *Militants or Partisans: Labour Unions and Democratic Politics in Korea and Taiwan*. Stanford: Stanford University Press.
Lee, Y.-K. (2015). Sky Protest: New Forms of Labour Resistance in Neo-Liberal Korea. *Journal of Contemporary Asia, 45*(3), 443–464.
Lee, C. H., Lee, K., & Lee, K. (2002). Chaebols, Financial Liberalisation and Economic Crisis: Transformation of Quasi-Internal Organisation in Korea. *Asian Economic Journal, 16*(1), 17–35.
Lee, S.-K., & Han, T. (2006). The Demise of 'Korea, Inc.': Paradigm Shift in Korea's Developmental State. *Journal of Contemporary Asia, 36*(30), 305–324.
Lee, H.-S. (2012). Chaebol Under Siege. *The Korea Times* (online). Available at: http://www.koreatimes.co.kr/www/news/biz/2016/12/123_111085.html. Accessed on 8 March 2017.
Lee, Y.-L., & Hobday, M. (2003). Korea's New Globalisation Strategy: Can Korea become a Business Hub in Northeast Asia? *Management Decision, 41*(5), 498–510.
Lim, W. (2006). Korea FTA: A Mysterious Beginning and an Uncertain Future. *Asian Perspective, 30*(4), 175–187.
Liou, T.-H. (2008). South Korea's FTA Strategy. *Foreign Trade Review, 43*(1), 42–65.
Minns, J. (2001). Of Miracles and Models: The Rise and Decline of the Developmental State in South Korea. *Third World Quarterly, 22*(6), 1025–1043.
Mo, J. (2008). The Korean Economic System Ten Years After the Crisis. In A. J. MacIntyre, T. J. Pempel, & J. Ravenhill (Eds.), *Crisis as Catalyst: Asia's Dynamic Political Economy* (pp. 251–270). Ithaca and London: Cornell University Press.
Mo, J., & Moon, C.-I. (2003). Business-Government Relations Under Kim Dae-jung. In S. Haggard, W. Lim, & E. Kim (Eds.), *Economic Crisis and Corporate Restructuring in Korea: Reforming the Chaebol* (pp. 127–149). Cambridge: Cambridge University Press.
Moon, C.-I. (1994). Changing Patterns of Business-Government Relations in South Korea. In A. Macintyre (Ed.), *Business and Government in Industrialising Asia* (pp. 142–166). Crows Nest, NSW, Australia: Allen & Unwin.
Moon, S. (2009). The Cultural Politics of Remembering Park Chung Hee. *The Asian-Pacific Journal, 7*(19, 5), 1–33.
Mukoyama, H. (2013). *How Will the Economic Policies of South Korea's New Administration Influence Economic Relations with Japan?* (online). Available at: https://www.jri.co.jp/MediaLibrary/file/english/periodical/rim/2013/47.pdf. Accessed on 10 March 2017.

Mukoyama, H. (2015). Labour Market Reform Given Priority Among South Korea's Big Four Reforms—Trying to Reconcile Youth Job Creation with a 60-Plus Retirement Age. *Pacific Business and Industries, XV*(58).

Mundy, S. (2015). South Korea Aims for Creative Economy to End Reliance on Chaebol. *Financial Times* (online). Available at: https://www.ft.com/content/9203e38c-0dab-11e5-9a65-00144feabdc0. Accessed on 12 January 2017.

Nam, K. W. (1989). *South Korean Politics: The Search for Political Consensus and Stability*. Lanham: University Press of America.

Nohlen, D., Grotz, F., & Hartmann, C. (2001). *Elections in Asia and The Pacific: A Data Handbook*. Oxford and New York: Oxford University Press.

Oh, J. K.-C. (1999). *Korean Politics: The Quest for Democratisation and Economic Development*. Ithaca and London: Cornell University Press.

Oliver, C. (2011). Seoul Bolsters Small Companies in 'Tofu War'. *Financial Times* (online). Available at: https://www.ft.com/content/f59f279a-b133-11e0-a43e-00144feab49a. Accessed on 11 March 2017.

Pae, P. (2017). *South Korea's Chaebol* (online). Available at: https://www.bloomberg.com/quicktake/republic-samsung. Accessed on 1 September 2019.

Park, S.-H., & Koo, M. G. (2007). Forming a Cross-Regional Partnership: The South Kore-Chile FTA and Its Implications. *Pacific Affairs, 80*(2), 259–278.

Pirie, I. (2007). *The Korean Developmental State: From Dirigisme to Neo-Liberalism*. Abingdon and New York: Routledge.

Premack, R. (2017). Issue: South Korea's Conglomerates. *Sage Business Researcher* (online). Available at: http://businessresearcher.sagepub.com/sbr-1863-103804-2830718/20170821/south-koreas-conglomerates?type=hitlist&num=1. Accessed 25 June 2019.

Rhee, J.-C. (1994). *The State and Industry in South Korea: The Limit of the Authoritarian State*. London and New York: Routledge.

Roh, M.-H. (2003). Economic Vision. *Presidents & Ministers, 12*(3), 15–33.

Saxer, C. J. (2003). Democratic Transition and Institutional Crafting: The South Korean Case. *Democratisation, 10*(2), 45–64.

Seo, J.-Y. (2013). Park Urges Chaebol-SME Co-prosperity. *The Korea Herald* (online). Available at: http://www.koreaherald.com/view.php?ud=20130325000856. Accessed on 10 March 2017.

Seth, M. J. (2010). *A History of Korea: From Antiquity to the Present*. Lanham: Rowan & Littlefield.

Shim, J. H. (2003). Taking Care of Business Key to Roh Government. *Taipei Times* (online). Available at: http://www.taipeitimes.com/News/editorials/archives/2003/02/25/0000195888/1. Accessed on 1 February 2017.

Shin, J.-S., & Chang, H.-J. (2003). *Restructuring Korea Inc*. London: RoutledgeCurzon.

Sohn, C.-H. (2001). *Korea's FTA Developments: Experiences and Perspectives with Chile, Japan, and the US, Regional Trading Arrangements: Stocktake and Next Steps*. Trade Policy Forum. Paper presented at Regional Trading Arrangements: Stocktake and Next Steps, Trading Policy Forum, Bangkok, 12–13 June 2001.

Sohn, H.-K. (1989). *Authoritarianism and Opposition in South Korea*. London and New York: Routledge.

Suh, D.-S. (1982). South Korea in 1981: The First Year of the Fifth Republic. *Asian Survey, 22*(1), 107–115.

Vogel, E. F. (1991). *The Four Little Dragons: The Spread of Industrialisation in East Asia*. Cambridge: Harvard University Press.

Wang, S. (2012). *Business Interest, State Elites and Financial Regulatory Reform in South Korea and Taiwan*. PhD Thesis, Yale University.

Weiss, L. (2003). Guiding Globalisation in East Asia: New Roles for Old Developmental State. In L. Weiss (Ed.), *States in the Global Economy: Bringing Domestic Institutions Back In* (pp. 245–270). Cambridge: Cambridge University Press.

Wolf, C. (1962). Economic Planning in Korea. *Asian Survey, 2*(10), 22–28.

Woo, J. (1991). *Race to the Swift: State and Finance in Korean Industrialisation*. New York: Columbia University Press.

Yeo, J.-S. (2016). FKI Is Under Pressure to Disband. *The Korea Herald* (online). Available at: http://www.koreaherald.com/view.php?ud=20161006000825. Accessed on 9 February 2017.

Yoon, J.-H. (2010). The Asian Crisis of 1997–98: The Case of the Republic of Korea. *International Journal of Labour Research, 2*(1), 43–59.

Yu, H.-S. (1993). Industrial Structure and Labour Movement: Comparative Study of South Korea and Taiwan. *Korea Observer: a Quarterly Journal, 24*, 265–290.

Zeile, W. (1996). Industrial Policy and Organisational Efficiency: The Korean Chaebol Examined. In G. G. Hamilton (Ed.), *Asian Business Networks* (pp. 253–280). Berlin: Walter de Gruyter.

CHAPTER 3

The Non-Transformation of the Developmental State in Singapore

The previous chapter demonstrated how industrial structure and democratic transition played decisive roles in shaping the rapid transformation of the developmental state in South Korea. In this chapter, I aim to show that these two factors are also vital for understanding the non-transformation of the developmental state in Singapore. I argue that the state policy process in Singapore has been largely immune from the structural constraints generated by business elites and organised labour because of the country's industrial structure (with both high SOE and FDI), which gave rise to non-constraining economic interest groups (i.e. non-indigenous business interest groups, state-linked business interest groups and state-managed labour interest groups). I also argue that, as a result of the country's lack of a democratic transition and therefore lack of institutional constraints emanating from the middle class and business elites, the ruling elites remained single-minded in pursuing growth-first developmental agendas.

This chapter is organised into five sections. In the first section, I will explain the formation of the country's industrial structure. I trace the state's preference for a high level of FDI and SOE to the early period after the founding of the People's Action Party (PAP). I then show how the ruling elites' policy choices led to the formation of an industrial structure dominated by state-owned capital and foreign capital. The second section examines the transformation of the political foundation of the developmental state in Singapore. I will demonstrate a scenario in which

T. He, *The Political Economy of Developmental States in East Asia*,
https://doi.org/10.1007/978-3-030-59357-5_3

ruling elites are pushed to pursue a strategy of authoritarian co-optation in the absence of a democratisation movement. This political process is elaborated in three subsections. The first one concerns the preservation of the authoritarian structure of the country; the second concerns the PAP's adoption of an authoritarian co-optation strategy in response to the antagonism of the middle class; and the third section examines the PAP's heightened efforts in authoritarian co-optation following the party's 2011 electoral setback.

The third, fourth and fifth sections show how the FDI-SOE-dominated industrial structure and the lack of a democratic transition hampered the transformation of the developmental state in Singapore. The third section examines the formulation of the state's strategic economic vision in Singapore since the mid-1980s. I argue that, with the continuation of the authoritarian structure of the country, the economic performance of the country has remained the PAP's top priority since the early 1990s. The fourth section explains why the state's policy-making process has also been largely immune from the policy constraints produced by business elites. I argue that such an outcome was the result of both the lack of a democratic transition and the industrial structure of the country. The former has protected the state from the institutional constraints generated by business elites, while the latter has hindered the emergence of the structural constraints from business elites by producing non-constraining business interest groups. In the fifth section, I will examine the manner in which the high level of FDI led to the emergence of state-managed labour interest groups in Singapore. I will then show how the emergence of this type of non-constraining labour interests eventually allowed the state to manage organised labour in line with overall economic agenda.

How Elite Survival Shaped Singapore's Industrial Structure

The PAP's Struggle with the Leftist Movement

To understand the domestic origins of the Singapore developmental state, we must first examine the period of political difficulty facing the PAP, which culminated in a party split in 1961. Since its inception, the PAP was led by English-speaking political elites who lacked an electoral base in a city of Chinese speakers (Haggard and Low 2002; Rodan 1989;

Huff 1995). To secure political power, the PAP elites forged an alliance of convenience with the extreme leftists who had broad support from the local Chinese population (Turnbull 1977; Huff 1995). However, this marriage of convenience did not last long. In the early 1960s, significant conflicts between the two groups of political elites quickly escalated, particularly over the issue of merging with Malaysia, which precipitated the party's break-up in 1961 (Chan 1971; Turnbull 1977; Rodan 1989). The party split and subsequent formation of the Barisan Sosialis almost caused an annihilation of the PAP. Historian C. M. Turnbull (1977: 279) described the dangerous situation confronting the PAP in the early 1960s:

> When the split came in July 1961 most key figures in the party's branches defected to the Barisan, and at the lower level the PAP's organisation was almost crippled. Thirty-five branch committees resigned, and nineteen of the twenty-three paid organising secretaries defected. Large numbers of cadres quitted, and only 20 percent of the party's former members paid their subscriptions in 1962. Many branches were almost destroyed. Eleven had less than twenty-five members each and one had only ten. The PAP lost most of its active party workers and a great mass of supporters, many of whom were not pro-communist but the party was doomed and scrambled to leave the apparently sinking ship.

The dangerous situation following the party split in 1961 prompted the PAP elites to adopt a survival strategy that was based on a combination of political control and economic promotion. The task of imposing political control took several steps, first of which was to contain the spread of the leftist movement among the masses. In the late 1950s, the PAP saw the merger with Malaysia as the only short-term solution to the problem of the troublesome leftist opposition (Chan 1971; Rodan 1989; Turnbull 1977). With security in the hands of the central authorities, it was expected that the conservative Malayan government would take measures to eliminate the leftist threat (Chan 1971: 5; Turnbull 1977; Rodan 1989: 71). The proposed merger with Malaysia was accompanied by the PAP's political crackdown on the leftist movement. Following a referendum victory in September 1962,[1] the PAP banned the radical Singapore Association of Trade Unions (SATU) and granted legal status

[1] A referendum victory in September 1962 boosted the PAP's confidence in finalising the merger arrangement and dealing with the leftist groups at home.

to the National Trades Union Congress (NTUC), which sought government cooperation (Rodan 1989: 71). To remove any immediate electoral threat, the PAP launched two rounds of substantial political purging against the leftist groups. First, in February 1963, the Internal Security Council launched 'Operation Cold Store', involving the arrest of several Barisan Sosialis leaders, and in September and October of that year, immediately following the election, further steps were taken against 'extremists'. The arrests helped the PAP to consolidate its power by removing its political rivals (Turnbull 1977; Trocki 2006; Bellows 1970; Chan 1976).

The PAP's absolute political control commenced in late 1963. By then, the government's political crackdown had conclusively defeated the political threat posed by the leftist groups. An early election called for by the PAP after finalising the merger deal with Malaysia saw an infinite decline of the Barisan Sosialis, the only viable opposition party left (Turnbull 1977: 282; Kim 1985: 8). Having been pushed out by the PAP in the electoral arena, in 1968, three short years after independence, the Barisan Sosialis boycotted the general elections, leaving the PAP to monopolise the state decision-making process (Milne and Mauzy 1990). What was even more impressive was the fact that, despite the continuation of regular elections, there were no political opponents to challenge the dominant PAP. By the mid-1960, Singapore's political system transformed into a system of one-party dominance; there were no opposition members in parliament between 1965 and 1983 (Milne and Mauzy 1990; Trocki 2006; Bellows 1970; Chan 1976).

The political domination of the PAP in Singaporean politics could not have been possible without the creation of authoritarian institutions to impose political control in the country. One key authoritarian institution constructed by the PAP in the early 1960s to restrain political opposition forces was the Internal Security Act (ISA). The ISA allowed the PAP leaders to combat opposition groups in the name of national security (Trocki 2006; Ortmann 2010). Legislation was also enacted to make it virtually impossible for an independent group to amass the financial and public resources to organise a credible opposition party (Trocki 2006). Furthermore, the PAP considerably extended its control over educational institutions to curb radical ideas and took control of the mass media (see Rodan 1989: 97; H.-C. Chan 1976: 205). Two other political institutions for achieving PAP political domination were the Citizens' Consultative Committees (CCCs) and the community centres. The creation of these institutions led to a near saturation of the political arena and reduction in the political space for opposition parties to expand (H.-C. Chan 1976; Bellows 1970). More importantly, the co-option of people into the governmental grass-roots institutions strengthened the link between the ruling party and the masses, and cut into the potential recruitment source of the opposition (H.-C. Chan 1976). This ultimately led to the party's domination at the grass-roots level through a merger of the state and the party. As Chan Heng Chee (1975: 52) puts it, 'although these measures were initially enforced to suppress the communists, they have in fact resulted in the control and limitation of all political activity other than those of the ruling party'.

The PAP's efforts to impose political control went hand in hand with their determination to engineer a state-led development process. Prior to this, a national development plan had already been formulated in Singapore. The historical context for the development plan was a serious economic situation; in the immediate period after the PAP came to power in 1959, there was fear of massive unemployment due to high population growth rates, which were as a result of the declining mortality rate coupled with a high birth rate and migration from the Malay Peninsula to Singapore (Cheng 1991: 185). To promote job creation, in 1961 the PAP developed its first industrialisation initiative, the State Development Plan, 1961–1964, which involved a request to the World Bank for advice (Rodan 1989; Low 1998). However, similar to the South Korean case, the formation of a development plan did not mark the beginning of Singapore's state-led development process. Shortly after the plan's release, Garry Rodan (1989: 66) writes, 'The PAP was again preoccupied with urgent political questions which temporarily overshadowed the industrial programme'.

It was the party split of 1961 that ultimately intensified the desire of the PAP to launch their economic development programme. The government realised that rising unemployment could fuel the leftist movement; as Chan Chin Bock (2002) the former Economic Development Board (EDB) chairman recalls, 'Without jobs, the unemployed would roam the city streets, create mischief and become perfect targets for communist agitators. These were mostly Chinese-educated student activities who, as they joined the workforce, soon became politicised union members. The mandate of the newly-elected PAP government could be threatened by such unrest'. The urgency to contain leftist sentiment consequently pushed the ruling elites to shift all their energy to economic development. The renewed commitment of the ruling elites immediately led to the formation of the EDB in August 1961, shortly after the formation of the Barisan Sosialis. In this new state policy-making agency, the government's economic development plan was revived. As Garry Rodan (1989: 68) describes:

> One of the immediate implications of the split for the PAP government was that the State Development Plan, 1961-64, suddenly assumed even more importance than it already had. Lee's government would be heavily reliant on the Plan to take effect and thereby increase his government's electoral appeal. Not coincidently, from mid-1961 the implantation of the Plan rapidly gained momentum. After a very slow start in the first half of the year, by the end of 1961 M$85.78 million of the M$118.84 million, or 72% provided for economic development for the year had actually been invested. The EDB had also been established in August and wasted no time in assuming its intended role.

In the late 1960s, the PAP elites further strengthened their commitment to development during one particular historical event. In January 1968, the British Labour Government announced its plan to close all its bases in Singapore within the next three years. If not handled properly, the British pull-out could create a serious economic crisis for the country, as British spending in Singapore accounted for about 25% of its GNP, and the bases employed some 21,000 Singaporeans (Le Poer 1991). The withdrawal was expected to lead to an estimated loss of approximately 100,000 jobs (Rodan 1989: 87). The inevitable deterioration in living standards and the rising unemployment resulting from the British pull-out might further fuel leftist sentiment in the country. Consequently, the PAP believed it was necessary to intensify efforts to create economic opportunities for its people. With this heightened need for economic growth, the institutional capacity of the EDB in directing development was enhanced by the establishment of the Jurong Town Corporation (JTC) and the Development Bank of Singapore (DBS). The former had the dedicated role of providing infrastructure development, while the latter was formed to provide a financing function for industrial development (Rodan 1989; Perry et al. 1997).

Substituting the Domestic Private Capital

The previous section examined the rise of the developmental state in Singapore in the aftermath of the 1961 party split. The need for political legitimacy pushed the ruling PAP elites to create a dominant one-party system to achieve a political monopoly and formulate a combination of economic and social policies to generate performance-based legitimacy. In this section, I analyse how the PAP's policy choice led to the formation of an FDI-SOE-dominated industrial structure in Singapore.

When the PAP launched its industrialisation drive in the early 1960s, there was a dynamic and influential domestic business community that had emerged during the colonial period and was comprised of mostly small, family-owned firms and a number of large enterprises (Haggard and Low 2002). They could have become the agent of the PAP's industrialisation drive. However, for both economic and political reasons, they seemed incompatible with the PAP's political goal of rapidly creating jobs to contain leftist sentiment. Economically, they were not capable of helping the PAP jump-start the economy. PAP party leaders were convinced that the local business community, consisting overwhelmingly of small Chinese merchants and financiers, did not possess either the technologies and managerial skills to drive industrialisation or the willingness to embark on long-term development projects (Vogel 1991: 77; Haggard and Low 2002; Cheng 1991: 190). Politically, the Chinese merchants, who generally backed the Chinese state, spoke Chinese languages and followed Chinese culture, were also at odds with the English-speaking PAP leaders' political vision. The PAP was particularly suspicious of these indigenous capitalists for their political association with the leftist movement (Haggard and Low 2002; Regnier 1993; Huff 1995).

The unsuitability of the local private firms in relation to the PAP's development ambition pushed the PAP to attract FDI in order to jump-start the economy. As the PAP urgently needed an immediate boost in employment creation through rapid industrial development, the utilisation of foreign capital became inevitable.[2] This need for a quick fix of the economy was not seen in the cases of South Korea and Taiwan, in which the ruling elites opted for the promotion of an organically-orientated

[2] This point was confirmed by both Lam Keong Yeoh and Alexius A. Pereira during private meetings in July 2014 and July 2015, respectively.

industrial outlook.[3] In the words of Ezra Vogel (1991: 77), 'The PAP permitted a level of foreign control that Taiwan and South Korea, more confident of their own entrepreneurial talent, would have found unacceptable'. From 1961 to 1965, as the PAP leadership was hopeful that a common market with Malaysia would be established, the role of the EDB in promoting industrial growth was somewhat downplayed (Low et al. 1993: 64). The State Development Plan, 1961–1964, called for building Singapore into 'an attractive investment site in itself' (Rodan 1989: 64). The government attempted this by pouring a large amount of public investment into the construction of industrial estate. Special attention to the development of industrial estates in the early 1960s was due to two considerations: (1) with the high wage levels in the region, the government had to examine other cost-cutting ways to attract foreign capital, and (2) with Malaya's industrial town of Petaling Jaya, the government needed to provide a better industrial site to redirect the FDI towards Singapore (Rodan 1989: 65).

A series of events in the second half of the 1960s intensified the desire of the ruling elites to attract FDI. After the separation, the loss of Malaysia as an economic hinterland in August 1965 made the import substitution industrialisation strategy adopted by the PAP seem unlikely to be successful. Singapore's post-separation entrepot trade declined as both Malaysia and Indonesia pursued policies of greater economic self-reliance (Rodan 1989: 87). After separation, the PAP leaders had frequently embarked on world trips in search of new markets, with limited success (H.-C. Chan 1971: 15). By then, FDI promotion seemed to be the only possible strategy for the PAP. FDI would not only provide Singapore with high levels of technology and management skills to generate industrial growth, but more importantly also ensure the small island's access to global markets. As Lee Kuan Yew (2000: 75) recalled in his memoirs, 'Since our neighbours were out to reduce their ties with us, we had to link up with the developed world – America, Europe and Japan – and attract their manufacturers to produce in Singapore and export their products to the developed countries'.

[3]The ruling elites in South Korea and Taiwan certainly had many more domestic entrepreneurial resources at their disposal. In Taiwan, a number of mainland capitalists retreated with the KMT regime to the island. In South Korea, the domestic enterprises were even more developed as a result of the Japanese colonial legacy.

As the EDB stepped up its efforts to create jobs after 1965, the PAP began to consciously pursue a strategy of FDI promotion. Between 1965 and 1969, there was a surge of FDI promotion in the country. In late 1965, gross fixed assets of foreign investment were just $157 million. By late 1969, with the enhanced institutional capacity of the EDB, the figure had risen by $443 million, of which $297 million was invested between 1968 and 1969 in an apparent attempt to boost employment in the light of the British pull-out (Rodan 1989: 99). In the early 1970s, once the task of job creation was finished and the British pull-out had taken place smoothly, the Singaporean government began to adjust its FDI strategy to be more selective in attracting MNCs to facilitate the country's transition to higher value-added manufacturing (Rodan 1989; Low et al. 1993). In the late 1970s, in the aftermath of an economic recession, the PAP attempted to integrate the operations of local and foreign capital to enhance the competitiveness of the industry, with little success (Rodan 1989). In this context, limited financial resources and assistance were channelled to develop locally-based firms into a support network to facilitate the party's FDI strategy.

The ruling elites also committed to the creation of SOEs as another alternative to the development of domestic private capital. The government's direct public investment in the economy dates back to the very beginning of the country's industrialisation drive. Between 1960 and 1967, the total number of public investments in manufacturing enterprises was 18. In 1968, as many as 13 such enterprises were established and another eight were set up the following year (Rodan 1989). There were two main motivations for the PAP to set up SOEs. One of them was the initiative to take over various operations vacated by the British, as 'the government was not prepared just to hope that private enterprise would fill the gap' (Rodan 1989: 95). The other motivation was the lack of initiative from private companies; in the absence of any alternative capital promotion, the government recognised the commercial viability of SOEs and thus acted to ensure the survival of enterprises (Rodan 1989).

While the Taiwanese and Korean ruling elites either limited or promoted DPCC in the market, the Singaporean ruling elites substituted the domestic private capital with other forms of capital—FDI and SOE—to expedite the formation of a strong industrial base in the country. For both economic and political reasons associated with political survival, domestic business elites were excluded from the PAP's industrialisation project at the beginning of the development process. These political choices led to an industrial structure dominated by FDI and SOE instead of DPCC.

The domination of FDI in the economy was clear by the late 1970s. While foreign investment accounted for 78.5% of total gross fixed assets in manufacturing in 1978, wholly foreign-owned companies also accounted for 52.3% of all manufactured exports for 1976–1978, and companies with at least 51% foreign ownership accounted for 87.5% (Rodan 1989: 130). In the same period, the SOEs also became a backbone of the Singapore economy and contributed 76% to the country's growth in GDP (Rodan 1989: 148). In the early 1980s, as Singapore embarked on a 'second industrial revolution', the state reinforced the FDI-SOE two-legged developmental strategy by expanding the JTC and made more investment to expand and diversify GLCs through the creation of the government's three wholly-owned holding companies (Rodan 1989).

These rounds of policy promotion led to the formation of an industrial structure characterised by FDI and SOE. Table 3.1 compares domestic and foreign companies' share in Singapore's manufacturing. The contribution made by several large foreign enterprises has been steadily increasing since the beginning of Singapore's state-led industrialisation. Since the mid-1980s, foreign enterprises' share in output has remained

Table 3.1 Domestic and foreign companies' share in Singapore's manufacturing

	Share in the number of firms (%)		*Share in output (%)*	
Year	*Domestic*	*Foreign*	*Domestic*	*Foreign*
1968	88.3	11.7	53.9	46.1
1975	78.0	22.0	28.7	71.3
1978	78.3	21.7	28.5	71.5
1980	75.1	24.9	26.3	73.7
1983	79.0	21.0	28.5	71.5
1985	79.0	21.0	29.7	70.3
1988	77.4	22.6	25.0	75.0
1990	76.6	23.4	24.1	75.9
1992	78.2	21.8	25.8	74.2
1995	78.7	21.3	23.6	76.4
1999	79.1	20.9	22.2	77.8
2001	79.5	20.5	21.5	78.5

Source Akkemik (2009: 44)

Table 3.2 GLC's contribution to Singapore's GDP

	Value added (S$ billion)			*Share of GDP (%)*		
	1996	*1997*	*1998*	*1996*	*1997*	*1998*
GLC	13.7	15.9	17.9	10.6	11.3	12.9

Source Low (2002: 287)

above 70%. SOE also secured its position in the economy, as Table 3.2 shows that that GLCs have contributed to about 11% of Singapore's GDP.

Elite Decisions and Non-Democratic Transition in Singapore

Unlike in South Korea and Taiwan, rapid economic development in Singapore did not change the political system. The country's lack of democratic transition can be explained by the strategic choices of the ruling elites in response to the absence of a democratic movement. This section demonstrates a situation in which an absence of a democratisation movement leads to ruling elites' adoption of a strategy of authoritarian co-optation. The section consists of the following three subsections: (1) the continuation of the PAP's authoritarian rule in Singapore in the context of the lack of a democratisation movement; (2) the adoption of the PAP's strategy to co-opt the middle class after the mid-1980s electoral setback; (3) the PAP's intensified authoritarian co-optation efforts following the 2011 electoral setback.

The Continuation of the PAP's Authoritarian Control

Rapid socioeconomic development did not lead to a democratisation movement in Singapore. Since the late 1980s, the empowered society has alienated itself from the authoritarian party. As Catherine Lim (1994) notes, 'It is easily seen that the main criticisms levelled against the PAP point to a style deficient in human sensitivity and feeling – "dictatorial", "arrogant", "impatient", "unforgiving", "vindictive"'. The territory's small size made it extremely easy for the authoritarian government to control the rapidly-changing society. As Beng-Huat Chua observes (1995: 207–208), 'Being political opposition can be a perilous activity in a very small island city-state where the state is pervasive in every sphere of social life'. The PAP's strong control of society generated a deep climate of fear, which gave 'rise to the prevalent practice of self-censorship, to the extent that many avoid or even vilify participation in activities that are held in the public sphere' (Lee 2002; see Lim 2007). As most Singaporeans chose to stay out of the political sphere and focus solely on their private lives, widespread political apathy emerged in the affluent society during the 1990s. Consequently, the form of state-society relations in Singapore evolved into what Lim (1994) calls 'the Great Affective Divide':

> The Great Affective Divide has created a model of government-people relationship that must be unique in the world: solid, unbreakable unity of purpose and commitment on the economic plane, but a serious bifurcation at the emotive level, resulting in all kinds of anomalies and incongruities. A kind of modus vivendi appears to have developed, by which each agrees to live with the other's preference as long as both work together for the good of the country. Hence the Government continues to say: "we know you dislike us, but..." and the people continue to think: "We are totally grateful to you for the good life you've given us and will vote you again, but..."

More recently, Singaporeans' fear of the PAP regime has lessened to some degree, as evident in three developments in protesting against the government during the early 2010s. Firstly, some people resorted to forms of high-visibility, high-risk protest never seen before, such as graffiti writing on public buildings, persistent, strident online criticism and intensified public gathering at the Speakers' Corner in Hong Lim Park. Secondly, the protest was not confined to a small group of young dissidents empowered by the Internet, but was spreading to involve large segments of the population. Lastly, a few young and exceptionally qualified Singaporeans joined the ranks of the opposition to stand as candidates against the PAP (Lim 2014; Da Cunha 2012). Despite the fact that the Great Affective Divide had seemingly 'reached crisis proportions' (Lim 2014), there was still no conclusive evidence to suggest that there was any national sentiment among most Singaporeans for greater democracy and political freedoms that is comparable to the Minjung movement in South Korea and the Tangwai movement in Taiwan.[4]

Singapore's authoritarian structure has clearly continued to ensure the PAP's political control and domination over society. A distinctive strategy of control, which came to be known as the 'out-of-bounds (OB) markers' in the 1980s, worked effectively to enforce self-censorship in society (Lim 2007). The only space for freedom of political expression—the Speaker's Corner—is closely watched by the state (Rodan 2001: 161; Milne and Mauzy 2002: 164). Anyone who is willing to take the risk of openly criticising the regime is subject to severe punishment. This zero-tolerance policy was demonstrated in two highly-publicised cases. In 2012, Prime Minister Lee Hsien Loong sued a pro-democracy blogger for defamation, and in 2015, an Internet personality was arrested and jailed for publicly criticising the legacy of Lee Kuan Yew.[5]

In the political sphere, the opposition community is also under the tight control of the PAP. Since the 1980s, the PAP has made sophisticated use of defamation lawsuits to marginalise outspoken members of the opposition (Ortmann 2010). Since the election of J. B. Jeyaretnam, most opposition parties have repeatedly stated that they intend to be a constructive opposition (Ortmann 2010; Mutalib 2004).[6] With slightly increasing social support in recent years, the opposition parties are now more articulate than in the past.[7] However, they still suffer from two weaknesses. One problem is that the opposition have been extremely fragmented due to different leadership styles (Mutalib 2004; Ortmann 2010). As Derek Da Cunha (2012: 18) argues, 'The inability of key opposition personalities to work with each other under just one or two banners has been of great benefit to the PAP'. The fragmentation of the opposition parties is likely to continue as more small parties enter into the next

[4] Most public gatherings at the Speakers' Corner concern socioeconomic issues rather than political reform. At present, anti-PAP views are mainly confined to cyberspace.

[5] To justify its strict control by pointing to the achievement of high living standards, the PAP leaders have been keen advocates of a series of ideologies including 'meritocracy', 'elitism' and 'Asian Value', to generate regime support and promote social consensus (Trocki 2006).

[6] The only exception has been the Singapore Democratic Party, which has adopted a more aggressive approach against the PAP.

[7] This point was confirmed by several scholars during my visits to Singapore in July 2014 and July 2015.

general election in 2016 (Koh 2015). Another problem for the opposition parties is a lack of party ideology.[8] Professor Alan Chong points out that 'most parties are clones of the PAP, with some slight differences in terms of being more pro-welfare, pro-liberal or pro-Singaporean' (Koh 2015). The main opposition party, the Workers' Party, takes a moderate approach, as evident in its principles of political engagement: 'The Workers' Party's participation in General Elections seeks to ensure that our office-holders do not simply walk into office without contest'. The party's successful establishment of a beachhead in parliament in 2011 was based on its increasing public image of being very much like the PAP, only more democratic (Barr 2014: 135).

Consequently, there is no need for the ruling PAP to transform its political formula. While authoritarian institutions were replaced with democratic ones in South Korea, all political institutions that limit political rights have remained in place in Singapore. The controversial ISA is still the core of the authoritarian structure and considered important for maintaining political order.[9] Even though the ISA is rarely used today, its existence 'functions as a psychological restraint on individuals who are potentially willing to voice their opinion in public or even join opposition parties' (Ortmann 2010: 128). The PAP's authoritarian structure was further strengthened in 2009 with the construction of the Public Order Act, which further restricted political rights to peaceful assembly and enhanced policing powers to control public gatherings (Amnesty International 2009). The PAP's long-standing stringent control over traditional media has increasingly extended to the Internet through state regulation (Lee 2004). With the establishment of a new institution, the Community Development Council (CDC), in 1996, the PAP's existing grass-roots organisation in the country was also strengthened to mobilise mass support (Vasil 2000: 174).

[8] All opposition parties including the SDP emphasise their alternative policies to socioeconomic issues for generating social support. Political control alone certainly does not explain this phenomenon. The PAP's strategy of co-optation also played a role in preventing opposition parties from presenting themselves as a viable political alternative. This co-optation strategy will be discussed below.

[9] In 1987, the ISA was applied by the PAP during the so-called "Marxist Conspiracy" against civil society activists and opposition party members. In October 2011, Teo Chee Hean, the Deputy Prime Minister, justified the relevance of the ISA and its powers of preventive detention in Parliament.

The above discussion confirms my hypothesis concerning the emergence of a pattern of democratic mobilisation of the social classes—the absence of a democratisation movement. In Singapore, the state's ability to retain its dominance in the country, mainly because of the small territorial size, made it extremely easy for the PAP to control the empowered society (the middle class and the working class). As a result, neither the middle class nor the working class were willing to challenge the strong authoritarian power of the PAP regime. In this situation, the ruling elites clearly had no desire to end their authoritarian rule. The result was the continuation of the PAP's authoritarian political system. In the following section, I will show that the absence of a democratisation movement can motivate ruling elites to adopt a strategy of authoritarian co-optation.

The PAP's Strategy of Authoritarian Co-Optation

The political context for the ruling elites' adoption of an authoritarian co-optation strategy was the emergence of middle-class discontent in the socioeconomic arena. In the early 1980s, the middle class became increasingly assertive about their material benefits, and there was growing confidence among Singapore's educated middle class to publicly criticise government policy (Rodan 1989: 183–186). One example is the unpopularity of Lee Kuan Yew's thesis on eugenics. Rodan (1993: 58) writes that 'in the subsequent "Great Marriage Debate" ... the columns of *The Strait Times* were replete with letters of dissent and dismay from female graduates ...'. The middle class' desire to protect their interests from unfavourable government policies was reflected in a growing sympathy for opposition parties who were willing to challenge the PAP's policy. Rodan (1992: 4) reports an unprecedented expression of dissent when the PAP harshly treated and publicly denounced the opposition party; 'It was apparent that there was a public sympathy for the idea of an opposition as such, especially among Singapore's now sizable middle class'.

The increasing antagonism of the middle class clearly threatened the PAP's hold on power. In the electoral arena, with the functioning of regular democratic elections, the PAP's position was weakening. In the mid-1980s, the middle class turned its dissatisfaction into 'protest votes', which contributed to the PAP's declining electoral support in the 1984 general election (Milne and Mauzy 2002). The election was a watershed, as the PAP's share of popular votes declined to 64.8%. The ruling elites' weakened standing necessitated strategic adaption to the new political environment. One key concern for the ruling party after the 1984 election was the possibility of a 'freak' election, or too many voters casting their protest votes for the opposition without thinking that the PAP could be voted out of power (Milne and Mauzy 1990, 2002). As Chua (1995: 175) writes, 'Lee Kuan Yew, while appreciative of the electorate's political cleverness in pressing the PAP government without defeating it, raised a sinister scenario of a "freak" election: asking the electorate what would happen if instead of just being given a message, the PAP government were defeated'. Imagining this scenario in which ruling elites would lose power completely, the PAP was subsequently compelled to pursue a strategy of authoritarian co-optation.

One dimension of this strategy was to create new authoritarian institutions to contain the growth of the opposition parties. The PAP's first such institutional reaction was the introduction of the non-constituency MP (NCMP).[10] This can be labelled as an authoritarian adaption strategy, as the NCMP weakened any sentiment for voting opposition members into parliament and co-opted different political voices into the PAP decision-making process (Rodan 1993; Milne and Mauzy 2002). New electoral rules to manipulate the electoral process were created to strengthen PAP political dominance. The most important institutional invention by the PAP was the group representation constituencies (GRCs), introduced in 1988. Not only did the GRCs raise the threshold of votes needed by the opposition, but they also eliminated all ethnic parties from the country (Milne and Mauzy 2002; Chua 1995; Mutalib 2004). The creation of the GRCs was related to the subsequent establishment of Town Councils. As elected MPs became town councillors, the voters had to consider how the consequence of voting for the opposition candidates would affect their well-being. Since the early 1990s, the PAP has been threatening to withdraw government funding and services to areas where opposition members are elected (Milne and Mauzy 2002). A more recent response of the PAP was the introduction of a cooling-off day to curb the opposition parties' momentum built up during eight days of official campaigning (Da Cunha 2012).

Perhaps an even more important strategic response of the PAP was the building of consultative institutions. These consultative institutions aim to create a more open polity and adopt a less combative governing

[10]Without any constituency base, these appointed MPs were 'likely to be more moderate and to respond to the centre of the political spectrum' (Chua 1995: 176).

style that allows for greater consultation and popular participation to meet the expectations of the increasingly demanding middle class (Rodan 1992; Vasil 2000: 141–174). In its first expression of projecting a consultative image, the PAP established the Feedback Unit in March 1985 to gather input from the public.[11] At the grass-roots level, in keeping with the ruling elites' intention to build a consultative government, the National Agenda and Next Lap campaigns were launched in 1987 and 1991, respectively, to adopt Singaporeans' views into the PAP's policy agenda.[12] In addition to grass-roots outreach, the Government Parliamentary Committee (GPC) and the Institute of Policy Studies (IPS) were established to promote policy consultation with experts and professionals outside of Parliament. Another government initiative was the creation of a new category of MP in 1989—nominated MPs (NMPs), who brought non-partisan ideas and professional opinions from the public into the parliamentary debate process (Rodan 1992, 2006). The purpose of these consultative institutions was clearly to strengthen the party's political dominance in a new political environment affected by the discontent of the middle class. As Rodan (1996: 33) argues, 'The PAP's aim appeared to be to undercut the growing support for opposition political parties by demonstrating how unnecessary they were'.

These consultative mechanisms were essentially created to facilitate the PAP's strategy of co-optation. Furthermore, following the mid-1980s electoral setback, the PAP stepped up its efforts to provide material benefits through the formulation of new social policies. By the 1980s, as the middle class wanted more than just a roof over their heads, the state's provision of public housing was no longer sufficient to meet their material needs. Between 1984 and 1990, the PAP introduced loans for tertiary education, medisave (health care) and medishield (low-cost insurance against illness). To improve the value and quality of housing, a Housing and Development Board (HDB) flat upgrading programme was launched in 1984. Policies such as Central Provident Fund (CPF) housing grant, the building of Housing and Urban Development Company (HUDC) flats and HDB executive condominiums were also formulated to meet

[11] In 2006, the Feedback Unit was reconstructed into REACH (Reaching Everyone for Active Citizenry @ Home).

[12] This process continued after the 1997 and 2001 elections when two national public consultation attempts were launched: Singapore 21 (S21) in 1997 and Remaking Singapore in 2002.

the new demand of Singaporeans to purchase desirable properties (Low 1998; Milne and Mauzy 2002).

The adoption of this strategy of authoritarian co-optation enabled the PAP to consolidate their political power in the new political environment. Between the 1991 and 2006 elections, except for a landslide victory in 2001 when the PAP won 75% of the popular vote, its share of the vote usually fell somewhere in between 61 and 66%. From 1988 to 2006, the PAP marched through the elections without facing a single opponent in more than half of Singapore's districts due to the opposition parties' strategy to encourage 'worry-free' protest votes from people who had no intention of voting the PAP out of power (Milne and Mauzy 2002: 150). In the first fully contested election in 2006, the opposition finally fielded enough candidates to force the PAP to wait until election day to declare victory, but captured only two seats. The inability of the opposition parties to take control of any GRC suggests that an immediate end to the PAP's electoral domination remained a remote possibility.

The Enhanced Authoritarian Co-Optation of the PAP After 2011

The theoretical logic behind the East Asian ruling elites' adoption of an authoritarian co-optation strategy was, once again, vividly demonstrated in the aftermath of the 2011 electoral setback. The Singaporean elites' strategic response was made in the context of a deep unhappiness within the middle class. This unhappiness had grown in the late 2000s and stemmed from three socioeconomic conditions[13]: (1) the deep recession after the global financial crisis created more financial burden for society; (2) the ageing population was increasingly vulnerable at the time of the economic downtown; and (3) the influx of foreigners that were accused by the Singaporeans of making housing unaffordable, driving up living costs and overcrowding public transport. In this context, the PAP's social welfare measures, adopted in the aftermath of the 1984 election, became increasingly insufficient to meet the material needs of the middle class.[14]

[13]The first two socioeconomic factors were pointed out by Tan Ern Ser in a private communication in July 2015. The third factor was raised by a number of scholars including Gillian Koh, Donald Low, and Alexius Pereira. These conversations took place in July 2014 and July 2015.

[14]For a description of the middle-class discontent, see The Economist (2010a). Also see Economist (2010b) for a government response to the situation.

With an election approaching, the government responded to this backlash with the rhetoric of 'inclusive growth', offering more material support to the unhappy middle class and anyone who needed help (MOF 2010).

Just as had happened in the mid-1980s, the unsatisfaction of the middle class eventually resulted in an election upset in 2011. The pervasive socioeconomic dissatisfaction of the middle class provided opposition elites with new opportunities to mobilise social forces (see Welsh 2011; Kesavapany 2011; IPS 2011). The result of the election marked the PAP's worst performance since independence, as it lost 39.9% of the popular vote and a record six seats out of 87. More significantly, the ruling PAP lost one entire GRC—its own institutional invention to make it impossible for the opposition to win. The awakened electorates cleverly sent a clear message to the ruling elites that they wanted policy change. To them, putting more opposition members in parliament would make a difference. As Da Cunha (2012) observes, 'there is an increased desire by Singaporeans to ensure that the governing party does not hold an overwhelming dominance on power'.

The renewed political insecurity associated with the dissatisfaction of the middle class led to the PAP's decision to adopt an even more extensive authoritarian co-optation. Consequently, both the extent and the substance of the PAP's co-optation efforts greatly increased after the 2011 electoral setback.[15] One immediate strategy to woo middle class' interests was the resignation of the PAP's first- and second-generation leaders (i.e. Lee Kuan Yew and Goh Chok Tong) from the cabinet to allow the PAP to 'have a fresh clean slate' in May 2011. As these leaders explained their decisions, 'After a watershed general election, we have decided to leave the cabinet and have a completely younger team of ministers to connect to and engage with this young generation' (BBC 2011). The core of this round of co-optation was a year-long extensive national policy consultation campaign called Our Singapore Conversation (OSC) which aimed to inform government policy-making (see Guo and Phua 2014; Tan 2016). This public consultation facilitated the government's enhanced efforts to co-opt the middle class through material benefits. From 2011 to 2015, the PAP improved Singapore's transport system, slowed down the influx

[15] This was pointed out by Gillian Koh during a private conversation in July 2014. According to Koh, previous public consultation campaigns were largely top-down processes with little public participation. More public engagement was seen in the extensive public consultation carried out in 2015 and 2016.

of foreigners and formulated a series of social policies to address urgent concerns transport, health care, immigration and housing (Tan 2015, 2016). This extensive provision of social welfare led political commentators to label the government budget proposals a 'Robin Hood' budget, 'corrective budget' or 'bridging budget' (Palatino 2013; Chua 2015).

The PAP's extensive co-optation of the middle class in the aftermath of the 2011 election did, once again, effectively strengthened its political standing in Singapore. As Kenneth P. Tan observes (2015: 112), 'OSC might have given the electorate the impression that the PAP government was listening to them, and the policy changes suggested that their views mattered'. The result of this was a massive electoral rebound for the PAP in 2015 when the party's popular vote soared to 69.9% and one SMC seat was recovered from the opposition (Vasu and Cheong 2016). While the ruling party improved its results in all constituencies, the Workers' Party retained control of the Aljunied GRC, but with a far slimmer vote margin than in 2011. Handing over five parliamentary seats to the opposition in exchange for losing just one GRC was perhaps an optimal result for the PAP, as a parliament without a clear presence of elected opposition members would certainly make the middle class uncomfortable.

To summarise, the PAP's strategic adaptions since the mid-1980s confirm my hypothesis that East Asian ruling elites will opt for a strategy of authoritarian co-optation when they face an absence of a democratisation movement. The empirical case has shown how this strategic choice was made at two crucial moments of the PAP's political survival in a rapidly-industrialising Singapore. The PAP's strategy of authoritarian co-optation was first adopted in the mid-1980s and pursued more extensively in the aftermath of the 2011 election. As a result of this elite strategy, the state's institutional arrangements were enhanced by the creation of both authoritarian institutions and consultative mechanisms to deal with middle-class antagonism around the mid-1980s. The strategy was then upgraded after the 2011 electoral setback, when elites faced even greater middle-class discontent. As a result of the ruling elites' political strategy, their authoritarian power was boosted by the creation of new political institutions to contain opposition parties and consultative institutions to co-opt middle-class interests.

The Formulation of the State's Economic Visions in Singapore

While in Taiwan and South Korea, the state's economic vision was eventually eroded after democratic transition, the strengthened PAP regime maintained a good rate of economic performance. The formulation of the state's growth-first economic visions can be divided into two periods: the period from the mid-1980s to the late 2000s, categorised by an immigration-growth driven model, and the period from 2010 onwards, categorised by a productivity-driven growth model. Both periods were shaped by the PAP ruling elites' desire to ensure Singapore's economic performance and growth prospects.

The Global City-State and the PAP's Pro-Immigration Policy

The background of the formulation of these two distinctive economic visions is the PAP's desire to push the nation towards greater globalisation. Among the three East Asian states, Singapore is undoubtedly the most integrated with the global economy, as the PAP has acknowledged the need for international capital since 1965. The state's ambition to achieve global integration and liberalisation is perhaps best reflected in the 1991 Strategic Economic Plan (SEP), which called for Singapore to become a first-league developed country by 2030. The plan aimed to develop Singapore into a global city-state by enhancing human resources, becoming internationally oriented, developing manufacturing and service clusters, maintaining international competitiveness and reducing vulnerability (see MTI 1991; Chia 2001; Low 2006).

It should be noted that, while the PAP was pursuing the strategy of authoritarian co-optation, the PAP introduced party-led economic restructuring committees in a significant change to the state policy-making process.[16] These committees focused on formulating a new state strategic vision. Between 1985 and 2016, the state created five units: the Economic Committee (1985), the Committee on Singapore's Competitiveness (1997), the Economic Review Committee (2001), the Economic Strategies Committee (2009), and the Committee on the Future Economy (2016).

[16] This point was confirmed during a private communication with Donald Low in July 2015.

These economic policy committees have two notable characteristics.[17] Firstly, the building of a consultative government has extended into the economic policy-making arena. These economic committees operated on a large scale, in regard to both its membership and the extent of the policy ground it covered. The members of the committees include top PAP elites, senior civil servants, business elites, prominent academics and representatives from government-sponsored NGOs. They function through a main steering committee and several subcommittees. Each subcommittee is assigned to a specific task regarding restructuring the economy. The second noticeable feature of these committees is the PAP's leadership role. The chairman of the main committee is always a top PAP official. The main committees of the last four economic restructuring committees were chaired by either the Minister of Trade and Industry (1985, 1997) or Minister of Finance (2001, 2009). Three top PAP elites were the chairmen of the main committees: Lee Hsien Loong (1985, 2001), Lee Yock Suan (1997) and Tharman Shanmugaratnam (2009). The PAP also took leadership at the subcommittee level; in 2001, PAP elites chaired five of seven subcommittees; and in 2010, PAP elites or senior civil servants chaired or co-chaired all subcommittees.

With these two characteristics, it is easy to see how the formation of PAP-led economic policy committees enhanced the state's capability to formulate coherent national economic agendas, as part of a broader authoritarian consultative state. These committees have always been a sort of soul-searching event, invariably coinciding with economic recessions, as the regular state-led large-scale policy formulation exercises allowed the PAP to conduct thorough and comprehensive policy reviews and adjust accordingly (Choy 2010).[18] Nevertheless, the core of the state's economic vision—the establishment of a global city-state—has remained unchanged, which is reflected in the policy recommendations made by the economic committees since the early 1990s.[19]

[17] These two characteristics are based on my examination of the three committee reports compiled in 2001, 2009 and 2016.

[18] The only exception is the 2016 economic committee which was not formed in the wake of an economic crisis. The government's justification is that Singapore was facing a crisis-like situation in 2016 as the country was moving away from an immigration-driven growth model to a productivity-driven one (such economic shift will be discussed in this section below).

[19] Studies provide some discussion on the 1984 economic committee (see Milne and Mauzy 2002; Rodan 1989, 1992). Secondary sources on more recent economic

From the mid-1980s to late 2000s, an important component of the Singaporean state's growth-first economic visions was the PAP's pro-immigration policy. While the pro-globalisation state strategic vision was well preserved in order to stimulate long-term growth, the PAP also had to deal with a new consequence of being a global city-state. The country had to face periodical economic crises brought about by cycles of booms and busts in the global economy (Choy 2010). Between 1985 and 2010, the country weathered four major economic crises: the 1985 global recession, the Asian financial crisis of 1997, the bursting of the US dot-com bubble in the 2000s and the global financial crisis of 2008. To ensure shorter-term performance, the unavoidable business cycle that the country had to face as a global city-state required the PAP to seize growth opportunities when global economic conditions turn better (Auyong 2014). This point was well reflected in Lee Hsien Loong's philosophy of growing 'as fast as we can', as introduced in his 2006 National Day Rally speech: 'I think that when conditions are good and the sun is shining, we should go for it, as fast as we can, as much as we can. Get the growth, put it under our belt, and put it aside a little bit, so when the thunderstorm comes again, we will be ready' (Prime Minister's Office 2006).

To seize opportunities to expand the economy, the PAP elites had two policy options.[20] The first was to augment the labour force through importation of foreign workers (particularly because of Singapore's low fertility rate). The second was to maintain the size of the workforce and push for productivity growth. In comparison with the task of promoting productivity, the importation of foreign labour seemed to be the clear option for the performance-orientated PAP to allow businesses to obtain the workers that they needed, seizing opportunities to expand when the conditions are favourable (Auyong 2014). Consequently, the urgent need to maintain good economic performance pushed the ruling elites to adopt a pro-immigration policy.

As a result of the PAP's strategy, the inflow of unskilled workers into the country was very much dictated by business cycles. Right

committees are very limited. My discussion is based on information provided in either executive summaries or full reports produced by these committees.

[20]The discussion of the PAP's preference for the importation of foreign labour was raised in a private communication with Donald Low in 2015. Low points out that the PAP opted for an easy solution (the importation of foreign labour) to drive up growth in between crises.

before the 1985 recession, the government planned to completely phase out low-skilled foreign workers to put more pressure on industries to restructure. However, the disastrous recession of 1985 made the PAP realise that cheap foreign workers could be used as a buffer to deal with economic fluctuations (Auyong 2014; Rahman 2010). To manage the inflow of low-skilled foreign labour, since the late 1980s, the PAP has implemented a series of measures including the pre-existing quota system and a system of levies that businesses must pay to hire low-skilled foreign workers (Rahman 2010; Auyong 2014). Administrative control was relaxed during periods of economic boom, that is, the first half of the 1990s, and more recently in 2007, to reduce labour shortages in various sectors. Conversely, the inflow of such migrants was discouraged during periods of economic downturn in the 1980s, the later parts of the 1990s and the early 2000s. After a series of economic crises in the early 2000s, to further expand the economy, the government decided to attract middle-level skilled foreign talents in response to 'a changing economic landscape which generates greater demand for middle-level skilled workers' (Rahman 2010: 205).

As the PAP has retained control within the state's authoritarian structure, maintaining economic growth has remained at the top of its policy agenda since the late 1980s and it remained dependent on the promotion of an immigration-driven growth model until the late 2000s. The rest of this section will focus on a policy adjustment that occurred between 2010 and 2015 to transform the immigration-driven growth model.

An Urgent Policy Change: Reducing Foreign Labour Dependency

The government's shift away from a pro-immigration policy was not an indication of a compromise in its growth-first strategic vision; rather, it was motivated by the ruling elites' intention to strategically modify the existing economic programme to suit the new social, economic and political context that they faced. I will argue that this shift was not driven by populist policy-making,[21] but instead a transformation of the

[21] Many citizens and members of the opposition parties hold the view that the policy change was a populist response of the PAP after its 2011 electoral setback. In a private meeting in July 2014, Gillian Koh revealed that the PAP's strategic response in the post-election period to cut the inflow of foreign labour was considered a 'victory' for people by the public.

immigration-driven growth model to a productivity-driven one. The roots of this policy change are both political and economic.

Towards the late 2000s, the PAP began to face a dire political situation as its growth-first, pro-immigration policy began to directly conflict with the interests of the middle class. As the PAP enlarged the labour force in order to expand the economy, Singapore's population increased from three million in 1990 to four million in 2000 and to five million in 2010, while the percentage of Singaporean citizens decreased from 86 to 63% (Lim 2011: 28). The middle class complained about the influx of both middle- and low-skill foreign workers, including that they were stealing jobs from local Singaporeans, being bad neighbours, keeping the wage level low, causing overcrowding on public transport and causing social problems in public spaces such as littering, drunkenness and the use of illegal drugs (see Rahman 2010; Chong 2012; Vasu 2014).

An expression of discontent from the middle class soon broke out within Singapore's limited political space. In cyberspace, the middle class established online petitions and organised their own forums to protest plans for a foreign workers' dormitory in nearby factories (Chong 2012: 192). In 2014, a major backlash against foreign workers on social media even prompted Lee Hsien Loong to warn against 'hateful or xenophobic comments, especially online' (Fenn 2014). At the Speaker's Corner, the one designated space for free speech, a massive public gathering broke out in protest of the PAP's white paper that had just been approved by Parliament, which aimed to increase the population to 6.9 million by 2030 (Adam 2013; Vasu 2014). In Parliament, the moderate opposition party also relayed this sentiment, calling for an 'orderly growth within limits'. Arguing that the government went for a 'growing at all cost' strategy, the opposition party voiced the concerns of the middle class—'foreign immigrants are taking away the jobs of Singaporeans or opportunities that Singaporeans could have been better served' (Mokhtar 2014).

This discontent did not result in any immediate policy changes. To persuade the middle class of the merits of its strategy, the PAP stressed a trade-off between maintaining economic growth and reducing foreign workers; the state could reduce overcrowding on public transport, for example, by restricting the entry of foreign workers, but this would in turn reduce the government's ability to deliver economic growth to its citizens (Oon 2010; MOF 2010). The PAP also employed rhetorical strategies such as stressing 'survival' and 'vulnerabilities' to appeal to Singaporeans to understand the economic importance of this policy (Rahman 2010: 209–210).

Although it continued to argue that the pro-immigration policy was crucial for the economy, the PAP eventually began to make adjustments as it realised that this policy may not be conducive to sustaining long-term growth. The policy recommendation of the Economic Strategic Committee (MTI 2010) points out that the pro-immigration policy is not a sustainable strategy for two reasons. Firstly, the aggressive labour force augmentation reduced the incentive for employers to upgrade their operations and raise productivity. Secondly, the country would also run up against the social and physical limits that an ever-increasing proportion of foreigners in the workforce will bring. Once ruling elites acknowledged the downside of the immigration-driven growth model, the government began to push for a shift to a productivity-driven growth model. In the 2010 Budget Statement delivered in that year, the word 'productivity' was mentioned 72 times (Auyong 2014). The shift to a productivity-driven model was clearly a strategy to reduce the country's dependence on foreign workers without sacrificing its prospects for economic growth.

Consequently, there were two parallel sets of economic policies after 2010. The first pushed for a shift towards productivity growth, beginning with the establishment of a state development agency, the National Productivity and Continuing Education Council in April 2010. The National Productivity Fund was also set up in 2010 and expanded in 2011 to provide funding for the state's policy shift (MOF 2010, 2011). This effort was twofold: firstly, a major wave of investment in the labour force with Continuing Education and Training (CET) and special training support for professionals, managers, executives and technicians (PMETs), and secondly, to support enterprise investments in innovation and productivity, a 'Productivity and Innovation Credit (PIC)' was introduced in 2010 and enhanced in 2011 to provide tax incentives to enterprises (MOF 2010, 2011). These efforts were accompanied by an increase in foreign worker levies to control their inflow across the economic cycle. To narrow the gap between productivity growth and labour supply, the Special Employment Credit (SEC) was also launched to raise the employment level of older Singaporeans (MOF 2010, 2011).

The second set of state policies aimed at seizing growth opportunities at the end of the 2009 financial crisis to ensure Singapore's economic performance. The country's policy shift towards productivity growth in

2010 did not mean an abrupt end to its growth strategy of labour argumentation. For the performance-orientated ruling elites, while the push for productivity contributed to longer-term growth prospects, the party's pro-immigration policy remained a handy tool for boosting shorter-term economic recovery. This logic is evident in Prime Minister Lee Hsien Loong's National Day Rally speech on 29 August 2010, when he announced that there would be another influx of foreign workers that year. To justify his actions to the middle class, he repeated a standard PAP explanation:

> This year, with the booming economy, we will definitely need more foreign workers so that we can create more jobs in Singapore. A few months ago, I mentioned to the press that we could need more than 100,000 foreign workers more this year... Maybe, we will get by with a few less, perhaps 80,000 workers. But I said this to highlight the trade-off which we face and which we cannot avoid. You want higher growth which will benefit our workers, that also means accepting more foreign workers to come and work in Singapore. You choke off the foreign workers, the economy is stifled, growth is not there, our workers will suffer. (Prime Minister's Office 2010)

The PAP accelerated its effort to reduce the country's reliance on foreign workers in late 2011, mainly due to the political situation it faced after the 2011 electoral setback. The party's poor electoral performance made the ruling elites realise that their growth-first approach to the immigration issue was not a politically viable strategy for power consolidation. This realisation compelled the ruling elites to modify their policy agenda to suit the new political environment. On 14 August, at the first National Day Rally after the election, Lee Hsien Loong signified the PAP's intention to change the pro-immigration policy of the PAP:

> Last year I spoke of this at length in the Rally, so I will not repeat the explanations which I gave you, hopefully you remember what I said last year. I think Singaporeans understand the logic of the policy but the emotional impact, they still feel that and that still causes worry and concern. So I empathise with this and we are acting to relieve the pressure and to make clear that we are putting Singaporean first. (Prime Minister's Office 2011)

The PAP's shift from 'growth first' to 'putting Singaporean first' means that policy-makers could no longer rely on the possibility of importing foreign workers as an easy solution for dealing with economic fluctuations. To ensure economic growth and continue Singapore's ascent to a global city-state, they needed an alternative for the private sector's labour needs. The push for productivity growth to reduce the country's reliance on foreign workers became a natural solution for the party's urgent need to maintain balance between keeping the economy growing and making the middle class happy, as evident in the remarks made by Lee Hsien Loong in an August 2015 interview:

> If we have no foreign workers, our economy suffers, our own lives suffer. (If) we have a lot of foreign workers, the economy will do well, (but) we have other social pressures, other problems with our society, which are going to be very real, and which we have to take very seriously and which we cannot accept. Somewhere in the middle, we have a mix of evils; on the other hand, we may be able to find a spot where all things considered, this is something which balances our needs as well as our identity, as well as our economic requirements, and enables us to move forward. (Channel NewsAsia 2015)

Facing a heightened need to correct past policy mistakes, the PAP stepped increased measures to slow down the inflow of foreign workers. Between 2011 and 2014, the PAP continued to use foreign worker levies as a price mechanism to control the inflow and also introduced a numerical limit on the importation of foreign workers—a calibrated reduction of the Dependency Ratio Ceilings (DRCs) across all sectors and the Man-Year Entitlement (MYE) quotas in the construction and process sectors (MOF 2012). To minimise the economic impact of reducing the availability of cheap foreign labour, the PAP also stepped up efforts to boost the domestic labour force. Older low-wage Singaporean workers, housewives and potential part-timers were encouraged to rejoin the workforce (MOF 2012). To narrow the gap between the reduction in the number of foreign workers and the availability of domestic workers, the government accelerated its push for greater productivity growth with the enhancement of its PIC scheme, the introduction of PIC bonuses, promotion of the CET system and the adoption of information and communication technology (ICT) solutions in the private sector (MOF 2012, 2013, 2014). In addition, to appeal to the middle class, in September 2013, the government announced the Fair Consideration Framework (FCF), which required employers to consider local workers first before they hire foreign workers (Ernst & Young 2014).

The authoritarian political system of the country continued to shape the state's formulation of an economic vision after the mid-2010s. The episode of radical state policy adjustment in the post-2011 period came to an end in 2015,[22] as the PAP reconsidered its economic implications. Deferment of the foreign worker levy, as announced in the 2015 budget, was in recognition of the potential that 'tighter foreign worker policies may be threatening the survivability' of firms (Norton 2015). Maintaining economic performance clearly remained at the top of the ruling elites' political agenda, and 'push for innovation and internationalisation' replaced 'push for productivity' as the key themes of the state policy agenda (MOF 2015; Tay 2015).

Policy Constraints from Business Elites in Singapore

The Emergence of Non-Constraining Business Interest Groups

In Singapore, the state's policy-making has been largely immune from the policy constraints of business elites, due to the industrial structure and lack of the democratic transition. In this section, I will show how the high level of FDI and SOE contributed to the emergence of two types of non-constraining business interests—non-indigenous and state-linked business interests. My hypothesis suggests that neither of them have produced structural constraints on Singapore's policy-making.

The country's high percentage of FDI led to the growth of a large number of non-indigenous business interests during the development process. Given that foreign business elites have a greater ability to transcend borders and therefore particular state policies should they wish to, the state's collaboration with MNCs required the PAP's consistent efforts to assure foreign investors that they would profit by participating in Singapore's economic development. As Lee Kuan Yew wrote in his memoirs, 'If I have to choose one word to explain why Singapore succeeded, it is "confidence". This was what made foreign investors site their factories and refineries here' (Lee 2000: 68). Clearly, all these government

[22] The radical approach to reduce the country's reliance on foreign labour came to an end even prior to the general election in September 2015.

interventions in the form of administrative measures to reward or discipline the domestic industrialists, as was prevalent in South Korea, became insufficient for the political elites to tame private business interest in the Singapore case.

With the political elites' goal of building international confidence, the state policy-making process is characterised by the provision of customer-oriented services to enhance MNCs' business operations in and from Singapore—a distinctive element that was largely absent in the state policy process in Taiwan and South Korea. As Edgar Schein (1996: 18) notes, the EDB, the state policy-making agency, 'has elements of a typical sales organisation of a large consumer-oriented corporation, only in this case what is being sold is a country and the EDB mission goes beyond marketing into entrepreneurial and venture capital activities'. In short, the functioning of the state's policy-making depends on the PAP's ability to retain the cooperation and trust of non-indigenous business interest groups by providing excellent 'customer services' to ensure the profitability of their foreign 'customers' in the development process. The EDB has accordingly been viewed as a 'one-stop' government agency to promote industrial growth in Singapore. As Edgar Schein (1996: 42) describes:

> Operationally this meant that the EDB should locate foreign investors, sell them on coming to Singapore, help them to find land and facilities for building their factories, assist them in recruiting and training a labour pool at the required skill level, provide whatever infrastructure was needed, offer whatever financial incentives or tax breaks were necessary, even make investments if necessary, and solve all problems that might arise subsequently as the manufacturing operation expanded without, however, compromising any of its own strategies, rules, and principles.

The policy partnership between the PAP and the non-indigenous business interests is similar to a kind of company-client relationship, which is based entirely on the economic and commercial motivations of each partner. Staffed by the most talented bureaucrats available in the system and equipped with all sorts of advanced managerial skills and knowledge, the EDB and other state agencies approached foreign MNCs to effectively 'ascertain what they require in order to realise the state's transformative developmental objectives' (Dent 2003: 260; Schein 1996; EDB 2011). The material interest of the MNCs thus became incorporated into the country's overall development strategy. One attempt by the PAP to maintain this company-client relationship is demonstrated by the EDB's launch of four award programmes—the Distinguished Partner in Progress Award launched in 1991, the Distinguished Friends of Singapore Programme launched in 1998, the Friends of Singapore Award launched in 2000 and the Honorary Citizen Award launched in 2003—to recognise the contribution of foreign investors to the country (see Yuen 2008).

While the relationship between the state and indigenous businesses became increasingly confrontational, the policy partnership between the PAP and MNCs remained harmonious and cooperative in nature. After 1985, the state set up groups to facilitate its dialogue with foreign investors, including the Singapore Economic Review Committee (SERC) in 1985, the Singapore Competitiveness Committee (SCC) in 1997, another Economic Review Committee in 2001 and the Economic Strategies Committee in 2011. Although a large number of foreign business elites were invited to join these committees, the chairman and deputy chairman have always been top leaders from the PAP. The incorporation of non-indigenous business interests into the state policy process was further institutionalised with the establishment of the EDB's International Advisory Council (IAC), although the chairman of the IAC has similarly always been a top PAP leader. The IAC's input in policy-making was highlighted when Deputy Prime Minister Teo Chee Hean, then IAC Chairman as well, commented on the IAC's deliberations: 'the IAC has provided valuable inputs to help sharpen EDB's strategies as Singapore seeks to transform existing industries and to seize new growth opportunities' (EDB 2013). In addition, the consultative relationship between the non-indigenous business interests and the PAP has also been based on the state's links with executive personalities from foreign MNCs, which 'intensified after the 1997-98 regional financial crisis at the behest of the state' (Dent 2003: 260).

Since the material interests of non-indigenous business elites were well served by the development-oriented state, they had little interest in reshaping the direction of state policy-making. As a result, the PAP government managed to retain its leadership role in the strategic alliance between the government and foreign investors. This outcome was highlighted in a study by Christopher Dent (2003: 260):

> In approaching transnational business representatives for advice, the government does not come with a "blank page" but rather with an

> extensively pre-planned and sophisticated policy framework. In their dealings in such matters, interviewed business representatives all confirmed that the government mainly consults with them for fine-turning advice and ultimately endorsement of their policy strategies. Thus, Singapore's hosted foreign Transnational corporations (TNCs) do not directly shape the government's economic policies" but are rather invited by the state to "sit around the strategic table to supplement the government's own thinking". Moreover, "change is very much government-led" and "the state combines its own industrial intelligence with that of transnational firms based here".

Non-indigenous business interests were not the only non-constraining interests that emerged during Singapore's industrialisation. The country's large number of SOEs resulted in the emergence of state-linked business interests, who by nature were directly controlled by the PAP. Since the creation of the GLCs, the PAP has maintained a style of strong top-down leadership through the Directorship and Consultancy Appointments Council (DCAC) established in 1971. The DCAC, consisting of top ministers and leading civil servants of the PAP government, was in charge of making almost every appointment at board and executive levels across almost every GLC (Milne and Mauzy 2002: 29). Regardless of who was running the Council on a day-to-day basis, it is certain that the ultimate decision always rested with the prime minister because he chaired the Coordinating Board, the top state agency that oversees the operations of the DCAC (Vennewald 1994; Worthington 2003; Barr 2014). Furthermore, the appointed chairmen and directors in the GLCs are not ordinary bureaucrats; rather, they are all veteran politicians or senior bureaucrats selected from different ministries, including brigadier-generals from the defence ministry (Haggard and Low 2002: 317). The appointment of senior state personnel played a significant role in ensuring the implementation of policy at the state-controlled enterprise level. As Vennewald (1994: 33) describes:

> Chairmanships and directorships in state enterprise in Singapore are policy positions. Contrary to functional boards which consist of executives from within the company and represent operational functions (finance, administration, marketing etc.), GLC and statutory boards lay down general guidelines and concentrate on the performance of the company. The directors of the companies only rarely function as managers. Most of them are "watchdogs over the state's Investment". None of these technocratic

> "mandarins", however, are able to exercise real political power or use their administrative powers to influence policies beyond an implementary or company level – at least not yet. The rules of the game are still set by the political leadership.

After the mid-1990s, the power to appoint board members and non-executive directors of GLCs was transferred from the DCAC to Temasek Holdings. Significantly, this occurred at around the same time that the ruling Lee family and a few Lee loyalists became directly involved in the PAP's managerial control over the GLCs. Three individuals have played crucial roles in this regard (Barr 2014: 63; Low 2001: 428). The first is S. Dhanabalan, a Lee Kuan Yew loyalist that occupied the chairmanship of both Temasek Holdings[23] (from 1996 to 2013) and the DCAC (by 1998). The second is Lee Hsien Loong's wife, Ho Ching, who was appointed the Executive Director and CEO of Temasek Holdings (from the early 2000s to this date). They were assisted by Lee Kuan Yew's wife's nephew, Kwa Chong Seng, who was appointed Deputy Chairman of Temasek Holdings (from 1997 to 2013). The appointments of these highly-trusted individuals in Temasek Holdings consequently strengthened the PAP elites' ability to impose managerial control over the GLCs. Thus, despite an increasing number of individuals from the private sector having been appointed to GLCs, the investment decisions of the GLCs were still under close supervision of the PAP elites. In the words of Low (2001: 428), 'This perpetuation of the developmental state through managerial control ensured consensus in corporate policy in line with state macroeconomic direction'.

The above analysis involves two types of non-constraining business interest groups: non-indigenous business interests and state-linked business interests. Their emergence was a result of the functioning of FDI and SOE as the economy's main types of capital ownership. The high level of FDI led to the emergence of non-indigenous business interest groups, who could withdraw their investment from the host country at will and thus shaped the state-business cooperation for policy formulation in Singapore in a fundamentally different way than occurred in South Korea and Taiwan, as the PAP sought to ensure that these groups' economic interests were incorporated into government policies. Consequently, few

[23] In 2013, S. Dhanabalan was replaced by Lim Boon Heng, a retired senior PAP leader.

changes occurred to the close collaboration between the PAP and non-indigenous business interests during the development process. The high level of SOE also cultivated a number of state-linked business interest groups in Singapore. As these business elites were mainly close associates, royalists or even relatives of the PAP, they basically acted as the watchdog for state policies rather than challenging the state's policy-making.

The Continuation of State-Led State-Business Cooperation

The rest of this section aims to achieve two goals. First, I aim to demonstrate a negative effect of FDI and SOE on the structural constraints from business elites—that these types of capital ownerships diminish affects the ability of private domestic businesses to influence the state. I will thus examine the relationship between the PAP state and a third segment of Singapore's private sector: local SMEs. I will pay particular attention to the interactions between the PAP state and the Singapore Chinese Chamber of Commerce and Industry (SCCCI)—the supposed counterpart of the Korean FKI. Second, I will show how both Singapore's industrial structure and lack of a democratic transition led to an absence of policy constraints from business elites. This result was manifested in the process of Singapore's financial liberalisation and privatisation which, unlike the Korean and Taiwanese experiences, mainly followed the state's economic objective to enhance the economic performance of the country.

The presence of foreign and state-linked business interests inevitably diminished the influence of indigenous business elites in the state's policy-making. This effect of the domination of FDI and SOE was clear from the beginning of the state-led development process. In 1969, at the occasion of the swearing-in ceremony of the Singapore Chinese Chamber of Commerce (SCCC), the new Chamber leadership stressed 'the need to follow the lead of the government and to adhere to the modern orientation of the PAP party-state' (Visscher 2007: 191). During the export-oriented industrialisation (EOI) from 1966 to 1984, the SCCC transformed itself into the Singapore Chinese Chamber of Commerce and Industry (SCCCI) and put great efforts into 'modernising' the Chamber to bring it more closely in line with the expectations of the political elites (Visscher 2007: 177–241). This is not to say that the SCCCI had ceased to function as an indigenous business interest group; indeed, its primary objective was to win state support for local private businesses. Squeezed in between international capital and state capital, the local business chamber felt that 'local private business deserved to be treated better than, or at least equal to, foreign private business' (Visscher 2007: 210). However, it was easy for the political elites to ignore this demand after they formed a close partnership with the international capital. As Visscher (2007: 210) observes, 'protests of the SCCC were vocal and almost continuous, but had little effect. The government was convinced of its economic development strategy to which the contribution of the local trading sector was far from crucial'.

After the mid-1980s, the weak domestic private business interests were incorporated into the Singaporean state's policy-making mechanism as a result of two important developments. Firstly, the consultative mode of economic decision-making empowered the local business owners by offering them new channels to win political protection for their interests. In the mid-1980s, with the establishment of the Association of Small and Medium Enterprises (ASME), the demand of the majority of local SME owners for greater state assistance had turned into criticism that 'the government had simply taken the easy option by relying on foreign capital' (Chalmers 1992: 70). Secondly, policy consultation with the private sector through the establishment of the Economic Committee (EC) made the PAP elites realise that the contribution of the local businesses, particularly that of SMEs, was important to the economy of Singapore (Visscher 2007; Chalmers 1992). The PAP's re-evaluation of its economic strategy thus gave new opportunities to the indigenous business interest groups to demand more state support for local capital.

The negative effect of both FDI and SOE on the level of structural constraints generated by business elites is clear in the case of Singapore. Squeezed in between MNCs and GLCs, the local business owners had limited influence on the state's economic policy-making. In more recent years, these weak domestic private business interests have been more closely incorporated into the Singaporean state's policy-making mechanism rather than shaping them. The inclusion of local SMEs was furthered with the establishment of the Enterprise Development Centre (later expanded into the SME Centre), which was supported by the state's SME promotion agency SPRING. Since the mid-2000s, the establishment of these service centres in all five local business associations has provided institutionalised channels for the PAP to incorporate the policy opinions of SME owners into the formulation of the state's SME policy. The continuation of local business leaders as a junior partner of the state during the economic policy-making process was clear in the statement of Thomas Chua, President of the SCCCI[24]:

> SCCCI can serve as an effective bridge between government and business to facilitate consultation and communication. We welcome the government consulting businesses ahead of introducing and implementing new government regulations that impact the business community, so that their views and suggestions can be incorporated. (SCCCI 2014)

While the emergence of structural constraints from business elites was significantly hindered by the FDI-SOE-dominated industrial structure, the lack of meaningful democratic transition of the country also prevented the emergence of institutional constraints from business elites. The continuation of state developmentalism differentiated Singapore from South Korea and Taiwan during the economic liberalisation process of the 1980s and 1990s. In the latter two cases, the processes of financial liberalisation and privatisation of SOEs were not free from constraining business interests. As a result, domestic business elites were able to strengthen their economic power by obtaining newly-released economic resources from their respective states. This development did not occur in Singapore.

Without any structural or institutional constraints produced by business elites in the state policy process, the state-led state-business cooperation has remained largely unchanged. A clear indication of the state's continued strategic role in the economy is the fact that the economic liberalisation of the 1980s and 1990s entirely followed the PAP elites' strategy of generating growth; the privatisation process that began in the mid-1980s aimed to both broaden and deepen the Singaporean stock market, and allow the private sector to be the engine of growth (Low 1998, 2006). The PAP chose listing on the local stock market via initial private offerings as its mode of privatisation, which did not strengthen the economic power of the private capital. At the same time, the PAP has also practised rolling privatisation, which allowed the state to withdraw from

[24] A further indication of local business elites' low policy status is that the issue for communication between the government and the private sector that Thomas Chua referred to here was a trivial issue. This remark was made by him at a session organised by the SCCCI to give members a briefing on the government's decision to stop issuing permits for the placement of freezer/storage containers at factories due to fire safety concerns.

areas that deterred private initiatives and make new investment as a part of continual industrial restructuring (Low 1998, 2001, 2006).

Similarly, Singapore's financial liberalisation process also proceeded gradually under the direction of the PAP elites. It was only after the test of the Asian financial crisis that the PAP was confident enough to open up the domestic banking sector (Lee 2000: 101). The subsequent two rounds of financial reform in 1999 and in 2001 accomplished not only the political elites' goal of creating strong PAP-linked local banks—the Development Bank of Singapore (DBS), the Overseas-Chinese Banking Corporation (OCBC) and the United Overseas Bank (UOB)—but also the creation of a more conducive environment for impending FDI (see Lee 2000; Yeung 2005; Chong 2007; Hamilton-Hart 2000). This strategy allowed the PAP to succeed in improving the international competitiveness of the country while still retaining control over financial resources in the banking system. In contrast to the South Korea and Taiwan cases, these PAP-directed liberalisation reform processes provided the independent local business elites with no opportunity to strengthen their financial muscles, instead enhancing the country's market efficiency while renewing the state's strategic role in the economy.

Since the mid-1980s, the Singapore developmental state has not deviated from its MNCs-GLCs growth strategy. While working closely with the MNCs and GLCs in research and development (R&D) and innovation activities, the PAP also pushed these enterprises to aggressively expand into overseas markets (see Wong 2011; Tsui-Auch 2004; Tsui-Auch et al. 2014; Pereira 2000, 2008; Chong 2007; Low 2006). Once political elites realised the importance of SMEs to the economy, they were able to co-opt input from SMEs to strengthen SME growth strategies and maintain the resilience of the developmental state. The Local Industry Upgrading Programme (LIUP) was established in 1986, the first project of the PAP to forge closer ties between MNCs and SMEs (see Chalmers 1992; Coe and Perry 2004). The 1993 Regionalisation Strategy externalised the LIUP by providing opportunities for local SMEs to expand overseas as associates of MNCs and GLCs (Low 2001, 2006). Ever since the first SME Master Plan in 1989, the productivity and capabilities of SMEs have also been boosted by a series of SME policy packages to 'achieve quality growth' (see Low et al. 1993; Chalmers 1992; MTI 2013).

Policy Constraints from Organised Labour in Singapore

PAP's Control of Organised Labour

Policy constraints from organised labour are also absent in Singapore, since organised labour has been tightly controlled by the PAP since the very beginning of the development process due to the state's focus on attracting foreign investment. In this section, I will show that a high level of FDI leads to the emergence of state-managed labour interest groups. I expect to find that the high level of FDI motivated the ruling elites to develop a distinctive pattern of industrial relations to manage labour interests during the development process. This concept was first shaped by the 1961 report of the UN Mission, which highlighted the importance of labour incorporation for Singapore's FDI-dominated economy:

> In our opinion Singapore has the basic assets for industrialisation. With the resourcefulness of her people, an active industrial promotion programme by the government, and – this is the main point – close cooperation between employers and labour, Singapore can successfully carry out the expansion programmes proposed in this report to achieve their basic objectives...The cooperation between employers and labour must come about...If not, labour will suffer for it. Capital can go to other countries. Enterprise can quiet down or escape. Labour has no escape possibilities. It needs employment here and has no time to wait. (Cited in Schein 1996: 37)

As the country stepped up its project of attracting FDI in the wake of independence, the need to create a stable pattern of industrial relations became even more urgent. In the first move towards this goal, in 1965, the National Trade Union Congress (NTUC) was called on to commit itself to a tripartite 'Charter for Industrial Progress' between the government, the NTUC and the Singapore Employer's Federation (SEF). This agreement stipulated that 'all partners in the industrialisation programme ... must pool their efforts and strive for a continuing increase in productivity and output in all enterprises' (Cited in Rodan 1989: 91). The ratification of the Charter essentially denied the traditional role of labour unions as legitimate interest groups and paved the way for incorporating organised labour into the state policy process.

The full cooperation of the organised workers in the state's policy process required the state's control over labour. As Lee Kuan Yew moved to win over the union, a few 'irrational' and 'ignorant' union leaders were soon arrested (Lee 2000). What followed was the legislation of new labour laws aimed at disciplining the labour unions, via the Trade Union Bill in 1966, the Employment Act and the Industrial Relations Act in 1968, the latter limiting labour costs, expanding managerial autonomy and increasing the cost of industrial actions (Rosa 1990; Coe and Kelly 2002; Rodan 1989; Leggett 2007). With these new laws, the labour unions ceased to engage in collective bargaining in the development process. As a result, the number of work stoppages reduced from a high of 161 in 1961 to zero in 1969 (Haggard 1990: 111). The pro-business labour laws, coupled with fear of an economic crisis, led to the decline of trade union movements in terms of membership, revenue and morale from 1965 to 1970 (B.-H. Lee 1995). The 1969 NTUC seminar was a turning point; as the unions creased to represent the interests of workers, the PAP allowed the NTUC to attract the loyalty of the union members by delivering a range of services to its members. In the 1970s, consumer cooperatives were established to offer essential commodities at low prices; taxi cooperatives were established to provide jobs to unlicensed taxi drivers; and an insurance scheme was set up to offer insurance coverage to workers. The union's strategy indeed worked as the decline of membership halted (B.-H. Lee 1995).

To a considerable extent, the PAP's successful control over organised labour was a result of the development of a close relationship between the party and the union. At the 1969 NTUC seminar, the development of a 'symbiotic' relationship between the PAP and the NTUC was first mentioned. The heart of the PAP-NTUC relationship was the formal and informal connections between the PAP and NTUC leaders. The first secretary-general of the NTUC, Devan Nair, an old unionist friend of Lee Kuan Yew, was urged by Lee to return to Singapore to lead the union. As Lee (2000) wrote, 'It was an enormous advantage for me to have Devan as secretary-general of the NTUC. He coordinated and fine-tuned my policies and inculcated positive work attitudes in the unions'. As a result, the NTUC 'entered into the ultimate collective agreement – compliance with, and subservience to, the state, in exchange for a seat at the table of government and the promise of continued rapid development' (Coe and Kelly 2002: 352). One thing was clear after 1969: not only were the labour unions denied their traditional role as legitimate interest groups, they also became a strategic policy partner of the ruling party. As Garry Rodan (1989: 93) observes, 'Trade unionism was finished in Singapore. Labour was now part of the corporate structure of the Singapore state'.

Another significant aspect of Singapore's success in creating state-managed labour interests was the establishment of the National Wages Council (NWC). The NWC has long been responsible for managing Singaporean labour interests in line with the government's economic agenda. In fact, the background of its establishment was the growth of industrial workers' material interests in the 1970s. Until 1971, with the wage of workers frozen by the government, rapid industrial growth resulted in considerable economic inequality between the waged labour and non-wage sections of Singapore society (Rodan 1989: 106). Even the NTUC found it difficult to justify the wage freeze policy and campaigned for a more equitable share of profits. Workers' discontent also coincided with a growing labour shortage and therefore 'a continually improving bargaining position' (Rodan 1989: 106). As a result, there was an unusual increase in industrial disputes, all of which essentially centred on greater material gains for workers. By then, 'the government had come to share the genuine fears of employers that a wage explosion was a real possibility but had also concluded that a total clamp on wages was not only impossible but counterproductive to wage control' (Rodan 1989: 106). The NWC was subsequently formed to 'introduce a formalised institutional control over the process by which wage rises were arrive at' (Rodan 1989: 106).

The formation of the NWC entirely transferred the responsibility of the unions in advancing the material interests of its members to the PAP. The material gains of organised labour now had to be regulated by the PAP, in line with the overall economic development programme formulated by the development alliance between the PAP state and international capital. As Lee Kuan Yew wrote with some satisfaction in describing this outcome, 'strict laws and tough talk alone could not have achieved this. It was our overall policy that convinced our workers and union leaders to support our key objective: to establish international confidence in Singapore and attract investments and create jobs'. Garry Rodan (1989: 106) explains how the NWC incorporated the NTUC into the state's policy-making process:

> In February 1972 the National Wage Council (NWC) was formed. This ten-member tripartite body was comprised of equal representation of

capital, labour and government and included an independent chairman, who in 1972 was Professor Lim Chong Yah, an academic economist. Representatives of capital were drawn from the Singapore Employers' Federation (SEF), the National Employers' Council (NEC) and the Singapore Manufacturers' Association (SMA). Representation of capital thus tended to favour larger employers and, particularly, international companies which dominated these bodies. Labour representatives were drawn from the NTUC, and the government's representatives from its own departments. Under this structure the government's influence was quite pervasive since, apart from its own direct representation, the PAP's cross-fertilisation with the NTUC, and the absence of any independent union representation ensure that in practice the NWC would reflect government policy.

Strengthening the Control Mechanism

The same effect of FDI on deterring the emergence of structural constraints was once again observed during Singapore's process of industrial upgrading in the late 1970s, as the task of ensuring industrial peace became even more crucial. By then, the PAP's labour management mechanism displayed signs of uncertainty stemming from three sources. Firstly, because the special relationship between the party and the union was largely due to the personal ties between Lee Kuan Yew and C. V. Devan Nair, it was feared that it might be more difficult to sustain and enhance the relationship because the second generation of the PAP lacked contact with the unionist leaders. Secondly, the NTUC had acquired a huge amount of assets through its business operations in the 1970s. With this growing economic power, the labour unions might become more capable of questioning PAP control over them and challenge the PAP's policy-making. Thirdly, within the NTUC, a grassroots leader, Phey Yew Kok had developed strong personal support and even vowed to challenge the newly appointed secretary-general at the NTUC conference in 1979 (Rodan 1989: 156; Vasil 1989). While there was no indication that organised labour might turn the growing power against the PAP, the remote possibility of labour's defection motivated the PAP elites to take the necessary steps to ensure that the PAP's control over organised labour remained firm as the country moved up the economic ladder.

An even closer integration between the PAP and NTUC was consequently witnessed after the 1979 NTUC seminar on 'Progress into the 80s'. The following year, an NTUC-PAP Liaison Committee comprising top leaders of both the party and union was established. To strengthen this close relationship, the PAP initiated a strategy of bringing technocrats into the union's leadership (Leggett 2007; Rodan 1989; Vasil 1989; Milne and Mauzy 2002). Lim Chee Onn, who had no previous party or trade union experience, was brought in as secretary-general. In 1980, he was also appointed Minister without Portfolio. These practices of bringing in technocrats to lead the NTUC and combining the offices of secretary-general and government minister continue today.[25] Consequently, after 1980, the NTUC began to function as a de facto governmental organisation, as it became closely affiliated with the PAP and is led by a team of technocratic elites co-opted from the government. Union leaders who run for elections as opposition candidates will be sacked by the NTUC (Leggett 1993: 124). In the words of Cho-oon Khong (1995: 122), 'The NTUC's purpose appears to be to explain government policy to union members and mobilise their support behind government initiatives'.

In addition to placing technocrats into NTUC leadership, the PAP also tightened its control over the rank-and-file workers. In this respect, the authoritarian system has enabled the state to strengthen its control over labour interests. In the 1980s, when the NTUC moved from omnibus unions to industry-wide and house unions, partly to enhance the NTUC's effectiveness, a few strong unions strongly opposed the state's decision and resisted the reconstruction (Rodan 1989; B.-H. Lee 1995; Leggett 2007). However, it was clear that 'any attempt to obstruct the reconstruction of unions would meet the full force of the PAP state apparatus' (Rodan 1989: 159). In another effort to reinvigorate its effectiveness, the NTUC restructured again after 1997 when the power base of these large unions was mostly removed (Lee 2000: 113). In 1982, a legal redefinition of trade unions reemphasised the need for the trade unions to promote good industrial relations and achieve productivity, and made breakaway unions unacceptable (Leggett 2007). In the 2000s, organised labour's position as a subservient partner to the PAP state was further clarified by the government's harsh treatment of the Airline Pilots' Association of Singapore to attempt to replace pro-business union leaders (Rodan 2006: 157). Since 1985, the NTUC has also paid much attention to strengthening its membership base. Against a global decline in labour union movements, the NTUC's membership base saw a twofold increase

[25] The secretary-general Chan Chun Sing, who assumed office in April 2015, is also the Minister in Prime Minister's Office and formerly a Major General in the Singapore Army. His predecessor Lim Swee Say was appointed as the Minister for Manpower.

between 1995 and 2005. The unionisation rate also grew by 4%, from 23 to 27% from 2009 to 2013 (B.-H. Lee 1995).

In sum, the high level of FDI in Singapore resulted in the emergence of state-managed labour interest groups. To facilitate the creation of a suitable investment environment for foreign investors, the PAP incorporated organised labour—the NTUC—into the state policy-making process by developing close NTUC-PAP relations throughout the industrialisation process. Such efforts by the state to develop a sophisticated labour control mechanism were not seen in the cases of Taiwan or South Korea. As the imperative to attract FDI grew, the government accordingly upgraded its labour control mechanism through even greater integration of the NTUC and PAP, as well as coercive measures over the rank-and-file workers. The emergence of state-managed labour interests consequently contributed to the absence of policy constraints from organised labour in Singapore. This absence will be the focus of the next section.

The PAP's Management of Labour Interests

My hypothesis is that the negative effect of FDI on the structural constraints from organised labour is essentially a result of the state's ability to manage controlled-labour interests in line with economic agendas. In the case of Singapore, the NTUC was mobilised by the PAP to offer support to the state's economic strategies throughout the development process. The emergence of state-managed labour interests was evident in the comments made by the NTUC's labour chief Lim Swee Say in the aftermath of the 2009 global financial crisis. Instead of pushing for greater material advancement for workers, he declared that the NTUC 'will be working towards helping put on track a "Cheaper, Better, Faster (CBF)" economy in the next two years. The CBF strategy will help drive Singapore into the next phase of growth' (UNPAN 2009).[26] In order to achieve overall economic growth, 'the union must (be) pro-business'.[27] As labour interests have been managed by the state, there have hardly been any structural constraints from organised labour in Singapore.

[26] A 'cheaper, better, faster' economy refers to a strategy of promoting cheaper cost, better quality and faster adaptation to maintain Singapore's competitiveness in the global economy.

[27] Lim Swee Say made the 'labour must be pro-business' remark when talking about Singapore's tripartism at an event hosted by INSEAD on 6 November 2009.

While organised labour in South Korea and Taiwan have both begun to produce constraints on the state policy-making process since the 1980s, the material interests of organised labour in Singapore have been carefully managed by the PAP in line with its national development agenda. Since the 1980s, the advancement of labour interests in Singapore has been linked to the government's task of promoting high value-added production, accompanied by three forms of labour gains: wage increases, social security provision and labour's skill formation. With the recommendation of the NWC, the wage level has rapidly increased in Singapore. However, significant labour gains in the late 1980s were a result of the state's efforts to raise labour costs in order to discourage low-skill, labour-intensive investments (Rodan 1989). In addition to wages, the cost of labour also included employers' contributions to the compulsory national superannuation scheme, the Central Provident Fund (CPF), and another payroll levy to the Skill Development Fund (SDF), which was established in 1984 for the training of low-skilled workers. The establishment of the SDF was a clear PAP strategy to upgrade the human capital of the workforce for higher value-added production (Rodan 1989).

While labour was awarded with a share of the country's economic growth, they had to bear the financial burden at times of economic hardship. To tackle the periodic fluctuations that began in the 1980s, the PAP state developed a mechanism to adjust the material gains of labour in line with economic performance through the preservation of a high degree of wage flexibility. In the mid-1980s, the seniority-based wage system was replaced by the flexible wage system. To ensure wage increases were commensurate with productivity gains, the NWC recommended that the companies use variable payments, including an annual variable component (AVC) and monthly variable component (MVC) to reward workers for their contribution to corporate performance. During difficult economic times, the state played a strategic role in adjusting the material gains of labour in order to reduce job losses. In response to the first four economic crises in 1973–1974, 1985, 1998 and 2001–2003, the NWC implemented wage cuts and CPF cuts to reduce costs for businesses and save jobs (C.-Y. Lim 2014; Tan 2004; Chew and Chew 2005; Leggett 2011).

There are two cases in which labour gains were decisively not the result of an increase in the structural constraints from organised labour. Although the pro-business 'cutting cost' strategy was not visible in the post-2009 crisis period, the government implemented a temporary Job

Credit Scheme to offer financial support to companies and help them avoid retrenchments.[28] In a similar case, after the 2011 election, a greater desire to please the middle class led to the formulation of the Wage Credit Scheme (WCS) through which the state provided financial credits to the private sector to increase the wage levels of low-income workers. This satisfied the desire of the middle-class workers for a wage increase without incurring additional costs for businesses (The Straits Times 2015).[29]

In addition to wage issues, the strategic management of labour interests was also expanded to other aspects of labour welfare provision. Since the early 2000s, as the country transformed itself from a manufacturing-based economy to a service-orientated one, it became increasingly crucial for the government to ensure job security for Singaporeans while maintaining industrial peace for businesses (Pereira 2008). To achieve this, the government's efforts to ensure the job security of workers consequently went hand in hand with its projects to upgrade labour productivity. This began with a decision in 2003 to heavily invest in a policy known as the 'Work Restructuring Scheme' to shift workers from the declining manufacturing sector towards the growing service sector (Pereira 2008). With the provision of comprehensive government-sponsored retraining programmes, the job security of workers could be secured only by upgrading their skills in line with the development agenda of the state-business alliance. This government upgraded this project in 2015 when, in line with the formation of the Committee on the Future Economy, it launched the SkillsFuture initiative to offer training programmes to the entire workforce and thus ensure job security for Singaporeans in the future economy (Saad 2015).

For development-orientated PAP elites, labour gains also had to be consistent with labour's contributions to the economy. The establishment of a workfare model by the government in 2007 was a clear indication that greater material interests of workers could only be achieved through hard work in the development process. With the introduction

[28] Lim Swee Say, the secretary-general of the NTUC at that time, noted that the government had to step into do more than just 'cutting costs' to rescue the country from the 2009 financial crisis.

[29] The economic logic behind the policy is that the state's financial assistance will help businesses cope with rising wage costs so that they can free resources to invest in productivity.

of a one-off Workfare Bonus and a permanent Workfare Income Supplement (WIS), the government incentivised low-income and older workers to remain in the labour force in order to receive the government's financial assistance (Ng 2011). In 2010, the Workfare Training Scheme (WTS) was introduced to provide government-funded training opportunities and help workers to be more self-dependent (MOF 2010). Self-reliance has remained the principle of the party's labour welfare model following the 2011 election, as evident in the introduction of the Progressive Wage Model (PWM) that links the material interests of low-paid workers to their skills upgrading and productivity improvements. The PWM ruled out the possibility of a pro-labour Minimum Wage Model which, in the government's view, is ineffective and populist (MOF 2014).

Summary of the Chapter

In the case of Singapore, we have seen how the non-transformation of the developmental state has been shaped by the FDI-SOE-dominated industrial structure and the absence of a democratic transition. This chapter explains that the FDI and SOEs' variables were both products of the strategic choices of the ruling elites in the process of economic and political development. The formation of the country's industrial structure was shaped by the PAP's urgency to kick off an industrialisation process and therefore prevent the revival of the leftist movement. The nation's move towards a consultative-authoritarian system since the mid-1980s was also an adaptive choice of the ruling elites to co-opt the interests of a growing middle class and consolidate the PAP's political power within a new socioeconomic environment.

The FDI-SOE-dominated industrial structure prevented the emergence of structural constraints from both business elites and organised labour, leading to the emergence of two types of non-constraining business interest groups. First, the country's high level of FDI led to the emergence of non-indigenous business interest groups. The PAP maintained a cooperative and nonconfrontational relationship with these foreign entrepreneurs and investors throughout the development process. Second, the country's high level of SOE produced a group of state-linked business interest groups. These state-linked business elites had no intention of challenging the state policy process, as many of them were close associates and royalists of the PAP. Subsequently, the large presence of FDI and SOE in the economy inevitably reduced the policy influence of the domestic business elites. The SCCCI—a supposed counterpart of the KFI—was firstly excluded and later incorporated into the development agendas of the PAP state. The Singapore case has also showed that a high level of FDI deters the emergence of the structural constraints imposed by organised labour. To create an attractive business environment, since the very beginning of the industrialisation process, the PAP made great efforts in managing organised labour in order to ensure industrial peace. Through the 1980s, the close relationship between the PAP and the NTUC further developed, paralleled by the formation of the NWC to manage the material interests of organised labour.

The industrial structure was just one side of the story. The Singapore case also demonstrates how the absence of a democratic transition prevented the emergence of institutional constraints from the middle class and business elites. With the continuation of its authoritarian structure, the PAP continued to place economic growth as a top priority of the regime. As I detailed in this chapter, the PAP's growth-first strategic vision since the late 1980s has been ensured by two supplementary policies. From the mid-1980s to the late 2000s, a pro-immigration policy was put in place to maintain the country's economic performance, but the immigration-driven growth model was later replaced by a productivity-driven growth model in order to adjust to the new economic and political environment after 2010. Because of the absence of both institutional and structural constraints from business elites, both the financial liberalisation and the privatisation that occurred in the 1990s followed the Singaporean state's objective to enhance economic efficiency.

References

Adam, S. (2013). *Singapore Protest Exposes Voter Worries About Immigration*. Available at: https://www.bloomberg.com/news/articles/2013-02-16/singaporeans-protest-plan-to-increase-population-by-immigration. Accessed on 1 October 2015.

Akkemik, K. A. (2009). *Industrial Development in East Asia: A Comparative Look at Japan, Korea, Taiwan, and Singapore*. Singapore: World Scientific.

Amnesty International. (2009). *Further Restrictions on Rights in Singapore*. Available at: http://www.amnesty.org.au/news/comments/20851/. Online access 3 July 2015.

Auyong, H. (2014). *Singapore's Productivity Challenge: Part II*. Singapore: Lee Kuan Yew School of Public Policy at the National University of Singapore. Available at: http://lkyspp.nus.edu.sg/wp-content/uploads/2014/11/

Productivity-challenges-in-Singapore-Part-3.pdf. Online access: 17 October 2015.

Barr, M. D. (2014). *The Ruling Elite of Singapore: Networks of Power and Influence*. London and New York: I.B. Tauris.

BBC. (2011). *Singapore Founding Father Lee Kuan Yew Resigns* (online). Available at: http://www.bbc.com/news/world-asia-pacific-13400296. Accessed on 17 December 2016.

Bellows, T. J. (1970). *The People's Action Party of Singapore: Emergence of a Dominant Party System*. Southeast Asia Studies Monograph 14. New Heaven: Yale University Press.

Chalmers, I. (1992). Loosening State Control in Singapore: The Emergence of Local Capital as a Political Force. *Southeast Asian Journal of Social Science, 20*(2), 57–84.

Chan, C. B. (2002). *Heart Work*. Singapore: Economic Development Board.

Chan, H. C. (1971). *Singapore: The Politics of Survival, 1965–1967*. Singapore: Oxford University Press.

Chan, H. C. (1975). Politics in an Administrative State: Where Has the Politics Gone? In C. M. Seah (Ed.), *Trends in Singapore: Proceeding and Background Paper*. Singapore: Singapore University Press for ISEAS.

Chan, H. C. (1976). *The Dynamics of One Party Dominance: The PAP at the Grass-roots*. Singapore: Singapore University Press.

Channel NewsAsia. (2015). *'I Owe Singaporeans a Responsibility' to Get Foreign Worker Balance Right: PM Lee* (online). Available at: http://www.channelnewsasia.com/news/singapore/i-owe-singaporeans-a/2023914.html. Accessed on 8 October 2016.

Cheng, S. H. (1991). Economic Change and Industrialisation. In E. C. T. Chew & E. Lee (Eds.), *A History of Singapore*. Singapore: Oxford University Press.

Chew, S.-B., & Chew, R. (2005). Wage Issues and Human Resources in Singapore. *Journal of Comparative Asian Development, 4*(2), 77–103.

Chia, S.-Y. (2001). Singapore: Towards a Knowledge-Based Economy. In S. Masuyama, D. Vandenbrink, & S. Y. Chia (Eds.), *Industrial Restructuring in East Asia Towards the 21st Century* (pp. 169–208). Singapore: Institute of Southeast Asian Studies.

Chong, A. (2007). Singapore's Political Economy, 1997–2007: Strategizing Economic Assurance for Globalisation. *Asian Survey, 47*(6), 952–976.

Chong, A. (2012). Disciplining Globalisation for Local Purposes? The Peculiarity of Contending Singaporean Economic Nationalism. In A. D'Costa (Ed.), *Globalisation and Economic Nationalism in Asia* (pp. 177–201). Oxford: Oxford University Press.

Choy, K. M. (2010). Singapore's Changing Economic Model. In T. Chong (Ed.), *Management of Success: Singapore Revisited* (pp. 123–138). Singapore: Institute of Southeast Asian Studies.

Chua, B.-H. (1995). *Communitarian Ideology and Democracy in Singapore*. London and New York: Routledge.

Chua, M. H. (2015). *Singapore Budgetm 2015: 7 Reasons Why This Year's Robin Hood Budget Matters* (online). Available at: http://www.straitstimes.com/opinion/singapore-budget-2015-7-reasons-why-this-years-robin-hood-budget-matters. Accessed on 8 December 2016.

Coe, N. M., & Kelly, P. F. (2002). Languages of Labour: Representational Strategies in Singapore's Labour Control Regime. *Political Geography, 21*, 341–371.

Coe, N. M., & Perry, M. (2004). Promoting Linkage to Foreign Transnationals in a 'Tiger' State: Singapore and the Local Industry Upgrading Programme. *Environment and Planning C: Government and Policy, 22*(3), 363–382.

Da Cunha, D. (2012). *Breakthrough: Roadmap for Singapore's Political Future*. Singapore: Straits Times Press.

Dent, C. M. (2003). Transnational Capital, the State and Foreign Economic Policy: Singapore, South Korea and Taiwan. *Review of International Political Economy, 10*(2), 246–277.

Economic Development Broad. (2011). *Heart Work 2- EDB& Partners: New Frontiers for the Singapore Economy*. Singapore: Straits Times Press.

Economic Development Broad. (2013). *Manufacturing & Digital Technologies Hub* (online source). Available at: https://www.edb.gov.sg/content/edb/en/news-and-events/news/singapore-business-news/Feature/singapore-from-strength-to-strength.html. Accessed on 10 June 2015.

The Economist. (2010a). Welfare in Singapore: The Stingy Nanny (online). Available at: http://www.economist.com/node/15524092. Accessed 12 December 2016.

The Economist. (2010b). Welfare in Singapore: Singapore Government Response (online). Available at: http://www.economist.com/node/15541423. Accessed on 12 December 2016.

Ernst & Young. (2014). *Singapore Implements Immigration Fair Consideration Framework* (online). Available at: http://www.ey.com/gl/en/services/people-advisory-services/hc-alert--singapore-implements-immigration-fair-consideration-framework. Accessed on 12 December 2016.

Fenn, M. (2014). *Singapore's Foreigner Problem* (online). Available at: http://thediplomat.com/2014/02/singapores-foreigner-problem/. Accessed on 6 December 2016.

Guo, Y., & Phua, C. (2014). *Our Singapore Conversation: Bridging the Great Affective Divide*. Singapore: Lee Kuan Yew School of Public Policy. Available at: http://lkyspp.nus.edu.sg/wp-content/uploads/2014/04/Our-Singapore-Conversation.pdf. Online access: 9 July 2015.

Haggard, S. (1990). *Pathways from the Periphery: The Politics of Growth in the Newly Industrialising Countries*. Ithaca: Cornell University Press.

Haggard, S., & Low, L. (2002). State, Politics, and Business in Singapore. In E. T. Gomez (Ed.), *Political Business in East Asia* (pp. 301–323). London: Routledge.

Hamilton-Hart, N. (2000). The Singapore State Revisited. *The Pacific Review, 13*(2), 195–216.

Huff, W. G. (1995). The Developmental State, Government, and Singapore's Economic Development Since 1960. *World Development, 23*(8), 1421–11438.

Institute of Policy Studies. (2011). *Singapore General Election in 2011: What Moves the Voters?* (online). Available at: http://lkyspp.nus.edu.sg/ips/wp-content/uploads/sites/2/2013/08/GK_CAB-GE2011_280411.pdf. Accessed on 10 December 2016.

Kesavapany, K. (2011). *Reflections on the Singapore General Election* (online). Available at: http://www.eastasiaforum.org/2011/05/12/reflections-on-the-singapore-general-election/. Accessed on 1 December 2016.

Khong, C. (1995). Singapore: Political Legitimacy Through Managing Conformity. In M. Alagappa (Ed.), *Political Legitimacy in Southeast Asia: The Quest for Moral Authority* (pp. 108–135). Stanford: Stanford University Press.

Kim, S. P. (1985). The Evolution of the Political System. In J. S. T. Quah, H. C. Chan, & C. M. Seah (Eds.), *Government and Politics of Singapore*. Singapore: Oxford University Press.

Koh, V. (2015). *Splinter Parties Point to Fragmented Opposition*. Available at: http://www.todayonline.com/singapore/splinter-parties-point-fragmented-opposition. Online access: 6 July 2015.

Le Poer, B. L. (1991). *Singapore: A Country Study*. Washington, DC: US Government Printing Office for the Library of Congress.

Lee, B.-H. (1995). Trade Union Growth in Singapore. *Asian Journal of Political Science, 3*(2), 90–111.

Lee, K.-K. (2004). Korea, Northeast Asian Economic Hub Country?: A Critical Study on the New Government Strategy. *Ritsumeikan International Affairs, 2*, 1–25.

Lee, K. Y. (2000). *From Third World to First: The Singapore Story, 1965–2000*. New York: HarperCollins.

Lee, T. (2002). The Politics of Civil Society in Singapore. *Asian Studies Review, 26*(1), 97–117.

Leggett, C. (1993). Singapore's Industrial Relations in the 1990s. In G. Rodan (Ed.), *Singapore Changing Guard: Social, Political and Economic Directions in the 1990s*. New York: St. Martin's Press.

Leggett, C. (2007). From Industrial Relations to Manpower Planning: The Transformations of Singapore's Industrial Relations. *International Journal of Human Resource Management, 18*(4), 642–664.

Leggett, C. (2011). Labour Markets in Singapore: Flexibility in Adversity. In J. Benson & Y. Zhu (Eds.), *The Dynamics of Asian Labour Markets: Balancing Control and Flexibility* (pp. 83–106). London and New York: Routledge.

Lim, C. (1994). *The PAP and the People—A Great Affective Divide*. Available at: http://catherinelim.sg/1994/09/03/the-pap-and-the-people-a-great-affective-divide/. Online access: 1 July 2015.

Lim, C. (2007). *An Open Letter to the Prime Minister*. Available at: http://catherinelim.sg/2007/11/04/an-open-letter-to-the-prime-minister/. Online access: 1 July 2015.

Lim, C. (2014). *An Open Letter to the Prime Minister*. Available at: http://catherinelim.sg/2014/06/07/an-open-letter-to-the-prime-minster/. Online access: 1 July 2015.

Lim, C.-Y. (2014). *Singapore's National Wages Council: An Insider's View*. Singapore: World Scientific.

Lim, S. (2011). Singapore as a Global City: A Balancing Act. In F. B. Yahya (Ed.), *Singapore Perspectives 2011: Our Inclusive Society: Going Forward*. Singapore: World Scientific.

Low, L. (1998). *The Political Economy of a City-State: Government-Made Singapore*. Singapore: Oxford University Press.

Low, L. (2001). The Singapore Developmental State in the New Economy and Polity. *The Pacific Review, 14*(3), 411–441.

Low, L. (2002). Rethinking Singapore Inc. and GLCs. *Southeast Asian Affairs*, 282–302.

Low, L. (2006). *The Political Economy of a City-State Revisited*. Singapore: Marshall Cavendish.

Low, L., Heng, T. M., Wong, S. T., Yam, T. K., & Hughes, H. (1993). *Challenge and Response: Thirty Years of the Economic Development Board*. Singapore: Times Academic Press.

Milne, R. S., & Mauzy, D. K. (1990). *Singapore: The Legacy of Lee Kuan Yew*. Boulder: Westview Press.

Milne, R. S., & Mauzy, D. K. (2002). *Singapore Politics Under the People's Action Party*. London and New York: Routledge.

Ministry of Finance. (2010). *Budget Speech* (online). Available at: http://www.singaporebudget.gov.sg/budget_2010/speech_toc/index.html. Accessed on 1 December 2016.

Ministry of Finance. (2011). *Budget Speech* (online). Available at: http://www.singaporebudget.gov.sg/budget_2011/budget_speech.html. Accessed on 2 December 2016.

Ministry of Finance. (2012). *Budget Speech* (online). Available at: http://www.singaporebudget.gov.sg/budget_2012/budget_speech.html. Accessed on 2 December 2016.

Ministry of Finance. (2013). *Budget Speech* (online). Available at: http://www.singaporebudget.gov.sg/budget_2013/budget_speech.html. Accessed on 2 December 2016.
Ministry of Finance. (2014). *Budget Speech* (online). Available at: http://www.singaporebudget.gov.sg/budget_2014/BudgetSpeech.aspx. Accessed on 3 December 2016.
Ministry of Finance. (2015). *Budget Speech* (online). Available at: http://www.singaporebudget.gov.sg/budget_2015/BudgetSpeech.aspx. Accessed on 3 December 2016.
Ministry of Trade and Industry. (1991). *The Strategic Economic Plan: Towards a Developed Nation (Adapted Executive Summary)* (online). Available at: https://www.mti.gov.sg/ResearchRoom/Pages/The%20Strategic%20Economic%20Plan%20-%20Towards%20a%20Developed%20Nation%20(1991).aspx. Accessed on 6 December 2016.
Ministry of Trade and Industry. (2010). *Report of the Economic Strategic Committee* (online). Available at: https://www.mti.gov.sg/ResearchRoom/Pages/Report-of-the-Economic-Strategies-Committee.aspx. Accessed on 12 December 2016.
Ministry of Trade and Industry. (2013). *Government Enhances Support for SMEs to Achieve Quality Growth* (online source). Available at: http://www.mti.gov.sg/NewsRoom/Pages/GOVERNMENT-ENHANCES-SUPPORT-FOR-SMEs-TO-ACHIEVE-QUALITY-GROWTH.aspx. Accessed on 18 June 2015.
Mokhtar, M. (2014). *Parliament: WP's Chen Show Mao and PAP's Cedric Foo Debate on Immigration* (online). Available at: http://www.straitstimes.com/singapore/parliament-wps-chen-show-mao-and-paps-cedric-foo-debate-on-immigration. Accessed on 5 December 2016.
Mutalib, H. (2004). *Parties and Politics: A Study of Opposition Parties and the PAP in Singapore* (2nd ed.). Singapore: Marshall Cavendish Academic.
Ng, I. Y. H. (2011). Workfare in Singapore. In C. K. Chan & K. Ngok (Eds.), *Welfare Reform in East Asia: Towards Workfare?* (pp. 131–148). London: Routledge.
Norton, H. (2015). *Tighter Foreign Worker Policies 'Threatening the Survivability' of Singapore Firms* (online). Available at: http://www.hrdmag.com.sg/news/tighter-foreign-worker-policies-threatening-the-survivability-of-singapore-firms-201619.aspx. Accessed on 13 December 2016.
Oon, C. (2010). *Citizen-PR Distinction Has Sharpened: MM* (online). Available at: http://news.asiaone.com/News/the%2BStraits%2BTimes/Story/A1Story20100219-199555.html. Accessed on 11 December 2016.
Ortmann, S. (2010). *Politics and Change in Singapore and Hong Kong*. London and New York: Routledge.

Palatino, M. (2013). *Singapore's 2013 'Robin Hood' Budget* (online). Available at: http://thediplomat.com/2013/03/singapores-2013-robin-hood-budget/. Accessed on 12 December 2016.

Pereira, A. (2000). State Collaboration with Transnational Corporations: The Case of Singapore's Industrial Programmes (1965–1999). *Competition & Change, 4*, 423–451.

Pereira, A. (2008). Whither the Developmental State? Explaining Singapore's Continued Developmentalism. *Third World Quarterly, 29*(6), 1189–1203.

Perry, M., Kong, L., & Yeoh, B. S. A. (1997). *Singapore: A Developmental City-State*. New York: Wiley.

Prime Minister's Office. (2006). *Prime Minister Lee Hsien Loong's National Day Rally 2006* (online). Available at: http://www.pmo.gov.sg/mediacentre/prime-minister-lee-hsien-loongs-national-day-rally-2006-english. Accessed on 12 December 2016.

Prime Minister's Office. (2010). *Prime Minister Lee Hsien Loong's National Day Rally 2010* (online). Available at: http://www.pmo.gov.sg/mediacentre/prime-minister-lee-hsien-loongs-national-day-rally-2010-speech-english. Accessed on 10 December 2016.

Prime Minister's Office. (2011). *Prime Minister Lee Hsien Loong's National Day Rally 2011* (online). Available at: http://www.pmo.gov.sg/mediacentre/prime-minister-lee-hsien-loongs-national-day-rally-2011-speech-english. Accessed on 10 December 2016.

Rahman, N. A. (2010). Managing Labour Flows: Foreign Talent, Foreign Workers and Domestic Help. In T. Chong (Ed.), *Management of Success: Singapore Revisited* (pp. 199–216). Singapore: Institute of Southeast Asian Institute.

Regnier, P. (1993). Spreading Singapore's Wings Worldwide: A Review of Traditional and New Investment Strategies. *The Pacific Review, 6*(4), 305–312.

Rodan, G. (1989). *The Political Economy of Singapore's Industrialisation: National State and International Capital*. New York: St. Martin's Press.

Rodan, G. (1992). Singapore's Leadership Transition: Erosion or Refinement of Authoritarian Rule? *Bulletin of Concerned Asian Scholars, 24*(1), 3–17.

Rodan, G. (1993). The Growth of Singapore's Middle Class and Its Political Significance. In G. Rodan (Ed.), *Singapore Changes Guard: Social, Political and Economic Directions in the 1990s* (pp. 52–71). New York: St. Martin's Press.

Rodan, G. (1996). Class Transformations and Political Tension in Singapore's Development. In R. Robison & D. S. G. Goodman (Eds.), *The New Rich in Asia: Mobile Phones, McDonalds and Middle-Class Revolution* (pp. 19–48). London and New York: Routledge.

Rodan, G. (2001). Singapore: Globalisation and the Politics of Economic Restructuring. In G. Rodan, K. Hewison, & R. Robison (Eds.), *The Political Economy of South-East Asia: Conflict, Cries, and Change* (pp. 138–177). Melbourne, VIC, Australia: Oxford University Press.

Rodan, G. (2006). *Singapore 'Exceptionalism'? Authoritarian Rule and State Transformation* (Working Paper No.131). Perth: Murdoch University.

Rosa, L. (1990). The Singapore State and Trade Union Incorporation. *Journal of Contemporary Asia, 20*(4), 487–508.

Saad, I. (2015). *Singapore to Build on SkillFuture Initiative in 2016* (online). Available at: http://www.channelnewsasia.com/news/singapore/singapore-to-build-on-skillsfuture-initiative-in-2016-8240776. Accessed on 16 February 2017.

Schein, E. H. (1996). *Strategic Pragmatism: The Culture of Singapore's Economic Development Board*. Cambridge and London: The MIT Press.

Singapore Chinese Chamber of Commerce & Industry. (2014). *Media Advisory: SCCCI Leads the Way to Facilitate Business-Government Communication* (online source). Available at: http://english.sccci.org.sg/Download.cfm?DObjID=4480&Mode=1&FN=/20141229%20Media%20Advisory%20on%20SCCCI%20as%20Facilitator.pdf. Accessed on 12 June 2015.

Tan, K. P. (2015). Singapore in 2014: Adapting to the 'New Normal'. *Asian Survey, 55*(1), 157–164.

Tan, K. P. (2016). Singapore in 2015: Regaining Hegemony. *Asian Survey, 56*(1), 108–114.

Tan, S.-S. (2004). Wage Reform and Tripartism: A Test of Trust at Work. *Ethos, 10*(3).

Tay, H.-B. (2015). *Budget 2015: The Push for Innovation and Internationalisation*. Available at: http://www.todayonline.com/singapore/budget-2015-push-innovation-internationalisation. Online access: 1 November 2015.

Trocki, C. A. (2006). *Singapore: Wealth, Power, and the Culture of Control*. Oxford: Routledge.

Tsui-Auch, L. S. (2004). Bureaucratic Rationality and Nodal Agency in a Developmental State: The Case of State-Led Biotechnology Development in Singapore. *International Sociology, 19*(4), 451–477.

Tsui-Auch, L. S., Chia, S., & Liu, A. (2014). The Changing Role of the Developmental State in Shaping Technological Development in Singapore. In U. Hilpert (Ed.), *Handbook of Politics and Technology*. London: Routledge.

Turnbull, C. M. (1977). *A History of Singapore, 1819–1975*. Singapore: Oxford University Press.

United Nations Public Administration Network. (2009). *Singapore: Labour Movement Working Towards Cheaper, Better, Faster Economy* (online). Available at: http://www.unpan.org/PublicAdministrationNews/tabid/115/mctl/Art

icleView/ModuleID/1467/articleId/20194/default.aspx. Accessed on 15 December 2016.

Vasil, R. (1989). Trade Unions. In K. S. Sandhu & P. Wheatley (Eds.), *Management of Success: The Moulding of Modern Singapore*. Singapore: Institute of Southeast Asian Studies.

Vasil, R. (2000). *Governing Singapore: A History of National Development and Democracy*. Singapore: Allen & Unwin.

Vasu, N. (2014). Singapore in 2013: The Times They Are A-Changin'. *Southeast Asian Affairs, 2014*, 275–289.

Vasu, N., & Cheong, D. D. (2016). Singapore in 2015: SG50. *Southeast Asian Affairs, 2016*, 295–314.

Vennewald, W. (1994). *Technocrats in the State System of Singapore* (Working Paper No. 32). Asian Research Centre (Murdoch University), Canberra: National Library of Australia.

Visscher, S. (2007). *The Business of Politics and Ethnicity: A History of the Singapore Chinese Chamber of Commerce and Industry*. Singapore: NUS Press.

Vogel, E. F. (1991). *The Four Little Dragons: The Spread of Industrialisation in East Asia*. Cambridge: Harvard University Press.

Welsh, B. (2011). *Soul Searching Singapore's 2011 General Election*. Washington, DC: East-West Centre.

Wong, J. (2011). *Betting on Biotech: Innovation and Limits of Asia's Developmental State*. Ithaca: Cornell University Press.

Worthington, R. (2003). *Governance in Singapore*. London and New York: RoutledgeCurzon.

Yeung, H. W. (2005). Institutional Capacity and Singapore's Developmental State: Managing Economic (In)Security in the Global Economy. In H. E. Nesadurai (Ed.), *Globalisation and Economic Security in East Asia: Governance and Institutions*. London: Routledge.

Yuen, B. (2008). *Singapore Local Economic Development: The Case of the Economic Development Board (EDB)* (online source). Available at: http://siteresources.worldbank.org/INTLED/Resources/339650-1194284482831/4356163-1211318886634/SingaporeProfile.pdf. Accessed on 12 June 2015.

CHAPTER 4

The Two-Phase Transformation of the Developmental State in Taiwan

This chapter explains how industrial structure and democratic transition shaped Taiwan's two-phase transformation process. I argue that changes in these two factors led to the variation between the state's minor transformation in the 1990s and its rapid transformation after 2000. During the first phase, while Taiwan's industrial structure deterred the emergence of structural constraints from business elites and organised labour, the country's democratic transition led to a relatively low level of institutional constraints from the middle class and business elites. During the second phase, Taiwan's transformed industrial structure resulted in significantly stronger structural constraints generated by business interests. At the same time, the effect of the democratic transition on producing institutional constraints heightened following the 2000 regime turnover.

This chapter consists of five sections. The first two sections analyse how ruling elites' strategic calculations shaped Taiwan's industrial structure and democratic transition. In the first section, I examine the manner in which the ruling elites' need for survival gave rise to the developmental state. I then show how the specific objectives of the ruling elites led to the formation of an SME-SOE development strategy, which subsequently shaped the initial industrial structure of the country. The second section examines the process of Taiwan's two-stage democratic transition to illustrate two theorised elite decisions: the decision to initiate democratic transition and the decision to introduce democratic elections. In the first stage, the ruling elites initiated democratic transition by announcing

T. He, *The Political Economy of Developmental States in East Asia*,
https://doi.org/10.1007/978-3-030-59357-5_4

the end of authoritarian rule in response to a middle-class-led democratic movement; but they were unwilling to introduce democratic elections in the context of their electoral dominance. In the second stage, Taiwanese rulers pushed for the introduction of democratic elections when their electoral dominance eroded gradually in the early 1990s.

The third, fourth and fifth sections show the transformation of the developmental state in three respects. In the third section, I examine the formulation of the state's strategic visions under four democratically-elected governments following the political opening in 1986. I argue that an erosion of the state's strategic visions began in the 1990s and accelerated after the 2000 regime turnover. The fourth section examines the policy constraints generated by business elites. I highlight two developments in this section. First, I show how the transformation of the percentage of DPCC led to the emergence of dispersed business interests in the 1990s and concentrated business interests in the 2000s. Second, I show how Taiwan's democratic transition failed to produce institutional constraints generated by business elites in the 1990s, versus the normalisation of these constraints after the 2000 regime turnover. In the fifth section, I examine how both the low level of DPCC and high level of SOEs diminished the structural constraints generated by organised labour by producing dispersed and state-sector labour interests.

How Elite Survival Shaped Taiwan's Industrial Structure

The Survival of an Émigré Regime

The origin of the policy choices of the Taiwanese ruling elites can be traced back to the domestic political situations facing the KMT after its relocation to Taiwan. During China's civil war, the KMT, led by Chiang Kai-shek, used Taiwan as a warehouse for their battle against the Chinese Communist Party (CCP); they never thought that the small island would be so important to their future political survival (Gold 1986). Within a single year, a combination of mismanagement and brutality by KMT troops dispatched to Taiwan had caused most of the pro-Chinese sentiments among ethnic Taiwanese to dissipate (Gold 1986; White 2009: 64). Ethnic tension escalated with the '2-28 Incident', during which troops responded to an anti-KMT protest by slaughtering thousands of ethnic Taiwanese residents. As Thomas Gold (1986: 51) writes regarding Taiwanese hostility towards the KMT regime:

> The "2-28 Incident" …had a profound effect on the Taiwanese people. They had already seen the mainlanders plunder and wreck their economy and lower their material and cultural standard of living, which under the Japanese surpassed that of nearly all of the rest of China. Now, they saw the government headed by Chiang Kai-shek break a pledge and send troops to Taiwan to support the rotten administration it had plagued them with in the first place. In the popular view, then, Chiang and all mainlanders were associated inextricably with Chen Yi and company. The masses lost faith in the regime.

When Chiang Kai-shek led the KMT retreat to Taiwan after being defeated on the mainland in 1949, the KMT elites began to focus on regime survival. As the KMT government in Taiwan was essentially an émigré regime, its only basis of legitimacy was the claim that it was the rightful government of all China (Gold 1986; Wade 1990). Such claim also implied the need to maintain the regime's mainland nature by excluding the majority of the islanders from the politics of the Republic of China (ROC) (Gold 1986). The KMT's arrival reinforced the impression that Taiwan was being put under the control of a barbarous outside power; mainlanders, who made up only 12–15% of the population, accounted for most of the government appointments, while few native Taiwanese were incorporated into the government (Wade 1990: 233).

The KMT's relocation to Taiwan motivated the regime to rebuild its political control mechanisms. These efforts began with KMT's party reform in 1950. Chiang believed that the old KMT had been plagued by factional struggle, corruption and low morale, and might soon fall apart; therefore, he must establish a new, solid, organisational system for his own and the party's survival (Myers and Lin 2007). His reform aimed to enforce organisational and ideological discipline, and establish a control mechanism revolving around Chiang himself. As the party's unchallenged leader, Chiang handed over his power to the younger generation that had a close relationship with him (Gold 1986). As Yun-han Chu (1994: 115) explains, 'The institutionalisation of the paramount leader in the party power structure laid the foundation for the autonomy and coherence of the party-state'.

KMT's party reform facilitated the state's creation of authoritarian institutions that allowed it to quickly impose control over Taiwanese society. 'The result was a renewal of its Leninist origins from the previous reorganisation in 1924. During 1950-52, the KMT created a network of party cells throughout the government, military and society to which each Party authority over the government bureaucracy and the military were reasserted', writes Bruce Dickson (1993: 56). As an émigré regime, the KMT did not have to respond to, and could instead control, vested societal interests in the society (Wu 2005). The emergence of an authoritarian state was evident in that the entire country was put under Martial Law for nearly forty years, until 1987. During this period, almost all civil liberties were tightly restricted, and a huge security and intelligence system was in place to monitor the whole political system as well as the entire society (Gold 1986; Wu 2005).

The KMT's imposition of political control went hand in hand with the creation of economic policy-making agencies. After the '2-28 Incident', it became clear that preventing dissent was not on its own a viable strategy for an émigré regime with little legitimacy in its new location (Gold 1986; White 2009). The KMT's regime survival was essentially dependent on its success to manage the ethnic divide between the mainlanders and islanders. In short, to generate social support for their hold on power, there was an urgent need for the KMT to create performance legitimacy to smooth ethnic tensions and retain the loyalty of both the mainlanders and islanders (Gold 1986; Wong 2003; Wade 1990; White 2009). As Wade (1990: 246) writes, 'The party leaders came to the realisation that economic development would soften the islanders' resentment of their exclusion from real power, and would allow the mainlanders to prosper on Taiwan without having to reclaim their position and assets on the mainland'.

Economic planning agencies were therefore created to carry out the regime's new priority for economic development. In the early period of KMT rule in Taiwan, the party had focussed on stabilisation and military development. To revive production, the Taiwan Production Board (TPB), chaired by the governor of Taiwan, was established as the state's most powerful economic organ. As the economic priority shifted to tackling inflation, the TPB was absorbed into the Economic Stabilisation Board (ESB). The ESB played an important role in formulating early industrial policy and establishing relations with the private sector in Taiwan. As the economy became stabilised by the late 1950s, the functions of economic planning and the utilisation of aid, as well as the task of industrial development, were shifted into the Council for United States Aid (CUSA), which became the new core economic planning agency in 1958 (Gold 1986; Wade 1990; Cheng et al. 1998; Wu 2005).

Beginning in the early 1960s, a number of economic policy agencies were created to guide an export-led growth process. In 1963, the CUSA was reorganised to prepare for the termination of US aid; its name was changed to the Council for International Economic Cooperation and Development (CIECD). In 1973, the CIECD was downgraded and renamed as the Economic Planning Council (EPC), and in 1978, it was once more upgraded to the ministerial rank and further reorganised into the Council for Economic Planning and Development (CEPD). The establishment of the CEPD marked the first institutionalised economic planning organ established to 'steer the process of industrial upgrading and an interest on the part of some technocrats in emulating the Japanese and Korean models of more centralised industrial planning (Cheng et al. 1998: 95)'.[1]

Limiting Private Capital Concentration in the Market

The KMT's regime survival strategy shaped the state's economic policy choices in regard to the percentage of DPCC and SOE. In the 1950s and 1960s, this link was manifested in dual policies of massive land reform and SOE promotion. The objective of land reform was closely linked to the domestic situation. Firstly, as a mainland regime, the KMT needed to prevent peasant upheaval and remove the economic and political base of the indigenous elite (Ho 1978; Dickson 1993; Gold 1986). A second imperative for the land reform was to generate social support. As the majority of the Taiwanese were peasants, land reform would not only promote agricultural development, but would also build support and promote development (Gold 1986).

The KMT had also learned an important lesson from its time on the mainland. The CCP's political and economic policies, especially those of land reform, had given it a strong base of social support that the KMT lacked (Dickson 1993: 57). The KMT now approached land reform on an unprecedented scale. Between 1949 and 1953, massive land reform was

[1] The CEPD was restructured into the National Development Council (NDC) in January 2014 to include a socioeconomic dimension of national planning.

carried out in three stages—the compulsory reduction of land rent; the sale of public land to farmers and the 'land to the tiller' programme. In all, about one-quarter of Taiwan's cultivated land was affected (Ho 1978; Chen 1961).

The massive land reform indeed accomplished what the KMT's goal of consolidating and stabilising political power on the island, as the majority of the population was satisfied with the reform. More consequential was that the reform removed the economic and political base of all the existing indigenous land-owning groups in Taiwan. Since this period, the landed class has never been a significant force in Taiwan's political economy (Gold 1986). Economically, the success of the reform helped the KMT push Taiwan onto a path of rapid industrialisation (Ho 1987). Reform was also supplemented by huge investments in agriculture to stimulate innovation in farming, which led to a very rapid agricultural growth that in turn created a major source of capital for the initial spurt of industrialisation (Clark and Roy 1997: 54). The reform also laid the foundation for the development of an SME-driven economy (Wong 2003).

While land reform was crucial for the KMT, the development of SOEs was equally important for the regime's political legitimacy. The first hint that the KMT wanted to try to prevent the growth of local capital came when the regime nationalised most of the enterprises previously owned by the Japanese following the end of World War II (Gold 1986; Wu 2005). The establishment of a large state-owned sector was linked to the immediate political urgency of the émigré regime to provide employment for their mainlander support base (Minns 2006: 206). As Karl Fields (2002: 129) assesses the function of SOEs in maintaining the regime's support from mainlanders, 'Faced with the task of employing and appeasing these effectively banished and potentially restive Soldiers, a number of firms within KMT, Inc. were reserved exclusively for retired military personnel'. To ensure the viability of these SOEs, during the period of US aid, around 90% of all US capital assistance went to the public sector. As a result of the government's deliberate promotion of state-owned capital throughout the early 1950s, SOEs accounted for nearly 57% of industrial production and 43% of domestic capital formation (Hsiao 1993: 151).

One consequence of the KMT's preference for SOEs was limited support to the private sector. To solidify its social base on the island, the KMT regime fostered a small number of private enterprises by providing government protection and access to government-controlled resources in the 1950s (Wu 2005; Gold 1986). Over the following two decades, these enterprises grew quickly and eventually became *guanxiqiye*, or conglomerates (Fields 1995). Yet the KMT adopted a more hands-off approach towards the rest of the private sector. During the period of US aid, only about one-third of US capital went to mixed public-private enterprises, and of this, only one in five dollars went to purely private businesses (McBeath 1998: 35). The SMEs therefore had to turn to the curb market for loans (Field 1995; Wu 2005). As the private sector divided into two, an industrial structure characterised by a low level of DPCC began to take shape by the early 1970s. As Wu (2005: 224) explains, 'A few large enterprises continued to grow and became business groups based on their domestic trade, whereas a large number of SMEs emerged and prospered through their activities in producing for the export market'.

After the mid-1970s, there was a strategic revision to the KMT's policy of preventing private capital concentration. The change was spurred by the global recession induced by an oil shock; the recession significantly slowed down Taiwan's economy, causing widespread discontent over government's inability to cope with the economic slump. The legitimacy of the regime was further undermined by several diplomatic setbacks, including the loss of its United Nations (UN) seat to the PRC, as well as de-recognition of the KMT regime by many countries (Chu 1992; Rigger 1996). By that time, the SMEs, mainly run by native Taiwanese, had proven their competitiveness as export champions (Wu 2005). In the wake of these economic and political crises, the KMT began to nurture these SMEs in order to maintain political legitimacy. To the KMT, this policy shift would not only win the political support of the majority of the Taiwanese people, but also promote export-led growth without sacrificing the egalitarian quality of Taiwan's economic development (Wu 2005).

In the context of this political calculation, the KMT state began to turn its attention to the development of SMEs. In 1974, the Credit Guarantee Fund for Small and Medium Businesses was established to help SMEs receive bank loans. Then, starting in 1976, the state began to form banks specifically for SMEs. In 1982, the state established the Department of Small and Medium Business (DSMB) and the United Service Centre to further support SMEs (Wu 2005). However, the KMT state was not ready to truly compromise on its goal of restricting the scale, concentration and influence of indigenous private business in Taiwan. Despite a wide range of measures to promote SMEs, between 1983 and 1990, loans from ordinary domestic banks to SMEs never exceeded 38% of total bank loans.

Even when the loans from SME-specific banks are factored in, the rate did not exceed 42% (Wu 2005: 295).

With the government's conscious policy intervention, Taiwan's low level of DPCC and high level of SOE capital were maintained. During the late 1970s and 1980s, while strengthening the role of SOEs in heavy industries, the KMT launched a 'joint project' with SMEs to upgrade high-tech industries and maintain Taiwan's economic competitiveness (Clark 1989; Gold 1986). As a result, the country's industrial structure came to be dominated by numerous SMEs. In 1981, 98% of the enterprises in Taiwan were privately-owned enterprises with fewer than 50 employees (Chen 1995: 86). In 1985, SMEs produced 65% of Taiwan's manufactured exports (Chou 1992). SOEs also retained their important position in Taiwan's industrial structure prior to the privatisation wave of the 1990s (Fields 2002). Located in between numerous SMEs and giant SOEs, Taiwanese business groups represented just over 10% of the total GNP (Fields 1995: 7).

In short, Taiwan's industrial structure was characterised by a low level of DPCC due to the domination of numerous SMEs in the economy. The dispersed industrial structure is significant when compared to the case of South Korea. Table 4.1 indicates that while SMEs contributed to 70% of Taiwan's export in the early 1980s, they only played a minor role (about 20% of exports) in South Korea. Although the domination of Taiwanese SMEs declined slightly by the mid-1980s, they still provided more than 66% of total exports in Taiwan versus a much lower figure in South Korea.

Table 4.1 Contribution of SMEs to export-Led growth in Taiwan and South Korea, 1982–90 (percentage)

Year	*Taiwan*	*South Korea*
1982	69.7	22.1
1983	63.4	20.0
1984	59.2	25.4
1985	61.2	27.3
1986	66.4	35.2
1987	67.1	37.7
1988	60.0	37.9
1989	61.6	41.8
1990	57.3	42.1

Source Abe and Kawakami (1997: 397)

Elite Decisions and Taiwan's Two-Stage Democratic Transition

The rapid development process eventually led to the transformation of Taiwan's political system in two stages: the removal of authoritarian institutions in the late 1980s and the introduction of democratic elections in the early 1990s. The long period of democratic transition, which was initiated in 1986 and accelerated in 1989, will confirm my theory in regard to elites' decisions to push for democratic transition in two dimensions. Firstly, the end of Taiwan's authoritarian rule in 1986 demonstrates a scenario in which the emergence of a middle-class-led democratic movement during the state-led development process can compel East Asian ruling elites to initiate democratic transition. Secondly, compared with the South Korean case, the Taiwanese case provides even more empirical support to the hypothesised relationship between elites' decision to introduce democratic elections and electoral threat due to internal variation. In the late 1980s, with no electoral threat to confront, the Taiwanese ruling elites were reluctant to introduce democratic elections. Only when an electoral threat became reality in 1989 did the ruling elites push for the introduction of democratic elections.

The First Stage of Democratic Transition in Taiwan: KMT's Liberalisation Without Democratisation

The Taiwanese experience represents a case in which the development process gave rise to the democratic mobilisation of the middle class without the working class as an ally. The democratisation movement in Taiwan was mobilised along lines of national identity. In the 1970s, the ROC's loss of the UN seat cut to the core legitimacy of the KMT regime. To the majority of the island's population, with the ROC's de-recognition in the international community, authoritarian rule could no longer be justified by the KMT's historical mission to retake the mainland (Rigger 1996; Chu 1992; Wu 1989). The loss of political status of the ROC awakened the political awareness of the emerging middle class, who 'began to evaluate from their own perspective Taiwan's international and political environment and contemplate possible reform' (Chu 1992: 34). Opposition liberal elites drew upon ethnic identity to break the KMT's power monopoly by linking Taiwan's diplomatic fate with democratic reform.

As Shelley Rigger (1996: 310) observes, 'For many ROC citizens, loosening the ruling party's political control meant self-determination for the majority ethnic group ... ethnic justice and political reform were inextricably connected, and together they formed the opposition party's ideological foundation'.

Despite rapid economic development, the working class remained largely absent within the democratisation movement. This is because Taiwan's decentralised economic development had deterred the growth of class consciousness (Minns and Tierney 2003; Y.-W. Chu 1996; Yu 1993). Prior to 1987, labour's discontent towards the regime was largely motivated by ethnic injustice concerning the mainlanders' control over Taiwanese workers in the SOEs rather than a desire for economic redistribution (Ho 2012b). On the other hand, the middle class had grown significantly as a political interest group during the 1970s. There were two segments of the middle class in particularly that constituted emerging political interest groups. The first one was urban professionals, particularly lawyers, physicians and intellectuals, who provided a leadership role in challenging the KMT party-state. The second was the numerous SME owners, who offered 'political funds and a fall-back career to leaders of the political opposition' (Rigger 1996; Cheng 1989; Chao and Myers 1998; Hsiao and Koo 1997). The empowered middle class 'made common cause with a handful of opposition-leaning politicians who had carved out niches for themselves within the realm of electoral politics', which soon gave rise to the Tangwai ('outside the party') movement (Rigger 2001: 945).

Bourgeoning democratisation pressure from the Tangwai movement in the late 1970s increasingly challenged the KMT's authoritarian rule. In the absence of an alliance with the working class, the Tangwai movement had to mobilise within the electoral arena (Rigger 1996). The willingness of the middle class to demand greater political rights from the state was demonstrated by two electoral campaigns that turned into the Chungli incident in 1977 and the Kaohsiung incident in 1979, respectively (Tien 1989; Tien and Shiau 1992; Rigger 1999). The KMT's subsequent crackdown generated even greater social support for the Tangwai movement among the middle class (Hsiao and Koo 1997). As several large pro-democracy rallies broke out in Taipei between May 1986 and September 1986, it was evident that the state could no longer retain its control in the country. As Chao and Myers (1998: 131) observe, 'For the first time in Taipei, there was a new pattern of political confrontation – Tangwai politicians eagerly took to the streets to demonstrate their cause and challenged the authorities to stop them. It would be repeated many times in late 1986 and continued through 1987 and 1988'. The Tangwai movement reached its climax in September 1986 when Tangwai candidates founded the Democratic Progressive Party (DPP), in defiance of the island's martial law (Chao and Myers 1998; Clark and Tan 2012).

Similar to the case of South Korea, the democratic mobilisation of the Taiwanese middle class played a crucial role in forcing the ruling elites to pursue a strategy of democratic transition. In Taiwan, the ruling elites' calculation of the formation of a new legitimacy formula through initiating democratic transition came much earlier than in South Korea, largely due to consistent pressure from the middle-class-led democratisation movement. As early as 1983, President Chiang Ching-kuo began to contemplate the idea of democratic transition to maintain the KMT's hold on power, assembling a team to put together a blueprint and strategy for democratic reform (Chao and Myers 1998). The formation of the DPP further highlighted that the old legitimacy pact between the state and society had run its course. If the KMT were to maintain power, the ruling elites needed a new form of legitimacy. As Bruce Dickson (1997: 213) reflects, 'The KMT would be better off allowing an organised opposition to participate within the political arena than risking continued chaos outside it'. It is therefore easy to understand why Chiang allowed the formation of the DPP, as democratic transition was the only option left for the KMT to remain its control over Taiwanese politics. This strategy was also evident in Chiang's speech during a Central Standing Committee meeting in October 1986:

> The times are changing, circumstances are changing, and the tide is changing. To meet these changes, the ruling party must push reforms according to new ideas, new methods, and based on constitutional democracy. Only then will our party be able to move with the tide and to be with the people all the time. (cited in Jacobs 2012: 65)

This elite decision soon led to the first stage of Taiwan's democratic transition—the removal of authoritarian institutions. In the last sixteen months of his life, Chiang Ching-kuo either allowed or actively promoted four major liberalisation reforms that paved the way for the KMT's democratic transition, including the acceptance of the formation of the DPP, the abolition of martial law, allowing ROC residents to go to Communist China and ending the restrictions on newspapers (Jacobs 2012). With this liberalisation direction, the KMT pushed for the removal of a series of authoritarian institutions that restrict the political rights of the people, such as loosening restrictions on the press, freedom of speech, and public demonstrations and the termination of temporary provisions effective during the period of the Communist rebellion in the late 1980s (Chu 1992; Tien 1989; Chao and Myer 1998).

The above discussion has covered the Taiwanese ruling elites' decision to initiate democratic transition. As Taiwan's decentralised economic development deterred the growth of class consciousness, the middle class was mobilised by opposition elites to lead a democratic movement, in response to which KMT elites pursued a strategy of democratic concession to transform their old legitimacy formula. However, compared to the relatively speedy transition in South Korea, in Taiwan, it took ten years from the point of the KMT's democratic concession in 1986 to the first direct presidential election in 1996. In the rest of this section, I argue that this slower transition process was because the KMT enjoyed strong electoral support at the time that it decided on democratic concession.

Despite the rise of the Tangwai movement, the KMT maintained its electoral dominance throughout the 1980s. One important factor contributing to the KMT's electoral resilience during this period was the party's 'Taiwanisation' programme, i.e. the recruitment of ethnic Taiwanese into the party's upper posts. The key imperative for this programme was the urgency of the mainland regime to make political concessions to the ethnic Taiwanese after the ROC's loss of diplomatic status (Tien 1975).[2] Proactive recruitment of Taiwanese into the upper ranks of the KMT represented a major departure from the party's mainland image (Winckler 1984; Tien 1975). In 1984, 12 of the 31 Central Standing Committee members and seven cabinet members were Taiwanese. At the local level, by 1985, the majority of the KMT cadres within the party's local branches had been born in Taiwan (Dickson 1996: 55). The proactive recruitment of Taiwanese undercut the ability of the opposition elites to mobilise the middle class along lines of ethnic identity during elections. As Hung-Mao Tien and Tun-Jen Cheng (1997: 18)

[2] Another motivation behind the Taiwanisation programme was Chiang Ching-kuo's intention to replace the old KMT leaders with young Taiwanese politicians, to achieve power consolidation when he took power in 1972.

write, 'Before the DPP was able to fully exploit the ethnic cleavage, the KMT had substantially indigenised itself and had thrown off its image as an externally imposed mainlander party'.

Another effective strategy of the KMT to retain electoral domination was the expansion of elections at the central level. In the 1970s, the Tangwai movement had combined two loosely organised camps with different strategic approaches; while the moderate camp believed the best way to increase the opposition's influence and bring about democratisation was to stand for election and use their power as elected officials to reform the system, other Tangwai activists believed protests to be the most efficient route to democratisation (Rigger 2001). In the early 1980s, the KMT gradually liberalised central elections in order to exploit the growing fissures within the Tangwai opposition (Winckler 1984). As a result, the difference between the two camps of the Tangwai movement was intensified, ensuring that the KMT's hegemony was not threatened electorally. The KMT's strategy to contain electoral threat from the opposition therefore paid off, at least in the early 1980s. As Edwin Winckler (1984: 498) notes, 'The principal reason the opposition did worse in 1983 than it did in 1980 was that evidently the radicals thought it more important to defeat the incumbent moderate than to defeat the Kuomintang'.

The KMT's electoral dominance was demonstrated in Taiwan's first true two-party contest in 1986; the party won 81% of the seats in both the Legislative Yuan and National Assembly. Dominating the state's two decision-making bodies, the KMT could now influence the passage of laws governing the pace and degree of democratic change to the political system (Chao and Myers 1998). With the ability to secure electoral victories, the ruling elites had no reason to pursue the second elite decision—introducing democratic elections. As J. Bruce Jacobs (2012: 67) observes, 'These final reforms of Chiang Chiang-kuo did contribute to Taiwan's ultimate democratisation, but in themselves they were not democratic. Chiang was never prepared to allow an opposition political party to defeat the Kuomintang'. Consequently, in contrast to the Korea case, the removal of authoritarian institutions was not accompanied by the installation of democratic ones.

In short, in contrast to the South Korean case, the KMT elites lacked the incentive to introduce democratic elections because they did not face an electoral threat at the time that they agreed to democratic concessions in 1986, and were capable of maintaining political power regardless. The

1986 case contrasts with that of the post-1989 period, when ruling elites pushed for a gradual introduction of democratic elections. What explains this internal variation was that the KMT now faced the real threat of being unseated by opposition liberals. Taiwan's internal variation thus verifies my argument that ruling elites introduce democratic election in response to an electoral threat. In the following section, I will assess how the growth of the ruling elites' willingness to allow democratic elections corresponded with the increase in the level of an electoral threat in the early 1990s.

Taiwan's Second Stage of Democratic Transition: The Introduction of Democratic Elections

By the late 1980s, the party's 'Taiwanisation' had resulted in a fierce internal strife between Taiwanese soft-liners and more conservative hardliners within the KMT. Following Chiang Ching-kuo's death in 1988, the power struggle became as much about the redistribution of power between mainlander hardliners and native Taiwanese elites as it was about control of the steering wheel for democratic reform and mainland policy (Chu and Lin 1995). The formation of two competing power blocs seriously eroded the KMT's ability to contain the expansion of the DPP. As Chu (1999b: 70) observes, during the 1992 election, 'a large number of mavericks, mostly from the non-mainstream faction, entered the race in defiance of the party central directives'. The KMT was further weakened by a party split in 1993, when a group of young KMT members left to form the New Party. The formation of the New Party greatly threatened the KMT's electoral viability. As Tien and Cheng (1997: 18) write, 'before the formation of the New Party, the KMT had appeared to be invincible, initially blunting and later decelerating the DPP's advance. The advent of the New Party threatened the KMT with political hemorrhage'. It became even more difficult for the KMT to achieve electoral dominance in 1991, when the DPP's factional dispute 'took a turn for better' as moderate and radical factions decided to cooperate for electoral battles against the KMT (Tien and Cheng 1997: 17).

The early 1990s saw a rapid decline of the KMT's electoral dominance in legislative elections, as indicated in Fig. 4.1. Prior to 1989, the KMT's share of the vote was always above 60%. In the 1989 and 1992 elections, the KMT's winning margin was cut from 55 to 30%. When the New Party split off from the KMT in 1993, the KMT's electoral edge eroded further

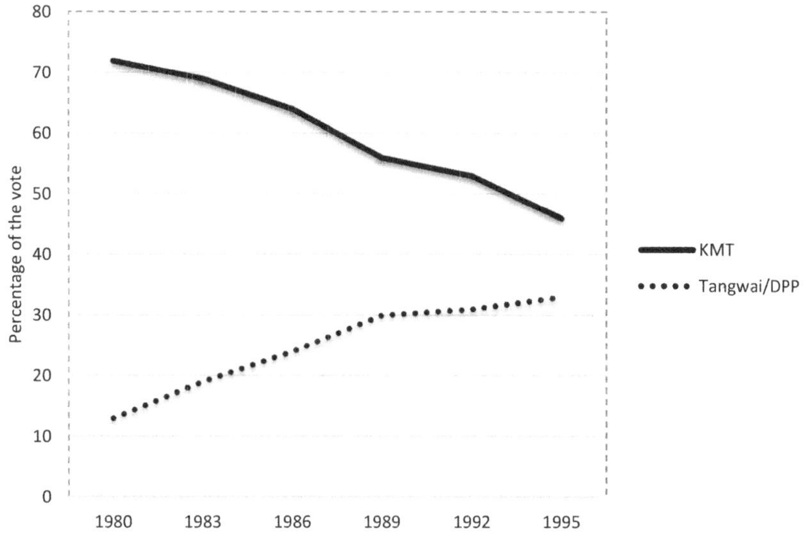

Fig. 4.1 KMT's electoral dominance and decline, 1980–95 (*Source* Clark and Tan [2012: 57])

and, by the mid-1990s, each party had carved out a fairly stable share of the electorate (Clark and Tan 2012; Chu 1999b). The ruling elites were already aware of the changing electoral arena they faced by the end of the 1980s. After the watershed election of 1989, KMT party chairman Lee Teng-hui 'lamented the election outcome, declaring that "we must say it was a defeat; because of the decisions made by all the voters, we cannot say the election outcome was unexpected or an accident". He urged that party to reform even more' (Chao and Myers 1998: 173). At that point, it became necessary for the KMT to introduce democratic elections in order to ensure that it would continue to hold a maximum amount of political power in the increasingly competitive electoral arena.

This strategic consideration pushed Lee Teng-hui to initiate the second round of democratic transition in the first half of the 1990s. After winning the presidency in 1990, Lee called for a National Affairs Conference (NAC) wherein political elites began the process of negotiating a blueprint for constitutional reform (Chao and Myers 1998; Jacobs 2012). Although the issue of direct presidential elections was not resolved during the NAC, the ruling elites and opposition parties forged a consensus on the direction of political reform (Chao and Myers 1998; Chu 1992; Jacobs 2012). New electoral rules were established for competitive elections in the two central parliamentary organs—the National Assembly and the Legislative Yuan. Thanks to its victory in the 1991 National Assembly election, the KMT was in a position to pursue these constitutional amendments without being vetoed by the DPP (Tien and Cheng 1997). With an alliance between the KMT mainstream and the DPP moderates during several rounds of constitutional amendments in 1992 and 1994, the National Assembly finally reached a consensus on the institutionalisation of direct presidential elections (Jacobs 2012; Tien and Cheng 1997). Taiwan's first direct elections were held for the National Assembly in 1991, for the Legislative Yuan in 1992 and for the presidency in 1996.

The KMT's strategic choice to introduce democratic elections indeed paid off. After the last piece of major democratic electoral rule—the direct presidential elections—was introduced in Taiwan in 1994, there was no longer a dominant party in Taiwan. Both the 1995 Legislative Yuan election and the 1996 National Assembly election produced a KMT majority that was too small to give the party effective control of these state decision-making bodies (Tien and Cheng 1997; Clark and Tan 2012). Although the KMT claimed Taiwan's first presidential election in 1996 with 54% of the vote, it could no longer lead the rest of the democratisation process in Taiwan. The electoral strength of the KMT and the DPP became increasingly more balanced during the 2000s and 2010s. When the KMT lost the presidency to the DPP in the wake of another party split in 2000, the existence of democratic institutions allowed the KMT not only to maintain its status as the largest party in the parliament between 2000 and 2008, but also to regain the presidency later in 2008. Although the KMT, facing even greater internal strife, suffered its biggest electoral setback in 2016, it remains a major opposition political party that has the chance to compete for political power in the politics of Taiwan (Rigger 2016).

In sum, Taiwan's second stage of democratic transition was facilitated by the KMT's electoral decline after 1989. A growing electoral threat provided the driving force for the KMT elites to push forward the introduction of democratic elections in the early 1990s. The internal variation between the cases of 1986 and 1989 offers further empirical support to my hypothesis that East Asian ruling elites introduce democratic elections in response to an electoral threat posed by opposition elites.

A Consequence of Taiwan's Democratic Transition: The Emergence of Identity Politics

To understand the political context in which Taiwan's economic decision-making occurs, one must trace the issue of identity politics following the democratic transition.[3] With the advent of democratic politics, political elites began to rally the support of their electorates along the lines of national identity and cross-strait relations. In the 1990s, the need for electoral support pushed elites to moderate their position particularly on the latter issue; a strong association with either unification or independence resulted was not conducive to votes, as citizens feared that either extreme would threaten Taiwan's social, economic and political success (Clark and Tan 2012: 64). Throughout the 1990s, there was a growing consensus among the major political parties to maintain Taiwan's status quo stance on political autonomy and to avoid provoking China. Such a consensus was reached during the National Development Conference of 1996 and the presidential election of 2000 (Clark 2002; Clark and Tan 2010, 2012).

This elite consensus did not last long. In the early 2000s, in order to maximise votes, the KMT and DPP both changed their political strategies to put more emphasis on appealing to base constituencies rather than to the median voter (Clark and Tan 2010, 2012). As a result of these strategic shifts, a deep partisan divide over cross-strait relations and national identity had come to dominate Taiwanese politics by the mid-2000s—a pro-China Pan-Blue coalition led by the KMT versus a pro-Taiwan Pan-Green coalition led by the DPP. As Clark and Tan (2010: 114) write, 'The Greens argued that they must "stand up for Taiwan" and accused the Blues of selling Taiwan out to China. In stark contrast, the Blues contended that the Greens were needlessly provocative and that a more accommodating policy could defuse the threat from China'. Given the saliency of national identity and cross-strait relations, the new political parties emerging during the 2000s allied in either the pan-blue or pan-green camps to mobilise voters, which had the effect of further polarising identity politics (Clark and Tan 2010).

[3] A similar division between political elites did not occur in South Korea, as socioeconomic issues lost their saliency among the middle class after the authoritarian government was removed (as explained in Chapter 2).

The Formulation of the State's Strategic Visions in Taiwan

With the emergence of institutional constraints from the middle class, the formulation of a viable economic vision became increasingly difficult in democratic Taiwan. For the past three decades, Taiwan's economic prospects have been closely tied to its economic relationship with China.[4] Regional and global economic trends have been the major driver of this development. In the early 1990s, China embraced globalisation and quickly became an important global economic player. The country's rising economic prominence in the regional and global economy was accompanied by rapid economic integration between the mainland and Taiwan. Driven by economic, social and political factors, both trade activity between the two economies and Taiwanese investment in China have been steadily growing since the early 1990s.[5] Taiwanese ruling elites have therefore faced an ongoing contradiction between promoting economic growth through cooperation with China and safeguarding Taiwan's national security from rising military threat from China. This section examines the economic strategies formulated by Taiwan's four democratically-elected administrations in regard to sustaining long-term economic growth. I will prove that with the emergence of institutional constraints, ruling elites have largely failed to formulate a viable strategy that can capture both the economic benefits of interacting with China and the task of safeguarding Taiwan's national security.

A Short-Lived Strategic Plan

The Taiwanese state's incapability to formulate a viable economic vision was already apparent during the Lee Teng-hui administration in the 1990s. The institutional constraints generated by the middle class produced two contradictory policies during this period. A strategic plan

[4] In almost all the interviews I conducted with academics, former politicians and former top bureaucrats, Taiwan's economic relations with China have been central to the discussion on the transformation of the state policy-making in recent years.

[5] Social factors include the geographic proximity, as well as cultural and language similarities. Economic factors concern the compatibility of the two economies. Political factors include the political calculations of the two governments. For a detailed discussion on the process of economic integration between Taiwan and China, see (Clark and Tan 2010: 129–135).

was formulated to further integrate Taiwan in the regional economy; recognising the increasing importance of the region for MNCs, the plan sought to transform Taiwan into an Asia-Pacific Regional Operations Centre (APROC). The idea has been attributed variously to Hsu Li-teh, a vice premier of mainland ethnicity, as one means to pre-empt pro-independence forces, and to premier Lien Chan, as a symbolic vision for his disjointed administration, among others (McBeath 1998: 201). Based largely on the assumption that mainland China would serve to develop Taiwan's economic hinterland, the strategic thinking of the Taiwanese policy-makers was to replace Hong Kong as a regional economic hub for the business operations of MNCs in the Asia-Pacific region; starting in 1995, this became the most daunting task for economic policy-makers for decades (McBeath 1998: 198–206; Ma 2001; Chou 2001).

Although Taiwan was eager to emulate Hong Kong economically, the Taiwanese public was certainly keen to avoid Hong Kong's political fate. As previously noted, the 1987 democratic transition resulted in a clear elite consensus among major political parties in the 1990s that maintaining the economic and political autonomy of Taiwan was the top priority, as it was also the preference of the middle class. This consequently pushed ruling elites to formulate a set of economic policies to deter Taiwan's economic integration with China. In the early 1990s, facing a surging outflow of capital to the mainland, Lee Teng-hui and other leaders were worried that the Taiwanese economy's increasing dependency on the mainland market was creating both economic and political risks (Chao 2002). Lee's solution to lessen this overdependence and diversify risks was the formulation of a 'southward policy', which attempted to reorient Taiwan's outflowing capital to Southeast Asia (Chao 2002: 193; Liaw and Wang 2009; Ku 1995).

The contradiction between promoting industrial upgrading and maintaining national security soon escalated as cross-straits relations worsened following the 1995–1996 missile crisis. In mid-August 1996, Lee voiced concern about Taiwan's overdependence on the mainland market and suggested that the APROC plan, which was oriented towards the mainland, should be redesigned (T.-J. Cheng 1997). The heightened need to ensure Taiwan's political sovereignty compelled the KMT leaders to step up measures to deter rapid economic integration between China and Taiwan. Following the missile crisis, Lee announced his 'No Haste, Go Slow' Policy, which was followed by administrative measures to monitor business investments and disallow those that exceeded US$50 million

(Myers et al. 2002: 78). Lee then called for 1996 National Development Conference to provide partisan endorsement of his policy to deter Taiwan's economic integration with China (Lin 2016).

Nevertheless, the ruling elites were aware of the importance of attracting MNCs and therefore endorsed the APROC by arguing that 'Taiwan has the skills and services necessary for exploitation of the mainland market' (McBeath 1998: 199). During a meeting with a delegation of the USA-ROC Economic Council in December 1996, Lee expressed his commitment to the success of the programme (US-Taiwan Business Council 1996). As the first democratically-elected KMT government's major economic vision, the half-suspended programme still had great significance for retaining the party's political power.[6] Eager to show off their economic strategies during campaigns, the KMT ruling elites subsequently pushed the APROC plan as their symbolic vision within the electoral arena. *The Economist* (1997) reports on the electoral significance of the KMT's economic plan:

> Although it is over two years away, President Lee Teng-hui's anointed successor, Lien Chan, the vice-president, has begun his campaign in all but name. After four years as prime minister, Mr Lien stepped down in August. During his term of office his only achievements were to launch a medical-care programme, now on the verge of bankruptcy, and APROC. Criticising APROC, therefore, amounts to weakening the ruling party's chances in an election that could be the hardest it has faced.

A rapid erosion of the state's capacity to formulate strategic visions was observed during the eight years of Chen Shui-bian's administration. Implementation of the APROC plan came to a complete halt after the DPP took power in 2000.[7] Although the APROC plan was shelved, Chen's government could not come up with a viable economic plan to replace it. As a result, the state lacked any clear economic vision to boost Taiwan's standing in the global economy. As journalists N. Hajari and M. Liu (2002) report, '[Chen] drops the usual buzzwords – research-and-development centre, regional hub – without providing any specifics

[6] The government's promotion website for the APROC plan is still accessible to the public.

[7] The APROC plan was replaced by a blueprint for building Taiwan into a 'Green Silicon Island'.

of how the island will reach those goals. His economic advisers have come up with ideas for dozens of reforms, but most have not been implemented'. Why was the Chen administration unable to formulate a strategic economic vision? As I will explain in the next two paragraphs, this was the result of the ruling elites' short-term political goals in the face of strong partisan competition after 2000.

During Chen's first term, suffering from deep political insecurity as Taiwan's first minority party president, he began to map out a strategy to secure political power during the 2001 parliamentary election and the 2004 presidential election. Economic performance was extremely important for the long-time opposition leader to boost his political standing in the country. To demonstrate his determination in reviving Taiwan's economy, Chen called for the Economic Development Advisory Conference in 2001 to endorse his new cross-straits economic policy, which he dubbed 'Active Opening, Effective Management' (Lin 2016). Chen's short-term economic vision was again demonstrated in 2003 when he appointed the KMT's Vincent Siew—the key architect of the APROC plan—as head of an economic advisory panel, another gesture to showcase his efforts to boost the economy (C.-Y. Lin 2003). Even to observers on the mainland, Chen's intention behind his clamour for 'three links' was crystal clear—to dominate the 2004 presidential election and gain an advantage over the pan-blue camp (Wang 2003). At the same time, Chen also made attempts to rekindle Lee Teng-hui's Southward Policy, which had largely been suspended because of the economic and political instability of the late 1990s (Li 2002).

During Chen's second term in office, as the DPP ruler changed his strategy for achieving short-term political survival, the formulation of an economic development programme took the backseat. By then, Chen's political power had become entirely dependent on the support of the Deep Greens rather than on the performance-orientated middle class (Clark and Tan 2010). Consequently, Chen moved to please core DPP supporters state by slowing down economic integration between the mainland and Taiwan, which began with Chen's announcement of a new policy to restrict Taiwan's investment into China—'Active Management, Effective Opening'—as the new guiding principle for governing cross-straits economic interactions (Lin 2016). In line with his anti-China stance, Chen also decided to cancel the second Economic Development

Advisory Conference (*Epoch Times* 2016).[8] The following year, Chen reiterated the government's cautious approach to China ties, contradicting calls by presidential candidates from both parties to fast-track the opening of the 'three links' across the Taiwan Strait.

Two Competing Economic Visions

The politicisation of the formulation of state strategic visions continued after 2008. Competition between the KMT and DPP pushed the ruling elites to adopt two competing state strategic visions. The formulation of these two highly-politicised policy visions, in line with their respective partisan identities, indicates the continued erosion of the state strategic vision in formulating a national economic programme for industrial upgrading. However, neither strategy was viable to enhance Taiwan's economic competitiveness within the global economy.

When the KMT returned to power in the late 2000s, they developed a controversial economic plan aimed at deepening economic integration with China. In order to revive the economy after a lengthy downturn under eight years of DPP administration,[9] Ma Ying-jeou, the newly-elected KMT president, linked the party's pro-China political formula to a national economic strategy (Wu 2013). Believing that access to the mainland market was the key to overcoming economic difficulties, Ma undertook a series of initiatives to deepen Taiwan's economic ties with China, including allowing direct flights across the Taiwan Straits, permitting Chinese students to study in Taiwan, launching institutionalised trade talks and, above all, the signing and implementing of the Economic Cooperation Framework Agreement (ECFA) in 2010. The obvious purpose of the ECFA was to deepen globalisation and liberalisation, with three objectives: (1) to promote cross-strait trade and economic relations; (2) to prevent Taiwan's economic isolation in East Asia; and (3) to enhance Taiwan's status as a regional investment hub. The ECFA

[8] By then, the Economic Development Advisory conference had become a synonym for closer economic integration with China.

[9] The rate of growth was significantly low between 2000 and 2007. During his 2008 presidential election campaign, Ma ran under the slogan of '633', i.e. goals of a six per cent annual GDP growth rate, US$30,000 per capita GDP and an unemployment rate of three per cent or less. Taiwan's growth prospect further dipped in 2009 as a result of the global financial crisis.

has since had two follow-up trade agreements: the Cross-Straits Service Trade Agreement (CSSTA) and the Cross-Strait Goods Trade Agreement (CSGTA).

However, Ma's economic vision was not a politically viable strategy and was deterred mainly by the middle class.[10] In order to execute Ma's highly-politicised and controversial strategy, the government had to influence the preferences of the middle class and create a policy consensus among the public.[11] To shape public opinions for the ECFA, the KMT launched a major propaganda effort in 2009. Syaru Shirley Lin (2013) analyses the ruling elites' efforts to influence the policy preference of the middle class:

> From April 2009, when the chairwoman of the government's Mainland Affairs Council (MAC) began campaigning for the ECFA, until President Ma's televised debate with DPP Chairwoman Tsai on April 25, 2010, the government spent considerable resources to increase public support to counter the impression that the ECFA was a "top-down" policy adopted without public consultation and that it would harm Taiwan's economic interests.

The government downplayed the public's security concerns and emphasised the trade deal's economic benefits. Its argument had three central points. Firstly, the ECFA focused entirely on economic issues and would not affect Taiwan's national sovereignty and political future. Secondly, the ECFA would generate growth and bring tremendous economic benefits to the country. Thirdly, if it did not sign the ECFA, Taiwan would be excluded from the process of economic integration in East Asia, not unlike North Korea (Lin 2016; Chow 2012; Tien and Tung 2011). These various justifications, coupled with a good economic recovery in 2010, were successful in convincing the performance-orientated middle class; survey data suggested that there was widespread and unambiguous support for the ECFA (Lin 2013; Clark and Tan 2012: 106–107).

Although there was consistent support at the grass-roots level to hold trade talks with Beijing, many Taiwanese remained concerned about the

[10] By the time Ma came to power, Taiwanese identity had become prominent in Taiwan. In 2008, for the first time, citizens considering themselves as Taiwanese rather than Chinese accounted for over half of the population.

[11] This point was learned during a private discussion with Yi-Ren Dzeng in February 2014.

negative economic impact of deepening economic integration with China, and furthermore China's political motivation behind such integration (Lin 2013, 2016). These concerns consequently led to collective actions from the middle class against the ECFA. Mobilised by the opposition party, the middle class demonstrated their discontent towards the ECFA with an eruption of social protests throughout the ECFA negotiations period, culminating in a large public demonstration that had the theme 'oppose a one-China market; hold a referendum' (Lin 2016; Gold 2010). As Gold (2010: 69) describes the sentiment of the middle class during a massive demonstration in Taitung in 2009:

> While Taiwan business groups and the political elite were pushing ECFA, many people at the societal level pushed back. They argue that Ma was selling out Taiwan's sovereignty and turning the economy over to the mainland, just as they had feared from the start. They predicted an influx of cheap (and possibly tainted) Chinese goods as well as labour, all to the determent of the island's economy and society...Although the Taichung talks produced a statement of intent to negotiate an ECFA, the actual content of such a pact has yet to be clarified, provoking more uneasiness and mistrust.

The government's single-minded push for a politicised economic strategic vision eventually ran into a direct clash with the interests of the middle class. On 19 March 2014, Ma's decision to force the CSSTA through parliament pushed disgruntled students to occupy the parliament building. The burst of middle-class interest soon turned into an unprecedented civil disobedience movement—the Sunflower Movement—to resist the government's plan for closer economic relations with China (Hsieh 2015).[12] One might argue that the China issue is not the only factor that triggered public opposition against the trade deal; however, it is almost certainly the most decisive factor. Ma's use of economic policy-making to push his political agenda angered the middle class, who were still concerned about the security threat posed by China and therefore intended to put a full stop to Ma's economic vision. As Shelley Rigger explains:

[12] The Sunflower Movement ended with an agreement that the government would pass legislation of an oversight mechanism for cross-strait agreements before a further review of the CSSTA.

> The existence of a clear political threat allows them to be less blinded than people in other countries by a neoliberal ideology that says these pathologies are inevitable and that there's nothing governments can do about them. Because China looms so large for them, both economically and politically, they have been able to brush aside the obfuscations and learned helplessness that are immobilising their counterparts in other countries and demand that their government protect them. (Wasserstrom 2014)

The return of the DPP government in 2016 brought about a completely different state strategic vision, and the KMT's strategic plan for deepening economic integration with China was scrapped in order to prioritise Taiwan's political autonomy and national identity.[13] The DPP formulated a new economic plan in 2016, a New Southward Policy plan that aims to 'strengthen Taiwan's trade and economic ties with members of the Association of Southeast Asian Nations (ASEAN), South Asian countries, as well as New Zealand and Australia' (Executive Yuan 2016). The new plan, as Tsai Ing-wen said in her presidential inauguration speech on 20 May 2016, will 'elevate the scope and diversity of our external economy, and bid farewell to our past over-reliance on a single market' (CNA 2016b).

Facing domestic challenges to stimulate the economy, Tsai's primary goal has been to stimulate the economy through participation in regional economic integration. The New Southward Policy promotion plan sets four clear tasks to achieve this goal: promoting economic collaboration; conducting talent exchanges; sharing resources; and forging regional links (Executive Yuan 2016). This economic ambition led to the creation of a state policy agency, the New Southward Policy Office, in June 2016 to coordinate the government's effort in rejoin the regional economic integration, which has been delayed for more than two decades (*Taiwan News* 2016).

Despite Tsai's outlook for regional economic integration, the state's economic agenda faces enormous political opposition from the mainland. The prerequisite for Tsai's government to implement the New Southward Policy is stable cross-strait relations, as Taiwan can only deepen integration with ASEAN members and India if China does not interfere. Tsai's government has acknowledged this point; the plan stresses the importance

[13] It is unlikely that Tsai or the current DPP-majority legislature, already unsettled by Taiwan's overreliance on the mainland, would ever approve the ECFA follow-up agreements leftover from the Ma administration.

of pursuing a 'well-intentioned interaction and cooperation' with China (CNA 2016b). Yet one question prevails: How will the DPP build a good relationship with the mainland without accepting China's bottom line for developing cross-strait relations—the 1992 consensus? The political need to maintain Taiwan's political autonomy and burgeoning national identity will clearly prove a major hurdle for the DPP to achieve its economic strategy in the years to come (Huang 2017).[14]

Policy Constraints from Business Elites in Taiwan

The Continuation of the State's Dominance Vis-à-Vis Business Elites

Prior to 2000, policy constraints from business elites imposed on the Taiwanese policy process were minor, having been shaped by a low level of DPCC that led to the emergence of dispersed business interests around in the country. These dispersed business interests consisted of a large number of SME owners, who played a key role in the economy. In the early period of Taiwanese industrialisation, which centred on low-skilled and labour-intensive industries, these employers were sometimes called 'black-hand bosses', as they had started off as machinists and apprentices and eventually became successful owners (Wu and Huang 2003). Having neither the capacity nor incentive to shape state policy-making, the SME owners largely operated outside of the policy-making process and were referred to by analysts as 'guerrilla capitalists' (Lam and Lee 1992). Between the 1960s and 1980s, these guerrilla capitalists took it upon themselves to search for market niches. This eventually enabled them to upgrade to the production of advanced electronics goods without needing deliberate nurturing from the state (Lam and Clark 1994; Fields 1998; Wu and Huang 2003).

The inability of these dispersed business interests to influence the state's economic decision-making began to show in the 1990s. With growing market competition from other Asian NICs, particularly from mainland China, SME owners struggled to survive on the small profit margins of export products (McBeath 1998: 121; Kuo 1998). They face an urgent need for state assistance with the expensive R&D needed to move into new market niches (McBeath 1998: 121). However, the SME

[14] That the New Southward Policy is infeasible because of China's strong objection is a point noted in many English and Chinese-language media commentaries.

owners were neither well organised nor politically powerful, and thus had little influence over economic policy-making within an increasingly democratic political system (Chu 1994; Clark and Tan 2012). Consequently, instead of confronting government policies, a large number of SME owners adopted an exit strategy by either closing down operations or moving abroad, particularly to China. Because of their small size and flexible production, SMEs soon found a second home in the mainland (Kuo 1998). Meanwhile, their relocation made SME owners even more distant from Taiwan's policy-making (Lam and Clark 1994).

Emerging large business interests were significantly weaker in Taiwan compared to the chaebol interests in South Korea. Unlike the chaebols, Taiwanese business elites lacked the structural power to challenge the state's policy-making during the 1980s. This weakness was vividly demonstrated within two strategic sectors that had enjoyed quick wealth accumulation as a result of rapid export-led growth. In the petrochemical industry, Taiwanese business elites managed to shape the policy direction in 1984 when they lobbied the government to reinstate the sector's strategic designation, which it had lost four years earlier (Wang 1996; Wu 2005). The government's eventual decision to reverse course, however, was not due to the structural power of private business elites. With limited economic and political resources, the business elites had to launch a joint lobby effort with SOEs in order to achieve their interests; it was in fact the SOEs' connection with the new premier that shaped the state's policy on the petrochemicals industry in their favour (Wu 2005: 160; Wang 1996). When the business elites did have the courage to launch a collective action against the state, the state doled out punishments accordingly. In the financial sector, for example, a powerful alliance formed by business elites, named the 'Thirteen Brothers', was broken up by Chiang Ching-kuo in 1985 (Wu 2005: 260–262; Kuo 1998).

The weakness of Taiwanese business interests continued after the democratic transition in 1986. Because of their inability to directly challenge the state, large Taiwanese business groups turned to new institutionalised channels to influence economic policy-making. Political liberalisation offered opportunities for these business interests to achieve their perceived policy goals (Chu 1994). The expansion of business influence and representation in parliament was significant during the late 1980s and 1990s.[15] As Yun-han Chu (1994: 126) observes, 'large corporations suddenly became the most sought-after patron of politicians and the local support factions'. The Taiwanese case therefore shows the incapability of dispersed business interests, emerging from a dispersed industrial structure, to influence the state's economic policy-making. While numerous SME owners opted to relocate to China following the democratisation of the state's economic decision-making, the remaining large businesses turned to institutionalised channels to exert pressure on the state in an increasingly democratic context during the 1990s.

Not only did business elites lack structural constraints upon the state, but they also failed to produce institutional constraints throughout the 1990s. This outcome was largely the result of the KMT's success in achieving financial independence from business elites by developing its own funding mechanism to compete in democratic elections—party-owned enterprises (POEs). During the period of economic liberalisation in the 1990s, the transformation of SOEs to POEs became an important component of the KMT's political survival (Chu 1994; Matsumoto 2002).

The creation of POEs was strategically important for the party's electoral viability. To the KMT, POEs could provide ample funding for the party's expensive electoral campaigns, and as a whole could serve as a mechanism for gathering votes (Fields 2002; Matsumoto 2002). In the late 1980s and early 1990s, POEs entered the construction sector, taking advantage of the real estate boom during the bubble economy and the Six-Year Development Plan, and set up new securities firms and banks in line with Taiwan's economic liberalisation (Chu 1994; Matsumoto 2002). In September 1992, the centrepiece of the KMT's funding mechanism was upgraded with the creation of seven holding companies after an integration and reorganisation of the KMT's businesses. There was a clear division of labour between the seven holding companies, with each one engaged in specific sectors (Matsumoto 2002). To maintain control over the POEs, in 1993 Lee Teng-hui set up a Business Management Committee (BMC) headed by his confidant Liu Taiying. The significance of the BMC was that it put POEs under the direct control of the KMT

[15] In the 1989, 54 out of 289 elected candidates received financial contributions from the business elites. With the increasing economic independence of the business elites, this number rose to 78 of out of 101 in 1992 and 92 out of 225 in 1998 (Shiau 1996: 223; Huang 2004: 55).

ruling elite. As Matsumoto (2002: 365) points out, 'The Lee-Liu system became the institutional basis that enabled the political use of the POEs'.

With an increasing demand for profits, the ruling elite launched an aggressive expansion plan to increase both the size and efficiency of the POE's capacity to generate funds. Under the Lee-Liu system, POEs shifted from being management centred to being investment centred, with investment focused on the high-tech and financial industries that were driving Taiwan's economic growth (Matsumoto 2002). The BMC also increased its reliance on stock trading, boosting the net profits of the seven holding companies (Matsumoto 2002). To further improve business efficiency, the POEs formed joint ventures with private firms as a strategy to acquire management resources from the private sector and reduce economic risks (Matsumoto 2002; Chu 1994; Fields 2002). The strength of the KMT's funding was particularly evident in 1998 when the party invested in 216 companies, increasing its total assets to NT$147 billion and its annual after-tax profit to NT$12.1 billion; this made the KMT business empire the fifth largest diversified business group in Taiwan (Cheng and Chu 2002: 47). The KMT's profit-generation capability subsequently left ruling elites immune to any institutional constraints from business elites in the 1990s. As Yun-han Chu (1999a: 195) observes, 'Unlike the Liberal Democratic Party in Japan or the ruling parties in South Korea, the KMT, which owns a huge array of business interests itself, relies little on political donations by the business community'.

As Taiwanese business elites produced neither structural nor institutional constraints, the nature of the state-led state-business cooperation remained largely unchanged in Taiwan in the 1990s. Chu (1994: 132) noted in the early 1990s that 'to date, the political ascent of the business elites has not reached the point of meaningful leverage over the top party leadership. While their financial leverage does now enable the business elites to capture individual lawmakers or even an entire local faction, the party leadership remains beyond their reach'. Consequently, the ruling elites continued to provide protection to the economic bureaucrats, who are empowered to operate with the perspective of long-term economic growth. Yun-han Chu (1999a: 195) describes the coherence of the state's economic policy-making process in the 1990s:

> Most vital economic measures, measures that have economy-wide ramifications, are still within the purview of the cabinet. As a last resort, economic officials can take their cases to the premier or the president and

> ask those figures to throw their weight behind key economic proposal that are deemed crucial to achieving priority development objectives. After all, under the existing institutional arrangements, the KMT's leadership still has a final say over nomination decisions, and no individual legislators is politically indispensable or electorally invincible.

The state's leadership role vis-à-vis business elites was manifested in the 1990s economic liberalisation. Compared to how business interests shaped South Korea's financial liberalisation in the 1980s, the large businesses' economic gain from Taiwan's liberalisation policies was largely the result of the government's pro-business outlook in the context of a power struggle within the KMT, which necessitated ruling elites' closer alliance with business elites in the early 1990s (Chu 1994; 1999a). Consequently, business groups were able to become full owners or part owners of new banks after Taiwan opened its banking sector in 1991 (Clark and Tan 2010: 117). The passage of the 1998 Trust Enterprise Law, aimed to diversify the banking and trust industry, further broadened financial sources for business elites (Clark and Tan 2010: 117). Business elites similarly succeeded in acquiring lucrative business profits by taking over SOEs, which had been concentrated in inward-looking sectors (Chang 2008). However, there were clear limitations in terms of how business elites could advance their economic interests. Having experienced the mainland regime's financial instability during the civil war, the Taiwanese government maintained absolute control over the financial system reform (Clark and Tan 2010; Tan 2001; Heo and Tan 2003; Chu 1999a).

Keeping the business elites in check, the government continued its developmentalism in the export sector. Just as it had previously promoted SMEs as the main agent for industrial upgrading and technological innovation, the government formulated various policies to stimulate their R&D (Lui and Qiu 2001: 83–86). According to Vincent Wang (1995), Taiwan's high-tech development in the 1990s was 'shaped by a dynamic trio of entrepreneurial state, guerrilla capitalism, and accommodative technologies'. In the midst of the 1997 Asian financial crisis, the KMT government adopted measures to help SMEs survive, including export guarantees, tax incentives and assistance in financing (Clark and Tan 2010). In short, as Lee and Chu (2008) write, 'In the 1990s, the KMT government maintained a precarious balance between taking into account distributional considerations and committing to developmental goals'.

To summarise, the emergence of policy constraints from business elites prior to 2000 resulted from two processes. The first is that the low level of DPCC produced dispersed business interests and thus weak structural constraints from business elites. In contrast to the South Korean case, large businesses were in no position to challenge the Taiwanese state's economic policy-making during this period. The second is the emergence of institutional constraints following the country's democratic transition. Unlike in South Korea, following Taiwan's democratic transition in 1987, Taiwanese business elites lacked institutional constraints because the KMT developed a mechanism to guarantee its own financial capability to compete in elections. As a result of the lack of both structural and institutional constraints, the Taiwanese state continued to formulate state economic strategies.

The Rise of Financial Conglomerates and the End of the SME Strategy

Drastic changes to state policy-making occurred after the regime turnover in 2000, shaped by an increasing level of DPCC during the process of financial liberalisation and therefore growing structural constraints from business elites, as well as by an increase of institutional constraints from business elites. Institutional constraints grew as the newly-installed DPP administration lacked the political funds to stay self-reliant. Unlike the KMT, who established a business empire for funding expensive electoral campaigns, the DPP emerged as a grass-roots political party largely dependent on SME owners for political donations. The KMT's huge financial advantage created a huge obstacle for the DPP's progress (Rigger 2001). Shelley Rigger (2001: 950) explains the huge gap between the KMT and the DPP in terms of their financial strength:

> According to the KMT's own estimates, its assets total about US$2.6 billion at the beginning of 2001. A Taipei Times report dated 1 March 2000 put the figure much higher, at US$6.7billion. The DPP, by contrast, has long suffered extreme economic straits. Until 1997, the party relied on individual donations for most of its income; it laboured under a burden of chronic debt and financial shortfall. In 1997 the situation improved when the government began paying subsidies to political parties. Nevertheless, in early 2001 the DPP reported assets of US$900,000, a tiny fraction of the KMT war chest.

In contrast to the KMT, the DPP had few institutionalised connections with the business community other than personal ties between DPP politicians and a few business donors and like-minded business elites (Lee and Chu 2008: 146). To build these personal relationships, the presidential palace, in the words of Lee and Chu (2008: 146), 'became the major agent in cementing intimate business-state relations'. As a result, whichever ruling elites were in power provided the business elites with easy access to the state's policy-making process. Given that the business elites largely came from inward-looking, non-tradable sectors, it was hardly surprising that the crucial policy suggestions made during Chen Shui-bian's 2001 Economic Development Advisory Conference were to review the tax-incentive system in order to bolster the property market and the construction industry (Lee and Chu 2008: 156).

As business elites produced more institutional constraints, they began to penetrate the state's policy-making. The most lucrative opportunity was to gain a share of state assets during the financial reform of the 2000s, as the reform was expected to result in the rapid conglomeration of Taiwan's banking industry as well as the privatisation of government-controlled financial institutions (Clark and Tan 2010). Although the government's strategy was to merge the existing banks and lending agencies to create financial institutions capable of international competition, the economic technocrats could not resist pressure from the business groups during the reform process (Clark and Tan 2010). In order to gain a position in the battle for privatisation and acquisition, the business elites mobilised to lobby legislators and high-ranking officials, including the first family. As Wu Yu-shan (2007: 991) describes:

> The major financial holding companies were at one another's throat for the grab. They mobilised legislators and used connections to high officials in the presidential office, even to the first family, to gain the upper hand. As one after another scandal was exposed, the public for the first time got a glimpse of the inner working of the business-government nexus. It appears that the bureaucrats were beholden to the politicians, who were in turn beholden to the top political leaders and private financial interests.

While the state could not accomplish its development goals because of business constraints, large businesses succeed in expanding their financial strength. As a consequence of the two rounds of hijacked financial reforms, the level of DPCC in Taiwan's industrial structure had increased

Table 4.2 Creation of financial holding companies in Taiwan in the 2000s

Company name	*Year of creation*
Hua Nan Financial Holdings Co., Ltd.	2001
Fubon Financial Holding Company	2001
China Development Financial Holding Corporation	2001
Cathay Financial Holdings	2001
Chinatrust Financial Holding Co., Ltd.	2002
SinoPac Financial Holdings Co., Ltd.	2002
E. SUN Financial Holding Co., Ltd.	2002
Yuanta Financial Holding Co., Ltd.	2002
Taishin Financial Holding Co., Ltd.	2002
Shin Kong Financial Holding Co., Ltd.	2002
Mega Financial Holding Company Ltd.	2003
First Financial Holding Co., Ltd.	2002
Jih Sun Financial Holding Co., Ltd.	2002
Waterland Financial Holdings	2002
Taiwan Financial Holdings	2008

Source Central Bank of the ROC (Taiwan), https://www.cbc.gov.tw/ct.asp?xItem=26986&ctNode=778&mp=2. Accessed on 21 April, 2018

by the late 2000s. The Financial Holding Company Law resulted in the rapid conglomeration of Taiwan's banking industry and the privatisation of government-controlled financial institutions. Most of these financial mergers and acquisitions had featured private financial holdings companies acquiring larger public financial holding companies or banks (Clark and Tan 2010; Wang 2012). Table 4.2 shows that 14 financial conglomerates emerged in the first half of the 2000s. One more was created in the late 2000s.[16] As a result of the emergence of these powerful financial conglomerates, a level of DPCC comparable to that of South Korea's chaebols had appeared in Taiwan by the late 2000s. The financial assets owned by the three most prominent family-owned business groups account for 64% of Taiwan's GDP (Tao and Chang 2008: 231). Consequently, there was an emergence of concentrated business interests in Taiwan. Having acquired substantial economic power, these business

[16]There are 16 financial holding companies as of 2017. Taiwan Cooperative Financial Holding Co. Ltd was created in 2011.

entities were capable of asserting their policy interests in the late 2000s (Wang 2012; Clark and Tan 2010).

Strong structural and institutional constraints generated by business elites on state policy-making were noticeable by the late 2000s. The KMT's financial advantage in electoral competition had faded after the 2000 regime turnover.[17] When the KMT returned to power in 2008, Ma Ying-jeou's administration could no longer shield the state's economic policy-making from major business interests. The decline of the state-led state-business cooperation was clear in Ma's tax reform policies. Since the mid-2000s, the government began to remedy the fiscal deficit by establishing a fairer taxation system (Ash et al. 2006). Although Ma's intention was to improve fiscal health, the Tax Reform Committee established in 2008 was dominated by business elites rather than by economic technocrats (C. Y. C. Chu 2015).[18] Raising taxes and withdrawing tax incentives could not be easily achieved, as such goals were undone by political lobbying.

The demise of the state-led state-business cooperation led to the end of Taiwan's SME strategy.[19] Constrained by large business interests, the ruling elites could no longer insulate the state's economic policy-making. SME owners now had to compete with strong economic and political actors to shape favourable policies. Given the SMEs' lack of political influence, these long-time drivers of export-led growth became increasingly marginalised in the policy-making process. As Clark and Tan (2012: 125) analyse the government's failure to promote an innovation-oriented industrial policy in advanced industries in line with the past strategy of SME promotion, 'While the official government position is to assist the SMEs toward these high-value added industries, the reality is that

[17] The profitability of the POEs, which had enabled the KMT's financial independence in the 1990s, declined after the regime turnover in 2000 (Huang 2004). In the 2000s, the KMT ran into trouble extracting dividends from its businesses in order to pay employee salaries and pensions. The KMT's financial trouble continued throughout DPP rule, as the DPP administration sought ways to force the KMT to disentangle from its business empire (see Mattlin 2011: 88).

[18] Two controversial tax cuts indicate the erosion of the state policy process by big business interests: the corporate income tax cut and the inheritance and gift tax cut.

[19] The SME sector has been the driver of Taiwan's economy and is crucial for its future industrial upgrading. I thank Dzeng Yi-Ren for pointing this out to me during a private communication in February 2014.

SMEs (by their structure and resources) are simply not equipped to take advantage of these plans'.

Policy Constraints from Organised Labour in Taiwan

In Taiwan, policy constraints emanating from organised labour have been limited since the late 1980s. The main factor hindering the capability of Taiwanese labour interests to challenge the state is that the country's initial industrial structure was characterised by a low percentage of DPCC and a high percentage of SOE. As this section will explain, these two industrial indicators have contributed to the weakness of Taiwanese organised labour.

The Rise of Dispersed Labour Interests

Taiwan's low DPCC rate gave rise to dispersed labour interest groups. The private sector has long been dominated by a large number of SME workers. During the KMT's one-party rule, this segment of industrial workers was controlled and organised by the authoritarian government along occupational lines. Occupational unions, in the words of Ming-sho Ho (2006a: 112), 'functioned as a residual category available to those who could not join industrial unions'. The primary reason for the enthusiasm of industrial workers to gain membership in occupational unions was that joining an occupational union was a prerequisite for SME workers to contribute to and receive various social insurance benefits (Ho 2006a).

Given the range of social status and economic conditions among members, occupational unions did not function as an effective channel for launching collective actions. According to Ho (2006a: 112), 'occupational unions in Taiwan functioned as officially licensed insurance agents and did not engage in activism on workers' behalf. It was not uncommon for the leadership of occupational unions to be in the hands of small-business owners who saw an opportunity to profit from the scheme'. Ho's observation proves that the occupational unions were not capable of standing up for workers; rather, they could only represent members with homogenous interests. Even after Taiwan's political opening, the large number of occupational unions remained under the leadership of the conservative Chinese Federation of Labour (CFL) that was 'less a representative of labour interests than an agent of the authoritarian party-state' (Ho 2006a: 123).

The changing political environment of the late 1980s did give rise to a burst of labour interests in the rest of the private sector. Within a year of the democratic transition, labour activists established 100 independent labour unions in a few large private enterprises by either organising non-union workers or seizing control of the KMT-sponsored unions. Efforts were also made to establish inter-union organisations to overcome the fragmented nature of newly emerged labour unions (S.-Y. Ho 1990; Y.-W. Chu 1996; M.-S. Ho 2006a; J. W. Y. Wang 2010). Although this episode of labour unionisation was impressive, unlike their South Korean counterparts, Taiwanese labour unionists had little organising experience. As Shuet Ying Ho (1990) observes, 'After the setting up of new unions, or after capturing union leadership, unionists found it difficult to develop their unions further'.

The weak organisational capability of private-sector workers, a result of low DPCC, was obvious by 1990. After a series of state crackdowns on labour activism, in collaboration with businesses, the pro-union drive stirred by the 1987 political reform had been nearly exhausted. The Taiwanese unionisation movement came to a clear end in the 1990s with the conclusive defeat of labour uprisings at the Far Eastern Chemical Fiber Company and Keelung Bus Company. Labour activists involved in these incidents were arrested and brought to court, where most were convicted (M.-S. Ho 2006a; Wang 2010). The defeat of the Keelung Bus Drivers' Union—one of the vanguards of the labour movement—marked the onset of the decline of the independent labour union movement.[20] Starting in the mid-1990s, another protest wave surfaced among workers who had been laid-off due to factory relocation to lower-cost China and Southeast Asia (Ho 2012a). However, these nonunionised workers were unable to pose a constant pressure on the state-business alliance. As Ming-sho Ho (2012a) explains, 'Although their protests tended to be highly disruptive, they failed to expand the organisational basis of Taiwan's labour movement since their activism usually came to an end when they were able to secure some compensation'.

[20] The number of workers involved in labour disputes reached a record high of 62,391 in 1989. It fell to 12,696 in 1991 and never rose again until the Asian financial crisis in 1997 and 1998 (Gray 2014: 100).

In contrast to the South Korean case, industrial workers' inability to organise forced them to shift their focus from grass-roots mobilisation to a partisan alignment in order to advance their economic interests. In the 1990s, organised labour chose to establish a strategic partnership with the DPP. Ho (2006b) argues that this partnership was inevitable for two reasons. Firstly, the DPP was an attractive outlet for discontented workers because of the workers' disillusionment with the KMT. Secondly, an alliance with organised labour provided the main opposition party with the possibility to develop their voter mobilisation system and therefore undermine the KMT's electoral dominance. With the alignment between labour and the DPP, a number of local federations of labour unions were established in DPP-controlled localities in the 1990s. This later formed the foundation for the Taiwan Confederation of Trade Unions (TCTU), which was granted legal status by the DPP in 2000 (Ho 2006b; Wang 2010; Lee 2011), to challenge the KMT-sponsored CFL.

However, the political alignment with the DPP further weakened the organisational basis of Taiwanese organised labour. In the early 2000s, both the number of unions and labour membership declined significantly. Ho (2006a: 126) points out two primary reasons for this outcome. The first was that as organised workers shifted their actions from the grass-roots level to the legislature, they found it 'increasingly difficult to mobilise lukewarm constituencies'. The second was that as organised labour became associated with the DPP, labour found it 'hard to attract other existing industrial unions as well as to build more local federations of industrial unions when Taiwan's politics polarised after 2000'. Although new labour leadership in 2006 stressed their political neutrality (Chiu 2011), the damage to the organisational strength of organised labour had already been done. By the mid-2000s, organised labour had lost its capacity to mobilise against state policy-making. As one labour activist explained, 'when the DPP failed to deliver what they promised, organised labour in Taiwan had no mobilisation strength to make their demand heard by the government' (Lee 2011: 85).

The Rise of State-Sector Labour Interests

The low level of DPCC was not the only factor limiting the structural constraints of organised labour in Taiwan. The organisational strength of Taiwanese labour was also affected by the strong presence of SOEs in the economy. The following section will test my hypothesis that the creation of SOEs facilitates the emergence of state-sector labour interests—which have a detrimental effect on the capability of organised labour to challenge the state.

The emergence of state-sector labour interests can be traced back to the early stages of Taiwan's industrialisation. During the authoritarian period, the economic interests of SOE workers were carefully managed by the KMT, who set up labour unions to co-opt labour interests. As Ming-sho Ho (2012b: 1026) argues, 'Labour unions were fashioned to generate maximal benefits and welfare without at the same time stimulating class consciousness among workers', and therefore 'in essence functioned as the human face of the KMT party-state'. To curb labour discontent, the regime also put in place specific political arrangements to keep the unions strictly under party control, including the installation of party branches to ensure that the party and unions were integrated at the basic level, the manipulation of union elections, monitoring of union meetings, as well as the dispatchment of party members to be permanent union staff (M.-S. Ho 2012b). With a combined strategy of co-optation and coercion, the KMT succeeded in achieving 'the seemingly self-contradictory mission of organising workers without empowering them' (M.-S. Ho 2012b: 1026).

Despite the KMT's efforts, labour interests among SOE workers were not completely absent in the authoritarian period. With the political relaxation of the 1970s, the growing labour interest brought about by the development process began to emerge in existing labour organisations in the state-owned sector. Ho (2012a: 139) explains that 'prior to the mid-1980s, the labour unions of Taiwan's SOEs had become de facto complaint centres that unfailingly processed and forwarded a plethora of demands to the company...Thanks to the incessant pressure from below, labour unions had burst out of the highly restrictive straightjacket designed during the repressive authoritarianism of the 1950s'. However, the subtle changes to the nature of labour unions should not be exaggerated. There were still great limitations on what SOE workers could achieve, as the unions remained in the control of staff who had been dispatched by management. In short, 'the shifting of union functions took place incrementally and was not always detectable because the KMT cadres appeared to have unions under their firm control' (Ho 2012a: 139).

Democratic transition finally provided SOE workers with the necessary political environment to pursue their material interests. However, the labour interests that emerged in the state-owned sector were fundamentally different from those of the private sector. Since the 1990s, the division of labour interest advancement between the state-sector labour interest groups and the private-sector labour interest groups has been demonstrated in two aspects. The first concerns the institutional channels created by the state for wage increases in the SOE sector. Unlike labour interests in the private sector, government agencies—the Ministry of Economic Affairs (MOEA)—oversaw the wage levels of Taiwanese SOE workers.[21] As the SOE workers could use these channels to achieve their perceived interests, the wage negotiation process was largely non-confrontational and did not require labour mobilisation. As Yoonkyung Lee (2011) writes:

> They try to coordinate wage negotiations within the SOE unions with a common proposal drafted by the TCTU or the CFL. Yet their bargaining strategy has been indirect but politicised by taking advantage of their linkage to elected politicians. In wage negotiations, unions contact their partisan allies, who are usually national legislators serving on the budget and economic committees of the Legislative Yuan. Unionists request that these legislators put pressure on MOEA officials in charge of SOE wage settlements.

The policy concerns of the SOE workers were also fundamentally different than those of the private-sector workers. A major focus of the SOE workers in defending their interests has been SOE restructuring and privatisation. In response to the threat of privatisation that first emerged in the late 1980s, the SOE workers quickly organised (M.-S. Ho 2012a). Their desire to mobilise culminated in 1999, when the SOE unions formed the Alliance of SOE Labour Unions. In addition to organisational strength, this also gave them political leverage over the ruling elites to shape the state's privatisation policy. Both the KMT and the DPP believed that the support of the SOE unions was of great importance to their respective power consolidation within the increasingly democratic

[21] It is worth mentioning an interesting fact pointed out by Dzeng Yi-Ren during a discussion in February 2014. According to Dzeng, Taiwanese SOE workers tend to consider themselves as public servants and socially superior to private sector workers. This perceived socioeconomic superiority is perhaps a by-product of the channels institutionalised for them to advance material interests directly with the state.

political system (Lee 2011: 236). With organisational strength and political leverage, the demands of the SOE unions consequently produced strong constraints on the state's privatisation policy process throughout the 1990s and 2000s (Lee 2011: 233–236).

In summary, due to the low level of DPCC and the high level of SOE, the 1990s saw the emergence of two types of labour interest groups—dispersed labour interest groups in the private-sector and state-sector labour interest groups in the SOE sector. The dispersed labour interest groups, dominated by SME workers, lacked a strong membership base from the inception of Taiwan's labour union movement. In spite of SOE unions' strong membership base, the emergence of state-sector labour interest groups did not contribute to the structural constraints imposed on the state by the organised labour. This is because the economic interests of state-sector labour were often achieved through direct institutional channels with the state and were therefore fundamentally different from those of the private-sector labour interest groups. As privatisation was underway, state-sector labour interest groups quickly emerged to protect their own narrowly-focused material interests. The following section will provide a detail description of the low level of structural constraints generated by labour interests in democratic Taiwan as a result of DPCC and SOE.

The Weakness of Organised Labour

The effects of the low level of DPCC and the presence of SOEs finally manifested in the early 2000s. Both the emergence of dispersed and state-sector labour interests resulted in weak organised labour. The formation of the TCTU as a national centre magnified the internal conflicts within the two groups of industrial labourers. Given the dispersed nature of the private labour unions, SOE unions took leadership of Taiwan's independent union movement (Ho 2012a). As the SOE unions stepped up their efforts to defend their material interests in response to the threat of privatisation, growing discontent among the workers in the private sector quickly emerged. As Yubin Chiu (2011: 68) explains, 'Local CTUs, whose affiliated unions were mainly in the private sector, soon began to complain that the TCTU was too focused on SOE issues and was neglecting the disastrous trend of casualization'. In 2007, after two consecutive walkouts, a few local federations of labour unions formed a loose alliance with other smaller, unaffiliated union federations—the Solidarity of Labour Unions (SLU).[22]

With a weak organisational base, organised labour had little policy influence in regard to the minimum wage increase. Since 1988, when the Council for Labour Affairs (CLA) was established to adjust the base wage level every year, Taiwan's wage negotiation has been an orderly process. In the late 1980s, Taiwan's contract manufacturing had the option to relocate to the Mainland or Southeast Asia, a move that would leave many local workers behind. Without the possibility of making an immediate transition to higher value-added production, both the government and businesses preferred a lower minimum wage to sustain the country's traditional developmental model. As journalists Eva Dou and Jenny W. Hsu (2012) write on the motivation of the government to sustain a lower minimum wage, 'Taiwan has found itself in a Catch-22 as it tries to shift away from contract manufacturing toward building its own brands: By traditionally working as contractors for slim profits, Taiwanese campaniles discovered they lacked the cash to make large research investments or to attract talent through high salary'.

Organised labour in Taiwan had neither the interest nor bargaining power to challenge government strategy on this issue. Consequently, the adjustment of minimum wage followed economic rationales. In the aftermath of the economic downturns in 1997 and 2008, the government made the decision to maintain the minimum wage from 1997 to 2007, and again in 2009 (CLA 2010; Hsieh 2001; Huang 2009). In 2010, the establishment of the Basic Wage Deliberation Committee brought labour, government and management to the negotiation table. Given labour's organisational weakness, the annual Basic Wage Deliberation committee meeting constituted a new occasion for the government to adjust the minimum wage level in line with socioeconomic factors including price indexes, economic growth data and the unemployment rate (CLA 2010). In 2012, even after labour convinced the committee to suggest a wage increase, the government decided not to adopt the Council for Labour Affairs (CLA)'s recommendation to increase the minimum monthly wage until the economy showed a further sign of recovery (Zeldin 2012). In 2013, the CLA decided to scrap the rule of holding an annual review on

[22]The SLU focused their unionisation efforts on organising irregular workers whose economic interests were yet to be represented by the TCTU. However, their efforts were largely unsuccessful.

minimum wages and to hold a future meeting only when the consumer price index (CPI) increased by 3% or more annually (*Taipei Time* 2013).

The structural weakness of the organised labour is also clear in the process of labour law reform since the early 1990s. With the parliament's increasing role in the state's policy-making process, the Taiwanese organised labour could directly participate in policy-making by using the existing institutionalised channels. In the early 1990s, organised labour successfully prevented a downward revision of labour laws and forced the state to backtrack a proposed adjustment that would increase labour's financial burden during the reform of the national health insurance system (Ho 2006b). As state decision-making democratised, organised labour could defend their economic interests from being taken away by the pro-business state. However, given their limited economic and political resources, labour activists could not compete with business owners when it came to political lobbying. Consequently, organised labour could only gain under three circumstances. Firstly, the partisan divide since the early 2000s allowed organised labour to cooperate with the opposition parties to advance their economic interests. In the early 2000s, organised labour took advantage of the partisan conflict between the DPP-led Executive Yuan and the KMT-dominated Legislative Yuan. For example, in 2000, with the help of the KMT who attempted to block all government policies initiated by the DPP, the organised workers succeeded in shaping the DPCC in regard to the regulation of working hours (M.-S. Ho 2006b).

Secondly, when the opposition parties were not available for cooperation, labour had to compromise with the state-business alliance. On two occasions, the weak organised labour had to accept the state-business alliance's proposal for greater labour market flexibility to help management stay afloat with the revision of the Labour Standard Law in the late 1996 and the Economic Development Advisory Conference in 2001. As a result of this labour compromise, businesses were given the right to calculate working hours with more flexibility in 1996. In 2001, night shifts for female workers were legalised and further flexibility in calculating working hours with granted. In return, organised labour also achieved great labour gains. In the first instance, more than two million white-collar workers were included in the protection of the Labour Standard Law. In the second instance, organised labour benefitted from passage of the Protective Act for Mass Redundancy of Employees and the Employment Insurance Law (Ho 2006b, 2008; Wang 2010).

Thirdly, when the state-business alliance was willing to advance labour interests, organised labour had to accept the terms and conditions set by the former. In 2015, the KMT government made the decision to shorten the maximum working hours from 84 hours per two weeks to 40 hours per week, while at the same time increasing the legal cap for overtime from 46 hours to 54 hours and reducing the labour's public holidays by 7 days. Without mobilisation strength, organised labour had to compromise in order to receive any gains. In response, non-TCTU labour activists stormed the Ministry of Labour, claiming that the 'TCTU does not represent workers' (CNA 2015). Although most public holidays were restored in 2016, the new DPP government quickly drafted another amendment to the Labour Standard Act, referred to as 'one flexible day off', to offset the negative effects of a wage hike that same year (Central News Agency 2016a). In exchange for this much-delayed minimum wage hike, labour had little choice but to accept the terms and conditions set by the state-business alliance.

In sum, because of Taiwan's political liberalisation following democratic transition, the Taiwanese organised labour was no longer a subordinate actor in the development process. However, policy constraints generated by organised labour were limited. The organised labour remained structurally too weak to influence the process of minimum wage adjustment and labour law reform. In several occasions, the Taiwanese organised labour had to reach compromises with the state-business alliance in order to achieve some limited advancement of their material interests.

Summary of the Chapter

This chapter explored how industrial structure and democratic transition shaped a two-phase transformation of the developmental state in Taiwan. In the first few sections, I traced the sources of the country's industrial structure to the strategic choices made by the ruling elites. The ruling elites' political objectives for preventing private capital concentration in the market resulted in a low level of DPCC and a high level of SOE in Taiwan's initial industrial structure. The country's two-stage democratic transition was also shaped by the strategic choices of the KMT, in particular two different calculations. The first was the decision to end authoritarian rule in response to the intensifying middle-class-led Tangwai movement. The second was to introduce democratic elections only when the party faced an electoral threat after 1989.

Both the industrial structure and democratic transition of Taiwan contributed to a minor transformation of the developmental state between 1986 and 2000. The low level of DPCC limited the structural constraints from business elites and organised labour by producing dispersed business and labour interest groups. The state was also immune from the institutional constraints from business elites in the 1990s as a result of the KMT's development of profitable POEs. As a result, the state was able to retain its dominance over the private sector and over organised labour during the period of rapid democratisation. The only constraints that emerged were institutional constraints from the middle class, as manifested in the state's contradictory economic visions of maintaining Taiwanese autonomy while promoting economic integration with the mainland market.

More significant changes occurred to the state's policy-making process after 2000. The policy constraints imposed by business elites increased significantly from two developments. The first was changes to the industrial structure as a result of the privatisation of SOEs that created concentrated business interest groups. The second was that the emergence of institutional constraints generated by business elites normalised and even heightened following the advent of partisan competition after 2000. Concurrently, the state's policy vision began to erode as the process of formulating an overall growth strategy became highly politicised. Consequently, there was an emergence of short-term, electorally-motivated economic visions between 2000 and 2008, and economic visions closely linked to partisan identity after 2008. While constraints imposed on the state increased drastically in these two respects, the policy constraints from organised labour remained low due to the presence of both dispersed and state-sector labour interests.

References

Abe, M., & Kawakami, M. (1997). A Distributive Comparison of Enterprise size in Korea and Taiwan. *Developing Economies, 35*(4), 382–400.

Ash, R., Lin, J., & Wu, C. J. (2006). The Economic Legacy of the KMT and Its Implications for Economic Policy Formulation by the DPP. In D. Fell, H. Kloter, & B.-Y. Chang (Eds.), *What Has Changed?: Taiwan Before and After the Change in Ruling Parties* (pp. 83–105). Wiesbaden: Harrassowitz.

Central News Agency. (2016a). *Labour Activists Urge Large Minimum Wage Hike* (online). Available at: http://www.taiwannews.com.tw/en/news/2977000. Accessed on 12 November 2016.

Central News Agency. (2016b). *Full Text of President Tsai's Inaugural Address* (online). Available at: http://www.chinapost.com.tw/taiwan/national/national-news/2016/05/20/466744/p2/Full-text.htm. Accessed on 12 November 2016.

Chang, T.-C. (2008). *Taiwan Jingji Ziyouhua de Zhengzhi Luoji: Dangguo Ziben Zhuyi de Zhuanxing Yu Zhengshang Lianmo* [The Political Logics of Economic Liberalisation in Taiwan: The Transformation of Party-State Capitalism and the Reconstruction of State-Business Relations]. *The Taiwanese Political Science Review, 12*(1), 101–145.

Channel NewsAsia. (2015). *'I Owe Singaporeans a Responsibility' to Get Foreign Worker Balance Right: PM Lee* (online). Available at: http://www.channelnewsasia.com/news/singapore/i-owe-singaporeans-a/2023914.html. Accessed on 8 October 2016.

Chao, C.-M. (2002). The Republic of China's Foreign Relations Under President Lee Teng-hui: A Balance Sheet. In B. J. Dickson & C.-C. Chao (Eds.), *Assessing the Lee Teng-hui Legacy in Taiwan's Politics: Democratic Consolidation and External Relations* (pp. 177–203). Armonk: M.E. Sharpe.

Chao, L., & Myers, R. (1998). *The First Chinese Democracy: Political Life in the Republic of China on Taiwan*. Baltimore: Johns Hopkins University Press.

Chen, C. (1961). *Land Reform in Taiwan*. Taipei: China Publishing Company.

Chen, M. (1995). *Asian Management Systems: Chinese, Japanese and Korean Styles of Business*. London and New York: Routledge.

Cheng, T. J. (1989). Democratising the Quasi-Leninist Regime in Taiwan. *World Politics, 41,* 471–499.

Cheng, T.-J. (1997). Taiwan in 1996: From Euphoria to Melodrama. *Asian Survey, 37*(1), 43–51.

Cheng, T.-C., & Chu, Y.-H. (2002). State-Business Relations in South Korea and Taiwan. In L. Whitehead (Ed.), *Emerging Market Democracies: East Asia and Latin America* (pp. 31–62). Baltimore and London: The Johns Hopkins University Press.

Cheng, T., Haggard, S., & Kang, D. (1998). Institutions and Growth in Korea and Taiwan: The Bureaucracy. *The Journal of Development Studies, 34*(6), 87–111.

Chiu, Y. (2011). Old Constraints and Future Possibilities in the Development of Taiwan's independent Labour Movement. *Capitalism Nature Socialism, 22*(1), 58–75.

Chou, Ji. (2001). Taiwan's Macroeconomic Performance Since, 1980. In C.-C. Mai & C.-C. Shih (Eds.), *Taiwan's Economic Success Since 1980* (pp. 47–86). Cheltenham: Edward Elgar.

Chou, T. C. (1992). The Experience of SMEs' Development in Taiwan: High Export Contribution and Export Intensity. *Rivista Internazionale Di Scienze Economiche E Commerciali, 39*, 1067–1084.
Chow, P. C. Y. (2012). The ECFA, Its Impact on Cross-Strait Relations, and Implications for the United State. In P. C. Y. Chow (Ed.), *National Identity and Economic Interest: Taiwan's Competing Options and Their Implications for Regional Stability* (pp. 67–91). New York: Palgrave Macmillan.
Chu, C. Y. C. (2015). *Zhaohui Taiwan Jingji Zhengyi Yu Huoli* [Reclaim Taiwan's Economic Justice and Vitality]. Taipei: Common Wealth Magazine.
Chu, Y.-H. (1992). *Crafting Democracy in Taiwan*. Taipei: Institute for International Policy Research.
Chu, Y.-H. (1994). The Realignment of Business-Government Relations and Regime Transition in Taiwan. In A. MacIntyre (Ed.), *Business and Government in Industrialising Asia* (pp. 113–141). Ithaca and London: Cornell University Press.
Chu, Y-H. (1999a). Surviving the East Asian Financial Strom: The Political Foundations of Taiwan's Economic Resilience. In T. J. Pempel (Ed.), *Politics of the Asian Economic Crisis* (pp. 184–202). Ithaca: Cornell University Press.
Chu, Y-H. (1999b). A Born-Again Dominant Party? The Transformation of the Kuomintang and Taiwan's Regime Transition. In H. Giliomee & C. E. W. Simkins (Eds.), *The Awkward Embrace: One-Party Dominance and Democracy* (pp. 61–95). Cape Town: Tafelberg.
Chu, Y.-W. (1996). Democracy and Organised Labour in Taiwan: The 1996 Transition. *Asian Survey, 36*(5), 495–510.
Chu, Y.-H., & Lin, T.-M. (1995). The Process of Democratic Consolidation in Taiwan: Social Cleavage, Electoral Competition, and the Emerging Party System. In H. M. Tien (Ed.), *Taiwan's Electoral Politics and Democratic Transition: Riding the Third Wave* (pp. 97–104). Armonk: M.E. Sharpe.
Clark, C. (1989). *Taiwan's Development: Implications for Contending Political Economy Paradigms*. Westport: Greenwood.
Clark, C. (2002). Democratisation and the Evolving Nature of Parties Issues, and Constituencies in the ROC. In P. C. Y. Chow (Ed.), *Taiwan's Modernisation in Global Perspective* (pp. 135–159). Westport: Praeger.
Clark, C., & Roy, K. C. (1997). *Comparing Development Patterns in Asia*. Boulder: Lynne Rienner Publishers.
Clark, C., & Tan, A. C. (2010). Taiwan Enters the 21st Century: A Rude Awakening to the Costs of Success. In W.-C. Lee (Ed.), *Taiwan's Politics in the 21st Century: Changes and Challenges* (pp. 103–129). Singapore: World Scientific.
Clark, C., & Tan, A. C. (2012). *Taiwan's Political Economy: Meeting Challenges, Pursuing Progress*. Boulder: Lynne Rienner.

Council of Labour Affairs. (2010). *Implementation and Adjustment of Taiwan's Basic Wage* (online). Available at: https://twlabor.tier.org.tw/en/ParagraphCont.aspx?PeriodicalID=24&ParagraphID=2. Accessed on 6 November 2016.

Dou, E., & Hsu, J. W. (2012). *Solving Taiwan's Wage Stagnation Mystery* (online). Available at: http://blogs.wsj.com/chinarealtime/2012/10/03/solving-the-mystery-of-taiwans-wage-stagnation/. Accessed on 2 November 2016.

Dickson, B. J. (1993). The Lessons of Defeat: The Reorganisation of the Kuomintang on Taiwan, 1950–52. *The China Quarterly, 33*, 56–84.

Dickson, B. J. (1996). The Kuomintang Before Democratisation: Organisational Change and the Role of Elections. In H. M. Tien (Ed.), *Taiwan's Electoral Politics and Democratic Transition: Riding the Third Wave* (pp. 42–78). Armonk: M.E. Sharpe.

Dickson, B. J. (1997). *Democratisation in China and Taiwan: The Adaptability of Leninist Parties*. Oxford: Clarendon press.

The Economist. (1997). A Sore Point (online). Available at: http://www.economist.com/node/102942. Accessed on 16 November 2016.

Epoch Times. (2016). *The Second National Economic Development Conference Cancelled, Sustainable Economic Development Conference to Be Held* (in Chinese) (online). Available at: http://www.epochtimes.com/b5/6/3/14/n1253402.htm. Accessed on 12 January.

Executive Yuan of ROC. (2016). *New Southbound Policy Promotion Plan* (online). Available at: http://english.ey.gov.tw/News_Hot_Topic.aspx?n=6147D180AD652D77&sms=B5449820D7077391. Accessed on 15 November 2016.

Fields, K. J. (1995). *Enterprise and the State in Korea and Taiwan*. Ithaca: Cornell University Press.

Fields, K. J. (1998). Is Small Beautiful? The Political Economy of Taiwan's Small-Scale Industry. In E. M. Kim (Ed.), *The Four Asian Tigers: Economic Development and the Global Political Economy* (pp. 159–182). San Diego: Academic Press.

Fields, K. J. (2002). KMT, Inc.: Liberalisation, Democratisation and the Future of Politics in Business. In E. T. Gomez (Ed.), *Political Business in East Asia*. London and New York: Routledge.

Gold, T. (1986). *State and Society in the Taiwan Miracle*. Armonk: M.E. Sharpe.

Gold, T. (2010). Taiwan in 2009: Eroding Landslide. *Asian Survey, 50*(1), 65–75.

Gray, K. (2014). *Labour and Development in East Asia: Social Forces and Passive Revolution*. New York: Routledge.

Hajari, N., & Liu, M. (2002). *See Chen Run* (online). Available at: http://www.taiwandc.org/nwswk-2002-01.htm. Accessed on 10 November 2016.

Heo, U., & Tan, A. C. (2003). Political Choices and Economic Outcomes: A Perspective on the Differential Impact of the Financial Crisis on South Korea and Taiwan. *Comparative Political Studies, 36*(6), 679–698.
Ho, M.-S. (2006a). Challenging State Corporatism: The Politics of Taiwan's Labour Federation Movement. *The China Journal, 56*(56), 107–127.
Ho, M.-S. (2006b). Neo-Centrist Labour Policy in Practice: The DPP and the Taiwanese Working Class. In D. J. Fell, H. Kloter, & B.-Y. Chang (Eds.), *What Has Changed? Taiwan Before and After the Change in Ruling Parties* (pp. 281–298). Wiesbaden: Harrassowitz.
Ho, M.-S. (2008). *Tizhihua Jiqi Buman – Ershinian lai de Taiwan Laogong Yundo*ng [Institutionalisation and Discontent—Twenty Years of Taiwan's Labour Movement]. In H.-Z. Wang, K.-C. Li, & I.-C. Kung (Eds.), *Kuajie: Liudong Yu Jianchi de Taiwan Shehui* [Step in Forbidden Zones: Twenty Years Social Transformation in Taiwan, 1987–2008] (pp. 312–333). Taipei: Socio.
Ho, M.-S. (2012a). *Working Class Formation in Taiwan: Fractured Solidarity in State-Own Enterprises, 1945–2012.* Hampshire: Palgrave Macmillan.
Ho, M.-S. (2012b). Beyond Tokenism: The Institutional Conversion of Party-Controlled Labour Unions in Taiwan's State-Owned Enterprises (1951–86). *The China Quarterly, 212*, 1019–1039.
Ho, S. P. S. (1978). *Economic Development in Taiwan, 1860–1970.* New Haven: Yale University Press.
Ho, S. P. S. (1987). Economics, Economic Bureaucracy, and Taiwan's Economic Development. *Pacific Affairs, 60*(2), 226–247.
Ho, S.-Y. (1990). *Taiwan-After a Long Silence.* Hong Kong: Asia Labour Monitor.
Hsiao, H. H. M. (1993). The Political Economy of State-Business Relations in Taiwan. *Acta Oeconomica, 45*(1/2), 145–171.
Hsiao, H. M., & Koo, H. (1997). The Middle Classes and Democratisation. In L. Diamond, M. F. Plattner, Y. Chu, & H. Tien (Eds.), *Consolidating the Third Wave Democracies: Themes and Perspectives* (pp. 312–333). Baltimore and London: The Johns Hopkins University Press.
Hsieh, C. (2001). *No Raise for Base-Wage Earners* (online). Available at: http://www.taiwantoday.tw/fp.asp?xItem=18770&CtNode=451. Accessed on 3 November 2016.
Hsieh, J. F.-S. (2015). Taiwan in 2014: A Besieged President Amid Political Turmoil. *Asian Survey, 55*(1), 142–147.
Huang, K.-B. (2017). *Taiwan's Southward Integration Faces a Long Uphill Battle.* East Asian Forum (online). Available at: https://www.eastasiaforum.org/2017/10/17/taiwans-southward-integration-faces-a-long-uphill-battle/. Accessed 7 November 2017.

Huang, S. (2009). *No Change to Minimum Wage, CLA Says* (online). Available at: http://www.taipeitimes.com/News/taiwan/archives/2009/08/15/2003451148. Accessed on 6 November 2016.

Huang, T.-H. (2004). *Taiwan Zhengshang Guanxi de Yanbian: Lishi Zhidulun Fenxi* [The Evolution of the State-Business Relations in Taiwan: An Analysis from the Perspective of Historical Institutionalism]. *Issues and Studies, 43*(4), 35–72.

Jacobs, J. B. (2012). *Democratising Taiwan*. Leiden: Brill.

Ku, S. C. Y. (1995). The Political Economy of Taiwan's Relations with Southeast Asia: The 'Southward Policy'. *Contemporary Southeast Asia, 17*(3), 282–297.

Kuo, C. T. (1998). Private Governance in Taiwan. In S. Chen, C. Clark, & D. Lam (Eds.), *Beyond the Developmental State: East Asia's Political Economics Reconsidered*. London: Macmillan.

Lam, D., & Clark, C. (1994). Beyond the Developmental State: The Cultural Roots of 'Guerrilla Capitalism' in Taiwan. *Governance, 7*, 412–430.

Lam, D. K. K., & Lee, I. (1992). Guerrilla Capitalism and the Limit of Statist Theory: Comparing the Chinese NICs. In C. Clark & S. Chan (Eds.), *The Evolving Pacific Basin in the Global Political Economy: Domestic and International Linkages* (pp. 107–124). Boulder: Lynne Rienner.

Lee, Y.-K. (2011). *Militants or Partisans: Labour Unions and Democratic Politics in Korea and Taiwan*. Stanford: Stanford University Press.

Lee, P.-S., & Chu, Y.-H. (2008). The New Political Economy After Regime Turnover in Taiwan: An Assessment of the First Chen Shui-bian Administration. In S. Goldstein & J. Chang (Eds.), *Presidential Politics in Taiwan: The Administration of Chen Shui-bian* (pp. 143–166). Norwalk: EastBridge.

Li, F. (2002). *Chen Rekindles Southward Investment Policy* (online). Available at: http://taiwantoday.tw/ct.asp?xItem=19581&ctNode=122. Accessed on 11 November 2016.

Liaw, B. C. K., & Wang, Y.-Y. (2009). Double-Track Decision-Making and the Failure of Taiwan's Asia-Pacific Regional Operations Centre Plan in the 1990s. *Tamkang Journal of International Affairs, 13*(1), 73–100.

Lin, C.-Y. (2003). KMT's Siew to Head Chen's Panel. *Taipei Times* (online). Available at: http://www.taipeitimes.com/News/front/archives/2003/05/24/2003052387. Accessed on 2 November 2016.

Lin, S. S. (2013). National Identity, Economic Interdependence, and Taiwan's Cross-Strait Policy. In W. Hu (Ed.), *New Dynamics in Cross-Taiwan Strait Relations: How Far Can the Rapprochement Go?* (pp. 31–46). Abingdon: Routledge.

Lin, S. S. (2016). *Taiwan's China Dilemma: Contested Identities and Multiple Interests in Taiwan's Cross-Strait Economic Policy*. Stanford: Stanford University Press.

Lui, F. T., & Qiu, L. D. (2001). Taiwan: Thriving High-Technology Industries and SMEs. In K.-S. Kwong (Ed.), *Industrial Development in Singapore, Taiwan, and South Korea* (pp. 56–117). Singapore: World Scientific.

Ma, K. (2001). Taiwan as the Asian Pacific Regional Operations Centre: Its Significance and Prospects. In S. Masuyama, D. Vandenbrink, & S. Y. Chia (Eds.), *Industrial Restructuring in East Asia: Towards the 21st Century* (pp. 239–255). Singapore: Institute of Southeast Asian Studies.

Matsumoto, M. (2002). Political Democratisation and KMT Party-Owned Enterprises in Taiwan. *The Developing Economies, 40*(3), 359–380.

Mattlin, M. (2011). *Politicized Society: The Long Shadow of Taiwan's One-Party Legacy*. Copenhagen: NIAS Press.

McBeath, G. (1998). *Wealth and Freedom: Taiwan's New Political Economy*. Aldershot: Ashgate.

Minns, J. (2006). *The Politics of Developmentalism in Mexico, Taiwan, and South Korea: The Midas States of Mexico*. South Korea and Taiwan, Basingstoke: Palgrave Macmillan.

Minns, J., & Tierney, R. (2003). The Labour Movement in Taiwan. *Labour History, 85,* 103–128.

Myers, R. H., & Lin, H. (2007). *Breaking with the Past: The Kuomintang Central Reform Committee on Taiwan, 1950–52*. Stanford: Hoover Institution Press.

Myers, R. H., Chao, L., & Kuo, T.-C. (2002). Consolidating Democracy in the Republic of China on Taiwan, 1996–2000. In B. J. Dickson & C.-M. Chao (Eds.), *Assessing the Lee Teng-hui Legacy in Taiwan's Politics: Democratic Consolidation and External Relations* (pp. 73–90). Armonk: M.E. Sharpe.

Rigger, S. (1996). Mobilisational Authoritarianism and Political Opposition in Taiwan. In G. Rodan (Ed.), *Political Oppositions in Industrialising Asia* (pp. 300–322). London and New York: Routledge.

Rigger, S. (1999). *Politics in Taiwan: Voting for Democracy*. London and New York: Routledge.

Rigger, S. (2001). *From Opposition to Power: Taiwan's Democratic Progressive Party*. Bolder: Lynne Rienner.

Rigger, S. (2016). Kuomintang Agonises: Party Politics in the Wake of Taiwan's 2016 Elections. *Orbis, 60*(4), 488–503.

Shiau, C.-J. (1996). Elections and the Changing State-Business Relationship. In H.-M. Tien (Ed.), *Taiwan's Electoral Politics and Democratic Transition: Riding the Third Wave* (pp. 213–225). Armonk and London: M.E. Sharpe.

Taipei Times. (2013). *Editorial: Safeguarding Workers' Basic Rights* (online). Available at: http://www.taipeitimes.com/News/editorials/archives/2013/09/18/2003572391. Accessed on 6 November 2016.

Taiwan News. (2016). *New Southward Policy Office Approved* (online). Available at: http://www.taiwannews.com.tw/en/news/2938198. Accessed on 6 January 2017.

Tan, A. C. (2001). Taiwan: Sustained State Autonomy and a Step Back from Liberalization. In S. Horowitz & U. Heo (Eds.), *The Political Economy of International Financial Crisis: Interest Groups, Ideologies and Institutions* (pp. 165–176). Lanham: Rowman & Littlefield.

Tao, Y.-F., & Chang, J.-J. (2008). *Zhengshang guanxi zai minzhuhua zhihou de Fazhan: Yi jinrong ziyouhua wei li* [The Transformation of State-Business Relations After Democratisation: The Case Financial Reform]. In H.-Z. Wang, K.-C. Li, & I.-C. Kung (Eds.), *Kuajie: Liudong Yu Jianchi de Taiwan Shehui* [Step in Forbidden Zones: Twenty Years Social Transformation in Taiwan, 1987–2008] (pp. 219–239). Taipei: Socio.

Tien, H.-M. (1975). Taiwan in Transition: Prospects for Sociopoltical Change. *The China Quarterly, 64*, 615–644.

Tien, H. M. (1989). *The Great Transition: Political and Social Change in the Republic of China*. Stanford: Hoover Institute Press.

Tien, H.-M., & Cheng, T.-J. (1997). Crafting Democratic Institutions in Taiwan. *The China Journal, 37*, 1–27.

Tien, H., & Shiau, C. (1992). Taiwan's Democratisation: A Summary. *World Affairs, Democracy in Taiwan: Part One, 155*(2), 58–61.

Tien, H., & Tung, C. (2011). Taiwan in 2010: Mapping for a New Political Landscape and Economic Outlook. *Asian Survey, 51*(1), 76–84.

US-Taiwan Business Council. (1996). *Report on the Meeting with President Lee Teng-hui* (online). Available at: http://www.us-taiwan.org/reports/print120996.html. Accessed on 5 December 2016.

Wade, R. (1990). *Governing the Market: Economic Theory and the Role of Government in East Asian Industrialization*. Princeton: Princeton University Press.

Wang, J. (2003). *Comment: Chen's 'three links' Plan Fails To Impress* (online). Available at: http://www.chinadaily.com.cn/en/doc/2003-09/05/content_261389.htm. Accessed on 10 November 2016.

Wang, J.-H. (1996). *Shei Tongzhi Taiwan?* [Who Controls Taiwan?]. Taipei: Juliu.

Wang, J. W. Y. (2010). The Political Economy of Collective Labour Legislation in Taiwan. *Journal of Current Chinese Affairs, 39*(3), 51–85.

Wang, S. (2012). *Business Interest, State Elites and Financial Regulatory Reform in South Korea and Taiwan*. PhD Thesis, Yale University.

Wang, V. W.-C. (1995). Developing the Information Industry in Taiwan. *Pacific Affairs, 68*(4), 551–576.

Wasserstrom, J. (2014). *Taiwan's Sunflower Protests: A Q&A with Shelley Rigger* (online). Available at: https://www.dissentmagazine.org/online_articles/tai

wans-sunflower-protests-a-qa-with-shelley-rigger. Accessed on 2 December 2016.

White, L. T. (2009). *Political Booms: Local Money and Power in Taiwan, East China, Thailand, and the Philippines*. Singapore: World Scientific.

Winckler, E. (1984). Institutionalisation and Participation on Taiwan: From Hard to Soft Authoritarianism. *The China Quarterly, 99*, 481–499.

Wong, J. (2003). Deepening Democracy in Taiwan. *Pacific Affairs, 76*(2), 235–256.

Wu, Y. (2005). *Political Explanation of Economic Growth: State Survival, Bureaucratic Politics, and Private Enterprises in the Making of Taiwan's Economy, 1950–1985*. Cambridge: Harvard University Press.

Wu, Y.-S. (1989). Marketization of Politics: The Taiwan Experience. *Asian Survey, 29*, 382–400.

Wu, Y.-S. (2007). Taiwan's Developmental State: After the Economic and Political Turmoil. *Asian Survey, 47*(6), 977–1001.

Wu, Y.-S. (2013). *From Identity to Distribution: Paradigm Shift in Taiwan Politics: A First Cut*. Paper presented at The 55th Annual Conference of the American Association for Chinese Studies. New Brunswick, NJ: The State University of New Jersey at Rutgers, October 11–13.

Wu, R. I., & Huang, C. C. (2003). *Entrepreneurship in Taiwan: Turning Point to Restart*. Paper presented at the US-Japan Dialogue on Entrepreneurship in Asia, Tokyo.

Yu, H.-S. (1993). Industrial Structure and Labour Movement: Comparative Study of South Korea and Taiwan. *Korea Observer: A Quarterly Journal, 24*, 265–290.

Zeldin, W. (2012). *Taiwan: Cabinet Approves Increase in Minimum Hourly Wage* (online). Available at: http://www.loc.gov/law/foreign-news/article/taiwan-cabinet-approves-increase-in-minimum-hourly-wage/. Accessed on 5 November 2016.

CHAPTER 5

Understanding the Transformation of the Developmental State

This book has analysed the transformation of Asian authoritarian developmental states. In the post-war period, these developmental states emerged in several East Asian countries almost simultaneously to drive rapid economic growth from the 1960s through the mid-1990s. The Asian financial crisis of 1997 was a major event indicating that the developmental state had transformed; indeed, the capability of the old post-war developmental states to direct economic development has been undermined by the rise of various societal interests in these newly-industrialised countries. The literature on the transformation of the developmental state model has pointed to the rise of two social actors, namely business elites and organised labour, to explain the state's reduced capability to direct economic development. Yet this explanation does not address variations in the transformation process, both across East Asia and even within a single country. This book therefore seeks to answer two questions in particular. The first is why, across the region, did some developmental states experience a rapid reduction in their capacity to direct the development process, while others took a more gradually declining route, and still others remained resilient to these changes? The second is why, within a nation-state, did changes to the developmental state occur more rapidly in specific time periods despite the country's consistent socioeconomic performance? Although there are numerous studies on the transformation of the Asian developmental states, they have largely set aside these variations.

T. He, *The Political Economy of Developmental States in East Asia*,
https://doi.org/10.1007/978-3-030-59357-5_5

This book has introduced a theory to account for the states' various transformation outcomes. Using existing insights on elite survival and state development institutions, trade and interest groups, socioeconomic development and regime transition, I conceptualised that the state policy process is a dynamic one constantly shaped by various policy constraints and the political environment faced by ruling elites. From the outset, the developmental state was created by authoritarian ruling elites to generate performance-based legitimacy (Doner et al. 2005). Therefore, the state's economic policy was a useful tool for elites to achieve political legitimacy. The developmental state is not static but transitionary in the development process. The very successes of their policies bring about two political processes that eventually cause their transitions. First, international trade gives rise to assertive business and labour interests (Rogowski 1989; Gourevitch 1986). Second, socioeconomic development leads to the emergence of pro-democratic political interest groups, i.e. the middle and working classes (Lipset 1959; Moore 1966; Rueschemeyer et al. 1992). While the former process produces social actors capable of directly shaping state policy-making, the latter process gives rise to social actors who have interests to alter the political context in which the state's policy-making occurs. Accordingly, I hypothesised that variations occur in two parallel dimensions: (1) the emergence of economic interests is affected by the industrial structure of a country, which is shaped by the policy preferences of East Asian ruling elites as they try to maintain regime survival; and (2) the process of (non-) democratic transition initiated by ruling elites in response to the democratic mobilisation of the two social classes. The variations in the types of economic interests and regime transition outcomes in turn affect the state's transformation process by determining the levels of policy constraints generated by social actors.

In this conclusion, I will firstly revisit the book's theory. The theory has sought to explain four processes: (1) how East Asian elites' policy choices, influenced by their political objectives associated with regime survival, lead to the formation of a country's industrial structure; (2) how the democratic mobilisation (or lack thereof) of the middle and working classes pushes ruling elites to make regime transition choices; (3) how the industrial structure of a country affects the emergence of economic interests; and (4) how the emergence of economic interests and (non-) democratic transition of a country leads to policy constraints on the state. After revisiting this theory, I will also consider two theoretical contributions of this study for understanding the transformation of authoritarian developmental states in East Asia: (1) the creation of non-constraining economic interests as a new category affecting state policy-making; and (2) the identification of the role of the middle class in transforming the developmental state model. I will then discuss the application of the theory to the largest Asian authoritarian developmental state: China. I will end the chapter with some final thoughts on the transformation of the developmental state in East Asia.

Revisiting the Theory of the Transformation of the Developmental State

The theory consists of four major components. The first part concerns the formation of a country's industrial structure. I argue that ruling elites' policy preferences, which are largely motivated by goals of political survival, can affect the industrial structure of a country in terms of DPCC, SOE and FDI. The second part concerns the transformation of the political foundation of the state's economic policy-making process. I argue that different patterns of democratic mobilisation of the two social classes emerging from a state-led development process, i.e. whether or not the middle class and working class participate, result in different strategic decisions by the ruling elites in terms of initiating regime transitions. Moreover, the pace of democratic transition allowed by the ruling elites is determined by the level of electoral threats they face. The third part concerns the emergence of different types of economic interest groups. I argue that the industrial structure of a country (in terms of the degree of DPCC, SOE, FDI) can affect the types of economic interest groups that emerge from a state-led development process. The fourth part concerns the process of the developmental state's transformation, as in how the emergence of economic interests and the process of (non-) democratic transition leads to structural and institutional constraints on the state.

The Rise of the Developmental State and the Industrial Structure of the Case Study Countries

The first component of the theory explores the formation of the country's industrial structure, which is an unintended result of the policy choices of East Asian ruling elites. The establishment of a linkage between ruling elites' strategic calculations and the formation of the industrial structure require us to revisit the historical roots of the developmental state model in post-war East Asia. In the 1950s and 1960s, the Taiwanese, Singaporean and South Korean regimes were all struggling for political survival. In Taiwan, the mainland-originated KMT had little legitimacy to rule the hostile local population. In Singapore, the PAP was almost annihilated by a leftist movement that had gained strong support from the majority of the Chinese-speaking population. In South Korea, the political situation was equally dangerous for Park Chung-hee and his junior coup associates, who had no pre-existing political standing in the country. The desire for political survival motivated the ruling elites in all three countries to create authoritarian institutions and state economic policy-making agencies in order to pursue a strategy of political control and economic promotion, which would give them a secure power monopoly. The adoption of this survival strategy consequently gave rise to the institutional arrangements for state-led economic development in East Asia.

As the developmental state was created to ensure regime survival, the policy choices generated within the state's institutional arrangements were also linked to ruling elites' political preferences. In Taiwan, as the KMT was concerned about the survival of its émigré regime, the ruling elites' policy preference was to prevent the concentration of DPCC. Instead, the KMT pushed an SME-led development model that maintained political peace, and also complemented its SME strategy with promotion of strong SOEs. In Singapore, the urgency for rapid industrialisation to create employment for the local population prompted the PAP to replace the backward domestic business community with more advanced foreign partners in commercial sectors, and with SOEs in strategic sectors. In South Korea, the promotion of the chaebols, the only viable economic actors at the time, became the centre of the state's economic programmes. The adoption of these varied sets of economic policies locked the three East Asian countries onto dissimilar development paths in terms of the utilisation of DPCC, SOE and FDI capital. Consequently, three very different types of industrial structures, each underpinned by their respective source of capital, had been formed in these successfully-industrialised countries by the 1980s. Taiwan's industrial structure was characterised by a low level of DPCC coupled with a high level of SOE. Singapore's industrial structure of the country was dominated by FDI and SOE. In South Korea, the rise of chaebols had allowed for a relatively high level of DPCC.

Variety of Economic Interest Groups in East Asia

The second component of my theory concerns the emergence of different types of economic interest groups in the three countries. Industrial structure proves a key factor to understand this process, as specific types of capital ownership can contribute to the emergence of specific economic interest groups.

The South Korean case demonstrates the emergence of two types of economic interest groups in the state-led development process—concentrated business interest groups and concentrated labour interest groups—as a result of the country's high level of DPCC. The powerful capability of the concentrated business interest groups to influence the state was evident in the fact that the chaebols were able to constrain state policy-making during the process of financial liberalisation, even prior to the 1987 democratic transition. The democratic transition, coupled with the financial independence of the chaebols, further escalated the structural constraints generated by business elites. The result was the rise of a 'Chaebol Republic' in South Korea in the post-1987 period. The concentrated labour interest groups in South Korea were also located within the chaebol sector; due to an organisational advantage resulting from the concentration of industrial workers, many large chaebol-based labour unions quickly emerged after 1987. Similar to chaebol owners, chaebol-based labour unions also possessed strong structural capabilities to achieve their perceived material interests within the development process, therefore collectively elevating their economic status and becoming 'labour aristocrats'.

The Singaporean case shows the presence of non-constraining economic interests that do not produce constraints on state policy-making. The country's high levels of FDI and SOE led to the emergence of non-indigenous business interest groups and state-affiliated business interest groups, both of which had little interest in shaping the state policy process. As the empirical case revealed, while the state policy agency—the EDB—had closely integrated the economic interests of major MNCs with the PAP's economic projects, the GLCs were placed under the supervision of the party's close associates and highly-trusted former bureaucrats, who predominantly acted as watchdogs of the state economic policies. The high level of FDI also led to the emergence of state-controlled labour interest groups. At the outset of the industrialisation process, the national labour union movement—the NTUC—was put under the direct control of the PAP state, and the NWC was also created to manage the interests of organised labour in line with government policies. These labour control mechanisms were subsequently upgraded in the 1980s by bringing bureaucrats into the NTUC leadership, as well as through other authoritarian means as the PAP embarked on its industrial upgrading projects.

The Taiwanese case indicates how a low level of DPCC leads to the emergence of dispersed economic interest groups, which in this particular case consisted of a large number of SME owners that lacked both incentive and capacity to influence state policies; and of a number of business elites that were incapable of challenging state economic policy-making. This was evident in the fact that while SME owners resorted to private adjustments such as relocation rather than collective actions to advance their material interests, the business elites used the new institutional channels created by the democratic transition to influence state policy decisions. As DPCC increased as a result of the privatisation process in the 1990s and 2000s, the dispersed business interest groups did eventually become more concentrated and therefore more capable of challenging the state. Taiwan's low level of DPCC and high level of SOE prior to the early 1990s had also created dispersed labour interest groups in the private sector and state-sector labour interest groups in the SOE sector. While the private-sector labour unions lacked a strong membership base due to the difficulty to organise numerous dispersed SME workers, the SOE labour unions had their own communication channels with the state to advance their material gains and were concerned about issues (e.g. privatisation) that were fundamentally different from those of the private-sector workers.

The (Non-) Democratic Transition Process of a Country: Democratic Mobilisation and Elite Responses

The third component of the theory concerns the country's democratic transition, which is instrumental in transforming the political context in which the state's policy-making occurs. This concerns another set of elite choices in regard to pushing for or resisting democratic transition. I locate the source of this strategic choice to four patterns of democratic mobilisation of the middle and working classes emerging from the state-led development process. Taiwanese state-led development gave rise to a democratisation movement led by the middle class. The absence of the working class was largely due to the country's decentralised economic growth model, which had hindered the mobilisation of the working class on issues of socioeconomic injustice. In Singapore, rapid state-led socioeconomic development did not produce democratic mobilisation of the two social classes. Democratisation failed to emerge because of the strong presence of the authoritarian state in almost all social and political aspects of the tiny island country. The experiences of South Korea illustrated two other patterns of democratic coalitions. In 1980, when the opposition elites failed to present themselves as a united liberal community, the working class was highly mobilised along class identity to push for democratisation, while the middle class chose to side with the authoritarian system in order to protect their socioeconomic gains against radicalised labour. In 1987, the emergence of a unified opposition liberal community finally convinced the middle class and the working class to form a cross-class democratic coalition on the issue of socioeconomic justice to challenge the authoritarian government.

Two patterns of democratic mobilisation compel East Asian ruling elites to push the political system in a democratic direction. The other two incentivise ruling elites to resist any democratic changes. In the cases of South Korea in 1987 and of Taiwan, facing the democratic mobilisation of the middle class, the ruling elites had strong incentives to transform the old legitimacy formula, which had been based on a combination of economic growth and authoritarian control that they could no longer maintain. In Taiwan, a democratic coalition formed between the opposition elites and the middle class successfully forced the KMT to transform its legitimacy formula by pursuing democratic transition. Similar to the case of Taiwan in 1986, South Korean authoritarian rule ended in 1987 when the ruling elites decided to pursue a strategy of democratic transition in response to the emergence of a powerful cross-class alliance.

In the other two cases of South Korea in 1980 and of Singapore, East Asian ruling elites pursued political strategies to preserve the authoritarian nature of the political systems. In Singapore, in the absence of a democratic movement, the ruling PAP had no incentive to change its old legitimacy formula of imposing political control and promoting economic development. To consolidate their power in an environment of middle-class assertiveness, the PAP built new political institutions aimed at co-opting middle-class interests. Ruling elites' strategy of authoritarian repression was shown in the case of 1980 South Korea. Facing a democratisation movement led by only the working class, the ruling elites could easily resort to authoritarian repression to suppress labour unrest. This strategy proved effective and social order was quickly restored in the country.

As authoritarian rule ends, one important part of a democratic transition is the introduction of democratic elections. This process is also shaped by the strategic choices of East Asian ruling elites. A key factor influencing these choices is the presence of an electoral threat from opposition elites during the time of democratic transition. The logic is that, in the context of an electoral threat, the ruling elites will benefit from the decision to introduce democratic electoral institutions because it would ensure them maximum political representation in the new political system. By this same logic, if ruling elites expect to retain electoral dominance no matter what, they will not be incentivised to push for the introduction of democratic elections that could invite the possibility of losing political power. Historical analysis of the two cases of successful democratic transitions supports my theoretical propositions. In the case of Taiwan, the KMT successfully retained their electoral dominance through a project of 'Taiwanisation' among other tactics to undermine the electoral strength of the DPP. In 1986, with no urgency to maximise political representation, the KMT implemented political liberalisation but delayed the introduction of democratic elections. Only when the KMT's electoral domination showed signs of decline in the first half of the 1990s did the ruling party push for the second stage of democratic transition. In contrast, in 1987 South Korea, as the elites' electoral strength faced serious challenges from the rise of middle-class voters, the leaders opted for an immediate introduction of elections to ensure their maximum political presence in an increasingly democratic country.

The (Non-)Transformation of the Developmental State

The aforementioned two processes—the emergence of economic interests and the process of (non-) democratic transition—contribute to the creation of structural and institutional constraints. At any given time, the levels of these policy constraints determine the outcome of the state's transformation process. In this study, I explained three distinctive processes of the state's transformation: the rapid transformation of the developmental state in South Korea, the non-transformation of the developmental state in Singapore, and the two-phase transformation of the developmental state in Taiwan.

The South Korean case shows how the combination of a high level of DPCC and a rapid democratic transition can result in the immediate transformation of the developmental state. To a large extent, this transformation was the result of strong structural constraints generated by Korean business elites and organised labour. Even before the democratisation of the state's decision-making, the Korean chaebols were already capable of constraining the policy process. Since the early 1990s, producing both institutional and structural constraints, the chaebol owners have dominated economic policy-making for structural reform and industrial upgrading. At the same time, with the presence of strong chaebol unions, organised labour also foiled the plan of the state-business alliance to negotiate through a series of tripartite organs. These strong policy constraints were only temporarily relaxed in the immediate aftermath of the 1997 Asian financial crisis, when both Korean business elites and organised labour allowed the state to focus on a rapid economic rebound. The emergence of institutional constraints from the middle class after 1987 also affected the formulation of the state's strategic visions. In democratic South Korea, the state largely failed to formulate a viable economic strategy throughout most of the 1990s, as ruling elites faced a contradiction between generating growth through the old chaebol strategy, and the more politically popular strategy of structural reform. Only when this contradiction disappeared after the 1997 financial crisis did the Korean state regain a coherent strategic vision. Consequently, structural reform became a priority for the government from 1998 to 2007, and a more balanced growth model emerged as the key for ruling elites' political consolidation after 2008.

The Singaporean case provides a clear picture on how an industrial structure characterised by non-constraining economic interest groups and a lack of democratic transition combine to free the state of policy constraints from business elites and organised labour, therefore leading to non-transformation of the developmental state. The PAP state subsequently continued to pursue global expansion and industrial upgrading projects in close alliance with MNCs and GLCs, while carefully managing the material interests of organised labour in line with the state's economic agendas. State economic strategy therefore remained coherent and unchallenged despite the advent of consultative institutions since the early 1980s. As the PAP single-mindedly prioritised economic growth, a growth-first agenda had emerged since the mid-1980s in the form of an immigration-driven growth model. This strategy was modified between 2010 and 2015, as the country moved from an immigration-driven growth model to a productivity-based one. As I documented, the modification of the labour-driven growth model was motivated by the strategic consideration of the PAP elites to adjust to new economic and political situations.

The Taiwanese case demonstrates a two-phase transformation of the developmental state. The first stage brought a limited transformation prior to 2000. The emergence of dispersed business interests coupled with the ruling KMT's financial independence sheltered the state from policy constraints produced by business elites. Consequently, the government was able to continue its SME strategy for generating export-led growth. In the same period, the state's strategic vision was impaired because of the growing contradiction between pursuing economically-beneficial integration with the mainland market and satisfying the desire of the middle class to maintain Taiwan's political autonomy. In the second stage, a more rapid transformation of the developmental state was observed as more concentrated business interests emerged to generate greater policy constraints on the state's decision-making process. As a result of the institutional and structural constraints from business elites, the state was no longer able to strategically promote the SME sector. The state's development vision was also highly politicised and thus greatly eroded under the three administrations between 2000 and 2016, during which the KMT and DPP alternated power. Throughout both stages of transformation, the policy constraints from organised labour remained limited largely due to the initial industrial structure's a low level of DPCC versus a high level of SOE. The emergence of state-sector and dispersed labour interests resulted in weak organised labour groups that have been unable to constrain the state-business alliance in Taiwan.

Explaining the Non-Transformation of the Developmental State in China

The three authoritarian developmental states featured in this book have often been compared with weak or predatory states in Africa, second-tier developmental states in Southeast Asia, politically captured states in Western and South Asia, and socialist states governed by Marxist-Leninist communist parties.[1] How are the cases of South Korea, Singapore and Taiwan relevant to other developing countries? My book examines the transformation of a specific type of developmental state that is authoritarian in nature and historically associated with the experience of the three East Asian tigers.[2] This type of developmental state is indeed rare.[3] Besides the three case studies presented in this book, China likely presents the only remaining case to test my theory of the transformation of the developmental state model. This section therefore widens the theory's empirical scope by analysing the largest developmental state's non-transformation to date.

The Rise of the Chinese Developmental State

The emergence of the Chinese developmental state occurred in the post-Mao period. Just like in the other three cases, the CCP was in desperate need of political legitimacy. In the late 1970s, lengthy political campaigns such as the Great Leap Forward and the Cultural Revolution had decimated society and left people questioning whether the party and its championed socialist ideology could bring the economic prosperity it had promise. There were deep frustration and discontent among the population over restrictions on their economic and social life, as well as worsening living standards. After the death of Mao, the CCP could no

[1] See Evans (1995) for the comparison with predatory states in Africa; see Doner et al. (2005) for the comparison with Southeast Asia states; see Naseemullah and Arnold (2015) and Waldner (1999) for the comparison with politically captured states in Western and South Asia (i.e. Turkey, Pakistan, Syria); and see Vu (2010) for the comparison with socialist states in China and Vietnam.

[2] Unlike Singapore, South Korea and Taiwan, the other tiger, Hong Kong, was never an authoritarian developmental state, retaining a liberal (though undemocratic) political system throughout the development process.

[3] The Southeast Asian countries—Thailand, Malaysia and Indonesia—nearly constitute a developmental state. However, in the absence of 'systematic vulnerability', they never established the same type of state developmental mechanisms seen in post-war Northeast Asia (Doner et al. 2005). The economic and political experiences of countries such as India and Brazil do not resemble those of the three Asian tigers. Although India attempted an extremely ambitious programme of state-led development, it lacked the institutional capacity to carry out rapid industrialisation (Chibber 2003). The Brazilian state similarly lacked the kind of 'embedded autonomy' that the East Asian countries had to pursue industrialisation (Evans 1995). Meanwhile, despite the existence of a communist system in Vietnam, the authoritarian state has not been very successful in facilitating industrialisation (Vu 2010).

longer sustain power through political mobilisation. The CCP's crisis was made even worse by the economic successes of its neighbours. Taiwan's economic miracle in particular threatened to greatly undercut the legitimacy of the CCP in the late 1970s (White 1993; Harding 1987; Shirk 1993).

In the three case studies, the adoption of a survival strategy based on a combination of political control and economic promotion led to the creation of authoritarian institutions and central economic policy-making agencies. In China, given that the pre-existing communist political system could sustain the state's domination in society, the ruling elites' need for survival was manifest in the state's push for market reform to accelerate economic growth.[4] This process began with Deng Xiaoping's economic policy of 'reform and opening-up' in the late 1970s. This impulse for development was further reinforced in the early 1990s, as the need for political legitimacy in the post-Tiananmen period generated more urgency for the state to carry out market reform, as evident by Deng's 'Southern Tour' in 1992.[5] The subsequent decades witnessed a 'more extreme version of Deng's original model of economic reform' (Clark and Roy 1997: 89). Since the beginning of the reform era, a series of economic agencies, which eventually evolved into the powerful National Development and Reform Commission (NDRC) have been in charge of China's market reform and economic restructuring.[6]

In short, the Chinese developmental state emerged at the end of the Cultural Revolution in 1976 and was reinforced in the aftermath of the Tiananmen Square protests in 1989. Just as had happened in the other

[4] See Qian (2017), for a discussion on how China succeed in generating economic growth by pushing forward market reform, or, in Qian's words, creating 'market compatible institutions'.

[5] In January and February 1992, Deng travelled to Southern China, where he called for the whole country to push ahead with rapid market-oriented changes.

[6] The origin of the NDRC can be traced back to the Mao period when China practised central planning under the direction of the State Planning Commission (SPC). After China began its structural reform, the Commission for Restructuring the Economic System was established in 1982 to direct efficient institution building while the SPC continued to be an important organ for administering the economy and researching various economic problems. In 1998, as the CCP further shifted it policy towards market development to accelerate economic growth, the SPC was renamed the State Development and Planning Commission (SDPC), which then merged with the Commission for Restructuring the Economic System and the State Economic and Trade Commission. In 2006, it was relabelled as the NDRC.

three cases, the Chinese state-led development process has driven export-led growth and created major socioeconomic transformation since the early 1980s. After nearly four decades of rapid economic development, the Chinese state still exhibits strong characteristics of the developmental state model. My hypothesis regarding different types of economic interest groups and the role of the middle class in transforming the developmental state can shed light on the current status and future prospects of the Chinese state's transformation.

Elite Decision, Industrial Structure and Democratic Transition

One source of the Chinese state's non-transformation so far lies in the composition of capital ownership. Several elite choices have shaped the formation of the industrial structure. China's industrialisation was kicked off by Deng's 1979 decision to establish Special Economic Zones (SEZs) to attract FDI; this proved a less destabilising approach than reforming the state sector and developing the private sector (Gallagher 2002). The CCP's FDI promotion accelerated in the early 1990s with the adoption of the Coastal Development Strategy (CDS), which aimed to generate political support from representatives of the coastal provinces (Naughton 2006).[7] The development of another form of capital—SOE—became central to the CCP's version of economic reform after 1989. In the 1990s, the CCP leadership decided to accelerate SOE reform by selling off most of the small SOEs, while keeping the big SOEs under government control with the intention of eventually creating huge conglomerates for major industrial sectors.

Similar to Taiwan, mainland China's capital ownership was never concentrated in the domestic private sector. The private economy took off in agriculture, where the CCP essentially duplicated Taiwan's land reform of the 1950s by informally creating small-scale privatised agriculture based on long-term leases (Clark and Roy 1997: 87). The boom of urban private businesses only occurred after 1999 when the government granted greater constitutional protection and legitimacy to the private

[7] In 1992, most cities along the Yangtze River and China's borders were granted special privileges as coastal cities, and in addition, Shanghai was granted even greater autonomy. As a result, numerous development zones were established to attract foreign and domestic investment.

sector. However, indigenous Chinese entrepreneurs who contributed the majority of China's industrial growth could not obtain sufficient capital and therefore had to turn to informal networks for private-sector capital (Tsai 2002).

The second source of the state's non-transformation lies in the lack of democratic transition. China's economic boom did cultivate a middle class with liberal democratic beliefs as well concerns about socioeconomic well-being and protection of property rights. However, the democratic aspiration of the middle class—the social actor crucial for forcing East Asian ruling elites to initiate democratic transition—did not emerge in China. The extensive party-state nexus of the CCP made it extremely difficult for the newly-emerging middle class to develop their independence from the authoritarian state. Consequently, as long as their perceived social and economic well-being is not undermined by the current political system, members of the Chinese middle class employed in the state-sector maintain their loyalty to the CCP, while the ones outside of the state-sector (in particular private business owners) withhold support for democratic change (Wu et al. 2017; Chen and Lu 2011; Chen 2013; Tsai 2007). Andrew Nathan (2016) has categorised the middle class' attitude towards the CCP into four types: the politically anesthetised, the acceptors, the ameliorators, and the alienated. None of these categories are willing to support a democratisation movement.

In this context, the CCP elites have had no incentive to change their legitimacy formula through democratic transition. Just as in Singapore, the CCP has pursued a strategy of authoritarian co-optation since the 2000s to deal with discontent in a tightly-controlled society. One part of this strategy is the inclusion and co-optation of a wide of range of new socioeconomic forces emerging from market reform, as justified by the government's formulation of the 'three representatives' ideology in 2000. Particularly, the government's co-optation efforts have targeted private entrepreneurs, co-opting them into the state's formal decision-making process (Dickson 2003).

The other part of the government's strategy has focused on addressing the socioeconomic wellbeing of the social classes. While the emergence of social discontent in Singapore was manifested mainly in declining support for the PAP, the dissatisfaction of the Chinese middle class combined with blue-collar discontent has been displayed in numerous social protests in urban and rural areas alike.[8] The CCP's intention to address the demands of the social classes was first reflected in Hu Jintao's 'scientific theory of development', which marked the beginning of the government's attempt to improve the formulation of public policy in the 2000s (Lam 2006). One significant CCP strategy was the establishment of a service-oriented bureaucracy to effectively respond to society's socioeconomic demands. New instruments of state surveillance and violence were also created to contain the spread of these 'mass incidents' and restore social stability by force.[9] The government's focus on socioeconomic growth continued throughout the 2010s with the formulation of the concept of 'China dream' to improve the country's overall living standards.

State Economic Visions, Business and Labour Constraints

With the continuation of an authoritarian system, the Chinese state has retained its strategic visions since the early 2000s. National economic programmes are linked to the state's dual goals of economic growth and political reform. From 2002 to 2012, Hu Jintao pushed an economic vision to generate public popularity and address defects of the Chinese economy associated with regional economic imbalance (Lam 2006).[10] In 2013, the Xi Jinping administration created an even more ambitious economic programme—the Belt and Road Initiative (BRI)—to deal with the acute issue of industrial over-capacity and speed up industrial restructuring, all the while generating nationalist popular support (Yu 2017).[11]

The Chinese developmental state has also maintained its dominance vis-à-vis business and labour actors. Businesses have continued to act

[8] The increasing number of social protests in the 2000s caught the attention of China observers around the world. The number of protests reportedly increased from 8700 in 1993 to 87,000 in 2005, and estimates for the number of public protests in 2010 range between 180,000 and 230,000 (Gobel and Ong 2012).

[9] One example of this political manoeuvring was in 2005, when police forces merged existing anti-riot and counter-terrorist units into new 'special police' tasked with responding rapidly to violent mass protests (*The Economist* 2005).

[10] Under this economic vision, China's Western Development Campaign was launched to redirect large amounts of central government spending, FDI, and international development funding to the country's western regions.

[11] The BRI involves the export of Chinese industrial good to carry out massive infrastructure building in nearly 60 countries, primarily in Asia and Europe.

as key allies of the state as China has embarked on a global economic strategy. China's low level of DPCC has precluded significant structural constraints from either business elites or organised labour. The vast majority of indigenous private businesses (mainly SMEs) are dispersed business interests that are uncapable of challenging the state's economic policy-making. Large and powerful SOEs, who occupy the top and most of the middle tiers of the Chinese economy, generally operate as instruments of the government to execute national economic plans.[12] Similar to GLCs in Singapore, Chinese SOEs constitute state-linked business interests. Not only was a special agency—the State-Owned Assets Supervision and Administration Commission (SASAC)—established in 2003 to manage them, but they are also overseen by NDRC, the main policy agency for economic decision-making. That the CCP retains substantial authority over the appointment of top executives in SOEs and the placement of Party members on the board of firms makes it quite unlikely that these business interests retain any independent policy agendas (Pearson 2011, 2015).

The continuation of China's authoritarian structure has also prevented the emergence of labour constraints. In the reform era, the empowerment of industrial workers has been mainly a result of the CCP's efforts to maintain industrial harmony as a part of a broad desire for social stability. Since the mid-2000s, the establishment of labour unions has proven to be a top-down process.[13] Since the early 2000s, as the government turned to address various societal tensions, the All-China Federation of Trade Unions (ACFTU) has helped it resolve labour conflicts and ensure social harmony (Chen 2011). Consequently, since the beginning of the reform era, labour gains have largely reflected the CCP's desire to maintain political power. Legislation of some of the world's most protective workplace laws has been linked to the CCP's political objectives of facilitating urbanisation, managing central-local government relations, and building trust among the public (Gallagher 2017).

[12] It is argued that China's political economy has three tiers—top, middle and bottom—corresponding to their strategic positions in the economy. On the concept of China's Tiered Economy, see Pearson (2011).

[13] In 2006, the CCP ordered the unionisation of many foreign-owned companies in China, including Walmart.

Re-Examining the Transformation of the Developmental State

The transformation of the Asian developmental states as a result of the rise of various social forces is a well-studied subject. Previous studies have introduced two main insights: (1) that the state's reduced capability to direct economic development is the result of the emergence of business elites and organised labour, who are capable of challenging the state's economic agenda; and (2) the capital concentration of a country's domestic industries can affect the level of policy constraints from business elites and organised labour by facilitating the emergence of either concentrated or dispersed economic interests (Heo and Tan 2003). This book aims to advance the current understanding of the state's transformation process in two broad areas.

Capital Ownership, Economic Interests and Policy Constraints

This book has revealed that the emergence of economic interest groups throughout the development process does not lead to the same constraints on the state in every case. The key factor shaping the level of policy constraints from economic interest groups is industrial structure. In this study, I have differentiated three forms of industrial structure based on three types of capital ownership, namely, domestic private capital, foreign capital, and state-owned capital. According to their influence on state policy-making, economic interest groups can be categorised as either constraining groups or non-constraining groups. While a country's promotion of domestic private capital can lead to the growth of constraining interest groups, like in South Korea and Taiwan, a reliance on FDI and the state's direct participation in the economy through SOEs can contribute to the emergence of non-constraining economic interest groups like in Singapore.

Scholars have differentiated these types of economic interests in the cases of the East Asian developmental state. Heo and Tan (2003) noted, for example, the existence of either concentrated or dispersed economic interests, depending on the degree of DPCC. This distinction has proven useful in understanding the different levels of policy constraints imposed on the South Korean and Taiwanese states in the 1990s. Following Heo and Tan's example, I created a new catalogue of economic interest groups, i.e. non-constraining economic interest groups, to differentiate groups that have no impact on the state's policy-making process from those that do. What produces non-constraining economic interests is not ruling elites' preference for the degree DPCC but rather the availability of FDI and SOE to initiate and engineer rapid industrialisation. The creation of this new catalogue of economic interest groups is particularly helpful to explain the weak policy constraints imposed on the state in Singapore, where the economy has been dominated by large-sized MNCs and GLCs, both of which are considered highly concentrated economic interests. It also explains why the structural power of Taiwanese organised labour was so weak despite the presence of large SOE unions that were able to demand favourable policies from the state.

Theoretical conclusion 1: In addition to economic interest groups that produce various constraints on the developmental state, East Asian state-led development can also cultivate a group of non-constraining economic interests that produce no constraints on the state's policy-making.

The Role of the Middle Class in Transforming the Developmental State

The second insight advanced in this book concerns the important contribution made by the middle class to transform the East Asian developmental state. Existing literature on the transformation of the developmental state has attributed the decline of the state's capability to direct economic development to the rise of business elites and organised labour (Minns 2001; Kim 1999; Heo and Tan 2003; Clark and Jung 2002; Tan 2008; Lim 2009; Pereira 2008). Echoing that the rise of these two social actors has led to the transformation of the developmental state, I highlight the important role played by another group of social actors—the middle class—in transforming the developmental state.

I argue that the democratic mobilisation of the middle class plays a pivotal role in determining the state's transformation outcome. This argument consists of two parts, the first concerning the transformation of a country's political system. I argue that the democratic mobilisation of the middle class can force East Asian ruling elites to transform the political system in a democratic direction. Without the middle class pushing for democratic transition, ruling elites will preserve and reinforce the existing authoritarian system. The three case studies have verified this hypothesis; only when the middle class became mobilised in the case of South Korea in 1987 and in Taiwan, with or without the working class as an alliance, did the ruling elites initiate democratic transition to transform their legitimacy formula. When the middle class withheld their support for democratic transition, the ruling elites pursued political repression to consolidate political power, as demonstrated with a strategy of authoritarian repression in response to a democratic uprising led by the working class in South Korea in 1980, and a strategy of authoritarian co-optation to deal with the material interests of the middle class in Singapore.

Unlike business elites and organised labour, the middle class does not directly produce institutionalised policy constraints to transform the developmental state model. The second part of my argument therefore concerns changes to the state's economic policy-making process after a democratic transition pushed by the middle class. A democratic transition initiated by ruling elites in response to middle-class mobilisation ultimately transforms the political foundation of the developmental state; not only does it facilitate the emergence of economic interests, but it also changes the context in which the state's economic decision-making occurs. In South Korea and Taiwan, the transformation of the state's political foundation after democratic transition, has produced policy constraints since the 1990s. In contrast, as Singapore did not experience democratic mobilisation of the middle class, the PAP has reinforced the state's authoritarian system and consequently made ruling elites immune to any policy constraints.

Theoretical conclusion 2: Compared to business elites and organised labour, the middle class plays an equally, if not more compelling, role in transforming the developmental state. While business elites and organised labour may challenge state policy, the middle class can demand that the authoritarian political system is changed, creating the conditions for a reduction of state's ability to execute national developmental projects.

Concluding Remarks: Understanding the Transformation of the Developmental State

The East Asian authoritarian developmental state, in which aggressive economic policy intervention is a key feature, has been central to our understanding of successful industrialisation in several East Asian economies. It is believed that these states, born out of East Asian ruling elites' desire for political survival, cannot last, as the effectiveness of the state in engineering rapid growth may inevitably be undermined by the rise of social forces in the development process (Castells 1992). The theory presented in this book has explained under what circumstances the developmental state model is transformed, pointing to two processes in particular. One is the emergence of economic interest groups that are capable of challenging the state's decision-making, and the other is the emergence of the middle class to push the political system in a democratic direction.

This book simultaneously stressed the importance of two factors: the concentration of domestic private capital in a country's industrial structure, and the occurrence of a democratic transition. My empirical chapters have detailed how these factors contributed to policy constraints in South Korea and Taiwan, while the lack of these factors led to an absence of policy constraints in Singapore. My brief analysis of China also reveals that the transformation of the Chinese developmental state has been delayed by the absence of a democratic transition and low levels of DPCC. It should be emphasised that the Singaporean and Chinese ruling elites did not intentionally plan their country's respective industrial structures and democratic transition outcomes to delay the state's transformation process. As I have argued, the two factors are linked to the ruling elites' strategic choices; in other words, the emergence of non-constraining economic interests and non-democratic transition were unintended consequences of the desire for political survival. Just as the developmental state model itself was born out of the need for political survival, so too does its transformation follow this same logic. In the cases of South Korea and Taiwan, elite adaptation to the changing political context led to the transformation of the developmental state. In the cases of Singapore and China, a different set of elite policies, namely authoritarian co-optation, has prevented transformation of the developmental state.

I must further clarify the implication of my comparison between the two outcomes of transformation and non-transformation. The cases of South Korea and Taiwan have shown that the two types of social pressure brought about by rapid state-led development led to such transformation and therefore reduced the states' capabilities to direct economic development since the early 1990s. In South Korea, the developmental state has continuously been constrained by powerful economic interests; a recent renewal of state developmentalism has been overshadowed by the assertiveness of business and labour actors. In Taiwan, economic interests played a minor role before the 2000 regime turnover, after which explosive transformation commenced as the strength of the state was increasingly undermined by large businesses as well as the divisiveness of identity politics. In contrast, the Singaporean experience presents a case of a resilient developmental state that has so far proven immune to the consequences of socioeconomic development. Both the economic interest groups and the middle class in Singapore have co-existed with the government since the early 1980s. The experience of the most recent East Asian authoritarian developmental state—post-1978 China—also negates the inevitability of the developmental state's decline. The evidence presented in the previous section suggests the emergence of a second resilient developmental state, just like that of Singapore.

This does not necessarily mean that state developmentalism cannot co-exist with a liberal democratic system. As documented in Chapter 2, South Korea's democratic system did successfully renew state developmentalism in the aftermath of the Asian financial crisis, as the state managed to strengthen its policy-making capability and rescue the country from the edge of a financial meltdown. A similar re-emergence of state developmentalism has also appeared in South Korea in more recent years. Since the early 2000s, the South Korean state has also used the democratic political environment to achieve central economic strategy in sectors such as telecommunications and renewable energy (Kim 2018). While the cases of post-authoritarian developmental states deserve more attention, the political histories covered in this book prove useful narratives to understand the constraints brought about on the post-war developmental state. By detailing these constraints, I hope that scholars and policy-makers can understand the emergence of a set of new political challenges to the formulation of successful industrial policies in democratic East Asia.

References

Castells, M. (1992). Four Asian Tigers with a Dragon Head: A Comparative Analysis of the State, Economy, and Society in the Asian Pacific Rim. In R. P. Appelbaum & J. Henderson (Eds.), *State and Development in the Asian Pacific Rim* (pp. 33–70). Newbury Park: Sage.

Chen, C. (2011). *The Politics of Labour Protection in Authoritarian Systems: Evidence from Labour Law and Enforcement in Post-Reform China*. PhD Thesis, UC San Diego.

Chen, J. (2013). *A Middle Class Without Democracy: Economic Growth and the Prospects for Democratisation in China*. New York: Oxford University Press.

Chen, J., & Lu, C. (2011). Democratisation and the Middle Class in China: The Middle Class's Attitudes Toward Democracy. *Political Research Quarterly, 64*(3), 705–719.

Chibber, V. (2003). *Locked in Place: State-Building and Late Industrialisation in India*. Princeton and Oxford: Princeton University Press.

Clark, C., & Jung, C. (2002). The Implications of the East Asian Flu for Developmental State Theory: The Case of South Korea and Taiwan. *Asian Affairs, 29*(1), 16–42.

Clark, C., & Roy, K. C. (1997). *Comparing Development Patterns in Asia*. Boulder: Lynne Rienner Publishers.

Dickson, B. J. (2003). *Red Capitalists in China: The Party, Private Entrepreneurs, and Prospects for Political Change*. Cambridge: Cambridge University Press.

Doner, R. F., Ritchie, B. K., Slater, D. (2005). Systemic Vulnerability and the Origins of Developmental States: Northeast and Southeast Asia in Comparative Perspective. *International Organisation, 59*(2), 327–361.

Evans, P. (1995). *Embedded Autonomy: State and Industrial Transformation*. Princeton: Princeton University Press.

Gallagher, M. E. (2002). "Reform and Openness": Why China's Economic Reforms Have Delayed Democracy. *World Politics, 54*(3), 338–372.

Gallagher, M. E. (2017). *Authoritarian Legality in China: Law, Workers, and the State*. Cambridge: Cambridge University Press.

Gobel, C., & Ong, L. H. (2012). Social Unrest in China. In K. Brown (Ed.), *China and the EU in Context: Insights for Business and Investors* (pp. 178–213). London: Palgrave Macmillan.

Gourevitch, P. (1986). *Politics in Hard Times: Comparative Reponses to International Economic Crises*. Ithaca: Cornell University Press.

Harding, H. (1987). *China's Second Revolution: Reform After Mao*. Washington, DC: The Brookings Institution.

Heo, U., & Tan, A. C. (2003). Political Choices and Economic Outcomes: A Perspective on the Differential Impact of the Financial Crisis on South Korea and Taiwan. *Comparative Political Studies, 36*(6), 679–698.

Kim, Y. T. (1999). Neoliberalism and the Decline of the Developmental State. *Journal of Contemporary Asia, 29*(4), 441.

Kim, S.-Y. (2018). Wither Developmentalism After Democratisation? In T.-J. Cheng & Y.-H. Chu (Eds.), *Routledge Handbook on Democratisation in East Asia* (pp. 457–470). New York: Routledge.

Lam, W. W.-L. (2006). *Chinese Politics in the Hu Jintao Era: New Leaders, New Challenges*. New York and London: M.E. Sharpe.

Lim, H. (2009). Democratisation and the Transformation Process in East Asian Developmental States: Financial Reform in Korea and Taiwan. *Asian Perspective, 33*(1), 75–110.

Lipset, S. M. (1959). Some Social Requisites of Democracy: Economic Development and Political Legitimacy. *The American Political Science Review, 53*(1), 69–105.

Minns, J. (2001). Of Miracles and Models: The Rise and Decline of the Developmental State in South Korea. *Third World Quarterly, 22*(6), 1025–1043.

Moore, B. (1966). *Social Origins of Dictatorship and Democracy: Lord and Peasant in the Making of the Modern World*. Boston: Beacon Press.

Naseemullah, A., & Arnold, C. E. (2015). The Political of Developmental State Persistence: Institutional Origins, Industrialisation, and Provincial Challenge. *Studies in Comparative International Development, 50,* 121–142.

Nathan, A. J. (2016). The Puzzle of the Chinese Middle Class. *Journal of Democracy, 27*(2), 5–19.

Naughton, B. (2006). *The Chinese Economy: Transitions and Growth*. Cambridge: MIT Press.

Pearson, M. (2011). Regulation and Regulatory Politics in China's Tiered Economy. In S. Kennedy (Ed.), *Beyond the Middle Kingdom: Comparative Perspective on China's Capitalist Transformation*. Stanford: Stanford University Press.

Pearson, M. (2015). State-Owned Business and Party-State Regulation in China's Modern Political Economy. In B. Naughton & K. Tsai (Eds.), *State Capitalism, Institutional Adaption, and the Chinese Miracle* (pp. 27–45). New York: Cambridge University Press.

Pereira, A. (2008). Whither the Developmental State? Explaining Singapore's Continued Developmentalism. *Third World Quarterly, 29*(6), 1189–1203.

Qian, Y. (2017). *How Reform Worked in China: The Transition from Plan to Market*. Cambridge: The MIT Press.

Rogowski, R. (1989). *Commerce and Coalitions: How Trade Affects Domestic Political Alignments*. Princeton, NJ: Princeton University Press.

Rueschemeyer, D., Stephens, E. H., & Stephens, J. D. (1992). *Capitalist Development and Democracy*. Chicago: University of Chicago Press.

Shirk, S. (1993). *The Political Logic of Economic Reform in China*. Berkeley: University of California Press.

Tan, A. C. (2008). From State Entrepreneurs to Political Entrepreneurs: Democratisation and the Politics of Financial Liberalisation. In P. Paolino & J. Meernik (Eds.), *Democratisation in Taiwan: Challenges in Transformation* (pp. 153–166). Burlington, VT: Ashgate.

The Economist. (2005). *Protests in China: The cauldron boils*. Available at: https://www.economist.com/asia/2005/09/29/the-cauldron-boils. Accessed on 16 September 2019.

Tsai, K. S. (2002). *Back-Alley Banking: Private Entrepreneurs in China*. Ithaca and London: Cornell University Press.

Tsai, K. S. (2007). *Capitalism Without Democracy: The Private Sector in Contemporary China*. Ithaca: Cornell University Press.

Vu, T. (2010). *Paths to Development in Asia: South Korea, Vietnam, China and Indonesia*. Cambridge and New York: Cambridge University Press.

Waldner, D. (1999). *State Building and Late Development*. Ithaca, NY: Cornell University Press.

White, G. (1993). *Riding the Tiger: The Politics of Economic Reform in Post-Mao China*. Basingstoke and London: Macmillan.

Wu, W.-C., Chang, Y.-T., & Pan, H.-H. (2017). Does China's Middle Class Prefer (Liberal) Democracy. *Democratisation, 24*(2), 347–366.

Yu, H. (2017). Motivation Behind China's 'One Belt, One Road' Initiatives and Establishment of the Asian Infrastructure Investment Bank. *Journal of Contemporary China, 26*, 105.

Index

T. He, *The Political Economy of Developmental States in East Asia*,
https://doi.org/10.1007/978-3-030-59357-5

The manufacturer's authorised representative in the EU is Springer Nature Customer Service Centre GmbH, Europaplatz 3, 69115 Heidelberg, Germany. If you have any concerns regarding our products, please contact ProductSafety@springernature.com

Printed and bound by CPI Group (UK) Ltd, Croydon, CR0 4YY
30/09/2026
02225461-0004